EXHUMATION
OF A MURDER

Now the case itself, as has been said to you, is a remarkable one, a deeply interesting one and I doubt whether any of us engaged here today have in recollection so remarkable a case in its incidents.

Mr Justice Darling

Herefordshire Winter Assizes
Thursday, 13th April 1922

On the rim of the twentieth century loom the Titans — Seddon, Armstrong, Crippen, G.J. Smith and Landru, and then, in the era of booze and bullets, art descends literally to hack-work.

Dorothy Dunbar,
Blood in the Parlor

EXHUMATION OF A MURDER

The life and trial of Major Armstrong

by **ROBIN ODELL**

Researched by J.H.H. GAUTE *and* H.B. TRUMPER

Foreword by RICHARD WHITTINGTON-EGAN

SOUVENIR PRESS

Dedicated to the wives who, through the years, helped and endured
so much with the researching and writing of this book:
to Frances Gaute and Joan Odell and in loving memory of
Frances Trumper

This edition published 1988 by Souvenir Press Ltd,
43 Great Russell Street, London WC1B 3PA
and simultaneously in Canada

ISBN 0 285 62849 6 hardback
ISBN 0 285 62844 5 paperback

Printed in Great Britain by
Billing & Sons Limited
Hylton Road, Worcester WR2 5JU

Foreword

The case of Major Armstrong, the celebrated Hay Poisoner, the only solicitor ever to hang, is one of those classic, old-fashioned English murders which hail from the heyday of court-room drama when, with the hangman lurking in the pine-and-panel wings and the black cap an object of horrifyingly alarming currency rather than mere symbolism, the loser in 'the black dock's dreadful pen' lost all. It comes straight out of the pages of George Orwell's essayed nostalgia* for the era of the Great British Murder, when, after a Sunday lunch of roast beef and Yorkshire, you put your feet up on the sofa and, with a good strong cup of mahogany-brown tea, read all about the latest 'good' murder in the *News of the World*. And the Armstrong case was unquestionably one of the best; right up there in the grand tradition of Dr Palmer of Rugeley, Neill Cream, Mrs Maybrick, Dr Crippen, Seddon, and George Joseph Smith.

It is now more than thirteen years since the first edition of this book appeared, and fully ten since it has been possible to go out and buy a copy of it. And that was a great pity, because it is one of the best murder monographs ever written.

I must confess, in a purely personal context, to an additional pleasure in welcoming this exhumation of the *Exhumation*, for it is a book with the making of which I was very much involved. I followed its progress step by step, and shared in the small frustrations and large triumphs of research and reconstruction endured and achieved by Robin Odell, Joe Gaute and Dr Hubert Trumper. I live through it all again, sitting here writing these words on the topmost of the nest of mahogany tables which formerly stood in Major Armstrong's drawing-room, and from which the famous 'scuse fingers' poisoned scone was dispensed to the Major's 'intended' — Oswald Martin. Those tables are now preserved, together with many another criminous relic, in the home of my friend, that distinguished and indefatigable crime historian, Joe Gaute.

* 'Decline of the English Murder' in *Tribune*

I remember, too, how the triumph of the original publication was tinctured with sadness for us because, after all the long years — nearly ten of them — of preparatory hard work and meticulous research, Dr Trumper died just *one week* before the first completed copy of the book arrived 'hot off' the press.

It is only relatively recently that the mortal remains of the Major have been seconded to a new and better 'posting'. The authorities decided to exhume the bodies of all those who had been executed at Gloucester Prison and buried within its precincts, and permit their reburial in more hallowed ground.

But in Hay, with its arched and pinnacled clock tower and anachronistic atmosphere, the spirit of the little Major seems to linger on. Oddly, old Hay folk speak of him, not as a murderer but, with affection, as a sort of benefactor. They rise fiercely to his defence if a stranger (that is anyone who has not lived for a minimum of 65 years in Hay!) shows lack of proper respect for his memory. They speak out strongly of his many acts of goodwill and kindness.

The town itself has not changed a great deal. Were he to return, the Major would surely not feel out of place in it today. Cusop Dingle is still beautiful and the water sings and gurgles. The old church nods on in bird-bowered slumber, poor murdered Katharine Armstrong lying beside it in her unmarked grave. Hay Police Station and its adjoining Magistrates' Court are now private residences. I regularly take a cup of tea with my friends, the Knights, in a bright and cosy living-room, one corner of which was once the police cell occupied by Major Armstrong. Its barred window is still preserved. Mrs Marina Knights is, incidentally, related to Inez Rosser, the young maid at the Armstrong house who gave evidence at the trial. And the happy laughter of the Knights' grandchildren echoes through another living-room, converted from the court where Armstrong was, first, Clerk to the Magistrates, and, subsequently, the occupant of his own dock there.

In Broad Street, time has come a strange full circle. A solicitor still sits at Armstrong's desk in Armstrong's old room and, as if to complete the circle, he and his family have just moved into the 'Big House' up at the Dingle, in which Armstrong lived. I know this young solicitor as a friend, and hasten to add that any resemblance to Armstrong is solely geographical!

It so happens that I am very frequently in Hay and am often asked: 'Can you possibly tell me where I can get hold of a copy of that Armstrong book?'

RICHARD WHITTINGTON-EGAN

Acknowledgments

THE ambition of the author and researchers has been to produce a work that is accurate and definitive. Many persons have contributed and their help is gratefully acknowledged.

A debt of gratitude is owed to the Home Office for the loan of the official transcript of the trial and for recognising that research takes years rather than months.

Thanks are expressed to Mr J.C.G. Hammond and Mr Richard Whittington-Egan for reading the MS at an early stage and for offering many helpful suggestions; to the late Mr Henry T.F. Rhodes for his analysis of Mrs Armstrong's alleged second will; to Mr Frank Maryfield for advice on Armstrong's accounts; to Mrs Vi Kynaston for typing the final MS and Mr Edgar Lustgarten.

For their advice on legal and medical aspects of the case, thanks are due to Lady Farrar, Mr E.A. Godson, the late Mr Trevor Griffiths, The Law Society, Mr E.K.W. Matthews, the late Mr G.R. Paling, Mr Walter Sharp, Professor C. Keith Simpson, Dr Gavin Thurston and Mr J. Williams.

For the loan of papers, documents and press cuttings — *The Brecon and Radnor Express,* Mr. R.C. Hansen, Mr Michael Harman, *The Hereford Times,* Mr Kendall McDonald, Mr. J.R.F. Thompson, Mrs E.S. Whiting, and Dr Philip H.A. Willcox.

For searching official records and helping to trace some of the principal participants in the Armstrong case — Mr R. Barton, Dr F.H. Brisby, Mrs Freda Darm, Mr W. Jack Field, Dr L. Heasman, Colonel P.A. Higham, Mr R. McCartney, Mr B.S.W. Taylor, Mr Michael Thatcher, Mr M.R. Trappes Lomax, Mr H. Treherne and Mrs E. Ward.

For reminiscences of Major and Mrs Armstrong — Miss May Lilwall, Mr William Paradise, Mrs Inez Samuel (nee Rosser), Mr F.W. Stokoe and Mr Eddie Williams.

Research is a mosaic of pieces, the cement for which is provided by countless questions answered and items of information unselfishly given by friends, acquaintances and strangers. We have sought to acknowledge every source of help but hope to be forgiven for any omissions.

Contents

page

	LIST OF ILLUSTRATIONS	ix
	RESEARCHERS' INTRODUCTIONS	xi
Prologue	ARREST	1
1	NO WINE FOR THE MAJOR	6
2	EXCUSE FINGERS	35
3	THE MAJOR HOLDS COURT	63
4	EXHUMATION OF A MURDER	83
5	MOTIVE AND MALADY	117
6	REX v ARMSTRONG— THE PROSECUTION	141
7	REX v ARMSTRONG— THE DEFENCE	162
8	APPEAL AND EXECUTION	186
9	LIVES AND LEGENDS	209
	APPENDIX: ARMSTRONG'S STATEMENT	237
	BIBLIOGRAPHY	242
	INDEX	247

List of Illustrations

ILLUSTRATIONS   *page*

Armstrong's Birth Certificate   10–11
Armstrong's signature   14
Armstrong's diary entry recording his wife's death   32
Announcement of Katharine Armstrong's death in the   32
    Morning Post
One of Spilsbury's cards   88
Webster's report   91
Mrs Armstrong's second will   131
Analysis of signature on second will   138
Curtis Bennett's note for a photo-   182
    grapher during Armstrong's trial.
Armstrong's note to Matthews   192
Excerpt from the *Hereford Times*   196
Armstrong's Death Certificate   198–9
End of Armstrong's statement   241

PLATES

                                          Between pages

His Finest Hour! Herbert Rowse Armstrong, T.D., MA.   50–51
Mayfield – home of the Armstrong family
With his wife Katharine on their wedding day
Lieutenant, Devon Volunteers
Freemason
Adjutant
Solicitor
Mayfield's study with bureau
The bedroom – scene of Mrs Armstrong's demise

Broad Street, Hay, where the two solicitors   82–83
    confronted each other
Davies's chemist shop where Armstrong bought
    his arsenic
Mr and Mrs Davies and John Rangecroft of the
    Clinical Research Association
The Police: Weaver, Paling, Sharp and Crutchett

The Doctors: Willcox, Spilsbury, Hincks and Webster
Spilsbury and Hincks
Constance and Oswald Martin
Madame X at Hay
Madame X when young
Arriving for his trial
The women in the case – Nurse Kinsey, Miss Rosser,
    Nurse Lloyd, Miss Pearce and Mrs Price

The two solicitors' offices in Broad Street, Hay   114–115
The magistrates at Hay
Superintendent Weaver leads Major Armstrong into
    the Hay Police Court
Exhumed coffin carried into Church Cottage, Cusop
Reburial
In the dock of his own court

Mr Justice Darling is driven to the Assizes at Hereford   146–147
The jury arrive too
For the Defence: Bosanquet, Toogood and Matthews
Defence and Prosecution, Curtis Bennett and the
    Attorney General
The crowds assemble for the trial at Hereford's
    Shire Hall
Defending himself in court
Leaving Shire Hall after sentence of death
The crowd assembles outside Gloucester Prison for
    the execution

Researchers' Introductions

The case of Herbert Rowse Armstrong had always intrigued me; not that it had ever occurred to me that one day I should find myself very deeply involved in it. The story of that involvement is one of rather odd coincidences, which, in retrospect, seem to have signposted the way.

Indeed, a signpost was literally the beginning; for it was while I was staying with friends at Llyswen that I came, quite by chance, upon one which pointed to 'Hay 9 miles'. I decided on impulse that I would drive to the little border-country town and have a look at the tiny hamlet of Cusop, the actual scene of those events which had for so many years caught my imagination. What I saw there made the case seem even more fascinating! Sometime later, there arrived on my office desk a manuscript sent in for my firm's consideration by a Dr Hubert Trumper. I saw that Dr Trumper lived at Cusop, and, with my visit still fresh in mind, wrote to him asking if he had ever thought of writing a book on the Armstrong case. By return of post came an invitation to go down to Cusop and spend a weekend with him.

Consequently, I found myself again travelling to Hay-on-Wye. The meeting with Hubert Trumper was a happy one. Not only did we find that we got on very well on a personal level, but it turned out that our ideas about Armstrong matched so closely that we decided there and then to become 'partners in crime'. The decision to write jointly what we then called 'The Armstrong Book' came into being.

Our first researches confirmed earlier impressions that this was an almost unbelievable story which had never been told in exactly the way it happened. Nowhere was it explained how the authorities came to be alerted about the events which ended with the respectable solicitor and Magistrates' Clerk sitting in the dock of his own court. Our aim, therefore, was to exhume every fact, visit the relevant scenes, interview everybody who had any knowledge of the events so that we could tell the definitive story of what even the judge described as 'so remarkable a case in its incidents'.

Even more disturbing we found that virtually every version of the Armstrong case contained errors about such fundamentals as dates, places and names; one writer, for example, quite incorrectly wrote that Armstrong, on the morning of his arrest, had a taxi waiting to take him to Paris and was prevented from going only by the arrival of the police. We therefore made it a prime objective to lay the ghosts of old legends which encrusted and distorted the truth. Indeed, in this case, it meant delving right down to bedrock, relying on no other printed account, going right back to the beginning. Authoritative sources were tapped and new discoveries were made; letters written to Armstrong by the woman he had at one time planned to marry and proof that he forged his wife's will are given here for the first time as is the reason for the attempted murder of Martin, which started the whole affair.

Notes, abstracts, official files, letters, records of interviews, birth, death and marriage certificates and countless other documents mounted steadily. Frankly for a busy publisher, and an equally busy medical practitioner, the material began to get out of hand. The mere classification and organization of it took on the proportions of a mammoth task. Trumper and I were buried beneath the fruits of our research. That was bad enough, but time was running out—we had not envisaged a centenary volume.

It was at this juncture, with the materials ready for assembly, every fact checked and rechecked, that Robin Odell came on the scene. A very dear friend, who had already published a highly successful study of Jack the Ripper*, he gallantly undertook the task of shaping the material which Trumper and I had spent the best part of ten years quarrying out—polishing it, refining it, and producing this finished product.

So, ultimately, 'The Armstrong Book' became the joint effort of a trio. Two minds, it is said, are better than one. *Three* then should satisfy the most exacting requirements.

Trumper had lived in Cusop almost opposite Armstrong's house; I have 'lived' with Armstrong; Odell has had to live with all three.

Pyrford, Woking.   J.H.H. Gaute

* *Jack the Ripper in Fact and Fiction*, Harrap, 1965.

You will read in this book the facts about Armstrong. To research and present these in a readable form has meant years of hard work. We have found things about the little man never before recorded. Most of these support the verdict of the jury; a few show Armstrong in a more kindly light.

He gave much practical help to young people out of work. Some years ago it was broadcast that I was an author of a forthcoming book on Armstrong. An elderly man, having heard the broadcast came all the way from the north to see me. He said, 'I was only a lad and I was damn near starving here in Hay at the end of the First War and I tried to get a job with one of the big houses. Major Armstrong couldn't take me on but he gave me a hot meal and got me a job as a stable-boy in Clyro. He saved my life. Put that in your book.'

Armstrong was a Master of the local Masonic Lodge, a regular churchman and attained field rank in the army. What's wrong with these things? Many say that they showed him to be a hypocrite. Even his appearance was held against him though I agree that light-blue eyes seldom go with a humble and a contrite heart!

No third party ever knows the exact relationship between a man and his wife and it would be foolish to try and define any mental or moral conflict between Armstrong and his wife.

Best of all in his favour and throughout his long ordeal, he never tried to put the blame on his servants or anyone else.

He went to his death with courage, dignity and military deportment. And that is more than can be said of many honoured men.

Cusop, Hay-on-Wye.   H.B. Trumper,
                              T.D. M.A. M.B. B.Chir. (Cantab.)

Prologue: Arrest

IN THE little Welsh town of Hay, surrounded by hills and snuggling close to the River Wye, the last day of the year 1921 dawned with bitingly cold weather. There was a hint of snow to come as the townsfolk prepared to greet the New Year with customary optimism.

Major Herbert Rowse Armstrong, T.D., M.A., solicitor and Clerk to the local magistrates at Hay, shared that mood as he said prayers before breakfast at Mayfield, his home in Cusop just outside the town. Armstrong, who was a widower, lived with his three children and servants in well-appointed surroundings. Despite the fact that it was New Year's Eve and a Saturday, the Major intended going to his office for the morning, although he didn't expect many clients would wish to see him. He planned to work at home in the garden in the afternoon and later to entertain guests to dinner.

Wearing riding breeches, trench boots and an army officer's British warm, the Major was well protected against the cold as he set off down the drive and headed for his office in Broad Street, Hay. During the mile-long walk he may well have reflected on what the New Year would have in store for him. He could not realize it then, but fate was already working against him and he was destined never to see his home again.

The dapper figure of Major Armstrong in his seemingly unusual garb excited no comment as he walked through the town. He was well known for his military style and respected for his correct and courteous manner.

On nearing his office, the Major probably cast a casual glance across Broad Street at the premises of Robert Griffiths, where Oswald Martin, the only other practising solicitor in Hay, had his office. He then entered his own office which consisted of parts of a converted shop. Armstrong walked through the ground floor office saying, 'Good morning' to his clerk, Arthur Phillips, and nodding to Una Baker, the teenage office girl. He went straight upstairs to his large private office.

His arrival was rather later than usual but his staff put that down to the fact that it was Saturday morning. Having to work for half a day was boring for them because there was not a great deal to do.

A few minutes after the Major reached his office, at about 10 a.m., the street door opened again and admitted three men. Phillips rose from his chair to greet them and recognized at once the uniformed figure of Superintendent Albert Weaver, Deputy Chief Constable of Herefordshire. The Superintendent's companions, strangers to Phillips, were in civilian clothes.

Superintendent Weaver asked if Major Armstrong was in. Phillips replied that his employer had just arrived. Weaver said that it would not be necessary to announce them and the three men walked quickly to the stairs; one of the strangers turned and instructed Phillips that no-one was to use or answer the telephone. At the head of the stairs the trio turned right to face the door of Armstrong's private office. Una Mary Baker, who by that time was working in a small office adjoining Armstrong's, heard heavy footsteps on the stairs and went to the door; she was just in time to see the three men walk straight into Armstrong's office without knocking.

They found themselves in a large room behind the door of which hung the solicitor's trappings; a gown and a blue bag for carrying legal papers. On the far side of the room, close to a window overlooking the street, sat Armstrong at a spacious desk. Superintendent Weaver introduced his two companions to the solicitor as Chief Inspector Alfred Crutchett and Sergeant Walter Sharp, both of New Scotland Yard.

Chief Inspector Crutchett, reading from a prepared statement, told Armstrong:

Inquiries have recently been made concerning the sudden illness of Mr Oswald Norman Martin after taking tea with you on the 26th October last at your house at Cusop. He was taken ill soon after he left you on that date, and was later seized with sickness and purging. A specimen of his urine was taken on the 30th October 1921, and arsenic was found in it. These symptoms point to arsenical poisoning. It is known that you have purchased arsenic, the last occasion being on the 11th January 1921.

It is, therefore, necessary to enquire whether, and, if so, how, and by whom, arsenic could have been introduced into the food taken at the tea party.

I would also tell you that on the 20th September, Mr Martin received by post a box of Fuller's chocolates, and on examination it was found that some of the chocolates had been tampered with and arsenic put into them. The box was packed at Fuller's on the 2nd September.

It may be that you would like to make a statement as to your own actions on the 26th October: why Mr Martin was asked to tea; as to what became of the arsenic purchased by you, and as to any facts that may throw light on the matter. Also as to your movements during the period from the 2nd to the 20th September: if away from Hay, where and with whom you stayed; how you were occupied during that period, and whether you bought any chocolates, but I must tell you that anything you do say will be taken down in writing and may be used in evidence hereafter.

Armstrong, hiding the shock that he must have felt, replied, 'Certainly; this is a very serious matter; I will help you all I can. I was not aware that arsenic had been found in Mr Martin's urine, and I appreciate that the circumstances call for some explanation from me. I will make a statement and tell you all I know.'

A statement was then made by Armstrong in a manner which Crutchett described in a report to his chief as 'very guarded'. This was taken down in long-hand by Sergeant Sharp. Weaver and Crutchett remained in the room and when it was completed Armstrong read the statement through, made some corrections and signed it*. Crutchett then told Armstrong, 'Mr Weaver now has something to say to you.'

Superintendent Weaver cautioned Armstrong and arrested him on a charge of administering arsenic to Mr Martin on 26th October 1921 at Mayfield, Cusop, with intent to murder him. In reply to the charge, Armstrong said, 'I am quite innocent.'

*The full text of the statement showing the corrections made by Armstrong is given in the Appendix.

Armstrong was then asked to empty his pockets; their contents were placed on the desk and loosely wrapped in a piece of brown paper. While the desk itself was being examined Armstrong was told to sit in a chair in the centre of the room. He complied readily and while the police officers were investigating other parts of the room he asked if he might have his tobacco pouch. This was given to him and a short while later he asked if he might sit at the desk and read some business letters. Not wishing to obstruct the solicitor's business more than was necessary, Crutchett granted Armstrong's request. At this point the senior police officers were joined by Sergeant Walter Worthing of the Herefordshire Constabulary. His instructions were to assist in the detailed searches of the solicitor's offices.

A short while later, Crutchett noticed that Armstrong had opened the brown paper containing the items taken from his pockets and was turning over some letters. The Chief Inspector stopped him at once, asking him to move away from the desk, and saw to it that the brown paper was made into a parcel and tied with string. This parcel was later handed to the sergeant at Hay Police Station in whose charge it remained until it was examined in detail a few days later.

The police officers had been with Major Armstrong in his office for over two hours but the solicitor's employees in the office below had no inkling of what was happening. There was no reason why they should for the Major frequently had professional dealings with the police. Finally, a little after midday, Armstrong left his office accompanied by the police officers. They walked the short distance to Hay Police Station: the arrested man was not handcuffed and he walked quietly with the detectives.

The station sergeant, James Williams, was fetched from a football match at which he was a spectator, and told the identity of the man who was about to become his prisoner. Armstrong was taken into the sergeant's private sitting-room where he was formally charged.

Armstrong was searched and all articles of personal property were taken from him and duly entered in the register: they were a silver watch, gold ring, a pair of gold cuff-links, fountain pen, pocket knife, nail cleaner, cigarette holder and twelve pounds sixteen shillings in cash.

The following entry was made on the charge-sheet.

C.S. No. 1	31st Dec. 12.30 p.m.	Herbert Rowse Armstrong Mayfield Cusop, Solicitor	On the 26th October 1921 at the parish of Cusop did unlawfully administer poison 'to wit' arsenic to one Oswald Norman Martin with intent to murder him.

The events of the previous two and a half hours had been sudden and swift moving, and there had been little time for Armstrong to understand the enormity of what was happening. Away from his office and subjected to the cold routine of police procedure, he must have felt apprehensive despite his calm behaviour.

Armstrong was permitted to contact a solicitor and he requested Thomas Alfred Matthews of Hereford to act for him. Following this the prisoner was placed in Hay Police Station's No. 1 cell which is still known as 'Armstrong's Cell'. This was a small room with the traditional barred window high up in one wall. There was a board bed along one wall, a wash basin in one corner and a WC in the other. When this required flushing, the prisoner had to ring a bell and the duty police officer would operate the cistern from outside the cell.

Major Armstrong saw out the old year and greeted the new with whatever mixture of thoughts his confinement brought to mind. One thing was certain. He was no longer in a position to influence his own future—circumstances had already overtaken him.

1 No Wine for the Major

It is local gossip that Armstrong was a henpecked man.
Dr Thomas Hincks

THE MARKET town of Hay is set high up on the right bank
of the River Wye and stands astride the border between
England and Wales. The border is marked by the Dulas
Brook which flows through the town, placing the railway
station in England and the greater part of Hay in Wales.
Rising to the south and hemming the town in against the
Wye are the Black Mountains whose modest peaks include
Hay Bluff and Lord Hereford's Knob.

Hay's main thoroughfare is Broad Street which runs parallel
with the river below. Its houses have a quaint and intimate air
and a solid looking clock tower stands guard over their
affairs. Most of the shops are in the High Town, a tiny maze
of streets behind the clock tower.

Just south of the town, about a mile from its centre, is a
pleasant residential area known as Cusop. The houses here
have large gardens which afford their owners splendid views
of the nearby countryside. The Church of St Mary nestles at
the bottom of Cusop Hill sheltered by several majestic yews
which are supposed to have been mentioned in the *Domesday
Book.*

This story begins in the early 1900s when Hay was a
bustling little market town of 1300 people. Then, as now,
practically all industry and trade were connected with the
land. The border farmers and landowners, some of whom
commanded over a thousand acres, looked to Hay to service
their needs. The most important day in their weekly calendar
was Thursday when the town throbbed to the life of the
street- and cattle-markets.

While the farmer made his deals and consulted his bank
manager, solicitor or estate agent, his wife shopped in
High Town. Others made their way to the doctor's surgery
which was usually packed with people who managed to nurse
their ills until market day.

The air was filled with the noise of penned sheep and
cattle, and good-natured conversation and laughter emerged

from the doors of the public houses. Here profits were praised, deals solemnly sealed, boasts tested and gossip exchanged.

In the community of the market-place everyone knew everyone else's business but each knew his place. The social order was well defined and few attempted to step over the dividing lines, for the trend to permissiveness and equality which followed the First World War was not yet apparent.

The titled landowners with their big houses and rolling acres were largely a class apart, except for their patronage of some local institutions. The gentry and professional class included the doctor, solicitor and parson. They lived comfortably in surroundings of varying prosperity which could be judged by the numbers of servants and gardeners they employed. Essential to the well-being of the community were the tradespeople—shopkeepers and farmers—whose common dealings in cash and kind earned them little status. Finally, there were the farm labourers, shop assistants and servants whom the system treated humanely but with due regard to their lowly position.

Everyone accepted that status was bestowed by class but the popularization of the motor car was beginning to change that in subtle ways. A few cars used Hay's streets but horses remained for long the best form of transport to the outlying areas in the hilly Border country.

* * * * *

In 1906 an insignificant-looking man stepped into the life of Hay and began a sequence of events which was to plunge the quiet town into sensation. His name was Herbert Rowse Armstrong. Nature had created him in a small mould. At the mature age of thirty-seven he weighed seven stone and stood five feet six inches tall. His passport description referred to his equally diminutive features: '. . . nose, *small*; chin, *small*; mouth, *small* . . .'. He was well-proportioned and everything about him was neat. He was vain about his appearance, being addicted to high collars and buttonholes, and he wore a heavy moustache which was waxed at the ends. The most striking features of this little man were his bright blue eyes and enormous, size seventeen collars.

Herbert Rowse Armstrong was born in Plymouth on 13th May 1869, the son of William Armstrong, a colonial merchant and Eleanor, whose maiden name was Rowse. The family lived at 23 Princess Square, Plymouth and later moved to Liverpool where Herbert was brought up in a respectable but not very well-to-do home in Durning Road, Edge Hill. The generosity of two aunts made it possible for Herbert, who was a moderately gifted youth, to go up to Cambridge University. He was a shy, bespectacled undergraduate at St Catherine's College where he was understudy to the Cambridge coxswain for the Oxford and Cambridge boat race.

He was apparently well-liked at university and struck up a friendship with Lisle Carr, a future Bishop of Hereford, who was outspoken about his kindness. In 1891 Armstrong graduated a Bachelor of Arts and four years later was enrolled as a solicitor and Notary Public.

He took his first job in 1895 as an articled clerk in the offices of Alsop, Stevens and Crooks, solicitors in the city of Liverpool. He worked hard, managed to save a little money and began some of the strongest attachments of his life. He became interested in the army during those early days at Liverpool and joined the Volunteer Forces. He was commissioned Second Lieutenant in the 1st Lancashire Royal Fusiliers in 1900.

He also began his association with the Church and started Sunday afternoon meetings for young people at St Georges. During this period it is said that Armstrong became engaged to a Liverpool girl but for unknown reasons the engagement was broken off. It was in Liverpool too that he met and established a lifelong friendship with Arthur Chevalier, another young solicitor.

Armstrong was making a good beginning to his career and impressed people by his hard work and pleasant personality. A contemporary described him as a delightful man, correct in his manners and popular with both sexes.

Armstrong moved to Newton Abbot in 1901 and by this time had gained valuable professional experience and social standing. The next six years which he spent as a practising solicitor with Hutchings and Co. in the Devon town were important ones. He joined the Devon Volunteers where he progressed to Lieutenant, and met Katharine Mary Friend, his future wife. Katharine, daughter of a printer, was a Devon girl in her late twenties. Armstrong, thinking of marriage, sought to enhance his professional career by finding a partnership in a legal practice.

His quest for the right opportunity took him to the Welsh border country and in 1906 he secured a position as managing clerk to Edmund Hall Cheese, an elderly solicitor with a busy practice in Broad Street, Hay. Edmund Cheese, who was sixty-three, did not enjoy good health. He was tired and worried about keeping his business going; the thought of retirement was not far from his mind. He and his wife took Armstrong into their home as a lodger and the prospects for the new man must have seemed attractive with the likelihood of an early partnership.

The following year on 4th June, after an engagement of three years, Armstrong married Katharine Mary Friend at the parish church in West Teignmouth, her home town. After a honeymoon in Switzerland, the couple quickly settled into a modest house called Rothbury at Cusop. Within three years Armstrong was made a partner in the firm and the brass plate outside the Broad Street office bore a new inscription, *Cheese & Armstrong, Solicitors.*

This professional success enabled the Armstrongs to aspire to a better home and in 1912 they moved into another, larger house. This was Mayfield which was a solidly-built detached house with a double frontage and large garden. It was set well back from the road and was approached by a broad gravelled drive; it spelled success. It was at Mayfield, in the fashionable residential area of Cusop, that Herbert and Katharine Armstrong worked out the drama of their lives. They had three children: two girls, Eleanor and Margaret, and a boy, Pearson Rowse. Katharine's first pregnancy at the age of thirty-seven was an anxious one.

Armstrong also progressed in his soldiering ambitions and gained promotion to Captain in the Volunteer Forces. Soon after coming to Hay he took command of the Hay Territorials, who were known as D Detachment, Brecknockshire Battalion, South Wales Borderers. He threw himself wholeheartedly into the life of the pre-war territorial army, attending regular camps and diligently sitting the examinations which would

18 69 .	BIRTHS in the *District* of *Saint Andrew*, in the County of *Devon*.				
No.	When Born.	Name, if any.	Sex.	Name and Surname of Father	Name and Maiden Surname of Mother
216	Thirteenth May 1869 23 Princess Square	Herbert Rowse	Boy	William Armstrong	Eleanor Cole Armstrong formerly Rowse

I Certify that the above written is a true copy of an entry in the Register

Witness my Hand, this Third *day of* June

Armstrong's Birth Certificate

secure future promotion.

The desire to be an officer and a gentleman and to associate with men of the highest rank in the local social structure was a strong urge in Armstrong. He became a member of the Order of Freemasons and completed the trio of interests that dominated his life: Army, Church and Freemasonry.

In 1910 he was Senior Deacon in the Loyal Hay Lodge and a group photograph of the time hung on the wall of the lodge anteroom showing the diminutive Armstrong flanked by representatives of the oldest families in the district, including a knight and the son of a peer. In due course he held the high office of Worshipful Master and later of Chaplain at the Hay Lodge.

As an important agricultural centre, Hay could boast two firms of solicitors, Cheese & Armstrong and Robert Griffiths, with offices opposite each other in Broad Street. There was sufficient work for both firms, most of it conveyancing for farmers and landowners, and between them they handled the legal business for miles around.

All this added up to a period of success for Armstrong, and life at Mayfield with its staff of a housekeeper, two maids and a gardener must have been very comfortable. But there was one flaw in this otherwise perfect setting and that was Mrs Armstrong. Katharine Armstrong was a very strong

Rank or Profession of Father.	Signature, Description, and Residence of Informant.	When Registered.	Signature of Registrar.	Baptismal Name if added after Registration of Birth.
Colonial Merchant	William Armstrong Father 23 Princess Square Plymouth	Third June 1869	James Baster Registrar	

Book of Births, in the District of SAINT ANDREW.

1869

James Baster
Registrar.

character and despite her husband's public status in the Army, Church and Freemasons, she dominated the little man and at home both he and the children conformed to the rules which she alone dictated.

Armstrong did not rebel against her domination although people in Hay increasingly came to recognize that he was henpecked. No doubt his outside activities acted as a counterweight to the pressures at home and life went on with all the appearances of normality.

Then came the year 1914, a momentous one for Armstrong as for many of his countrymen. On 26th April, Edmund Cheese, aged seventy-one, died of cancer of the prostate, to be followed in an extraordinary coincidence by his wife the following day; she succumbed to a heart attack. The whole legal practice immediately passed to Armstrong whose first thought was of the possibility of amalgamating the business with that of Robert Griffiths. But before he could really get to grips with the new situation, world events took a hand and Britain was at war with Germany.

Caught up in the whirl of mobilization, Captain Armstrong was posted to the 1st Wessex Field Company, Royal Engineers, based in southern England. He was engaged mainly in administrative duties for which his professional background ideally suited him. For a period he was Adjutant to the

2/1 Wessex Division, Royal Engineers at Iford Camp near Bournemouth. Postings such as this enabled him to keep in touch with business affairs at Hay although the late Edmund Cheese's nephew, A.C. Sampson, acted as his *locum tenens*.

Armstrong learned that Griffiths was going through a bad patch as the old man's health was going downhill and his son, Trevor, had broken off his legal training on being called up and sent to France. Perhaps Armstrong sensed an opportunity to eliminate a business rival or possibly he acted generously to assist a colleague at a time of need. Whatever his motive, he made a formal approach to Griffiths on the subject of combining the interests of the two firms. But the old man turned down the offer and Armstrong soldiered on enjoying camp life and the glamour of the officer's mess. He also smoked and drank—modest indulgences which would have been unthinkable at home. Herbert Armstrong's horizons were thus being broadened in many ways during these early war years.

This period of Armstrong's life gives an insight into two important facets of his make-up: he was an egoist who constantly needed acclaim and he had a passion for trivia. Letters written to him by senior contemporary officers pay glowing tributes to Armstrong's efficiency: 'I can say that as far as I was concerned, as Adjutant I always found your unit run in a most capable way . . . I have no hesitation in saying that during the time you were with the 58th Div. the administration and training was always most satisfactory', wrote one correspondent. Another said, 'I do recollect the excellent condition your portion of the camp was always in and it has always been a pleasure to come to see it on my tours of inspection.'

The point about these letters is that they were not truly unsolicited testimonials; Armstrong wrote to these men, and presumably to others also, seeking tributes, either to further his army career or his self-esteem—or perhaps both.

Armstrong's mania for detail comes out in other correspondence and particularly in a wrangle which he had with another army officer in 1916 over the handling of stores and equipment ledgers. Like a good administrator, Armstrong kept file copies of his letters and these allow us to probe into the mind of a paper soldier at the time when thousands of men were preparing for death on the Somme. 'I hear incidentally,' Armstrong wrote to the officer commanding 3/2nd Wessex Field Company, RE, 'that complaints have been made as to the removal of office stationery and rubber stamps. I only brought away sufficient stationery for immediate use, not even a red pencil for myself. I never saw, or used a rubber stamp of the 3/2nd Company so could not bring it away'. A good deal of correspondence was expended on this row and Armstrong pursued it with single-mindedness.

Underlying this skirmish on the Home Front was the thought in Armstrong's mind that his competence was in question. To be the subject of criticism was obviously likely to promote an over-reaction in one who set out to seek self acclaim, and he reacted indignantly. Trivial though it was, this incident showed how the little man's mind worked.

Whatever the official outcome of the rubber stamp inquest, it did not affect Armstrong's army career as he was promoted to Major shortly afterwards. For three months at the tail end of the war, Major Armstrong served in France. He was not sent to the Front but was engaged in routine duties at the RE Base Depot; his army records show that he was, '. . . fitted with a Box Respirator, small', at the Base Training Camp, Rouen, in September 1918.

In a letter to a friend relating news of her husband at this time, Mrs Armstrong wrote, 'He says he works eight hours, six days a week in the saddle from 9 to 5 o'clock and Sundays off. I think he's 1½ miles behind the lines, bombs and shells from air raids continually over him, one day he rode unwillingly to a village that was under fire.'

In October, he returned to England and his war was almost over. Armstrong's Army Book 439 recorded his periods of service, his promotions and decorations and his Commanding Officers' testimonials: 'This officer is very well suited for duty in a department of the Provost Marshal . . .', and, 'I have every confidence in recommending Major H. Rowse Armstrong for the appointment of Area Commandant. His administrative training makes him particularly suitable for a post of this kind'. There were no entries on the page headed, 'Mentions in Despatches and Rewards'.

Armstrong was demobilized in May 1919 and he returned to Hay to pick up the threads of his business there. He took a great interest in the local branch of the Comrades of the Great War and commanded the company of ex-servicemen which took part in the unveiling ceremony of the Hay War Memorial.

His military career had not afforded Armstrong the opportunity of being 'among the gongs' but he was determined to secure what rewards were going. Accordingly he began to send out worrying letters petitioning for the award of the Territorial Decoration. It may be fairly said that he had earned it with over twenty years' territorial service but he was not yet retired from the army. In any event, his pestering brought results and the award was duly announced in the *London Gazette* on 4th November 1919. 'The King has been graciously pleased to confer the Territorial Decoration upon the undermentioned officers . . . Major Herbert R. Armstrong . . . A copy of the *Gazette,* heavily marked in blue pencil was kept by Armstrong. This made a fitting caption to a photograph of the time which showed him mounted on horseback. The little man's pride is self evident and this must surely have been one of his finest moments.

He was officially retired from the army in 1921, having reached the age limit, and a letter from the War Office informed him, 'you will be granted permission to retain your rank'. Armstrong needed no second bidding, for he used his rank on every conceivable occasion and even embellished his signature on cheques with the title which meant so much to him — 'Major'.

On cheques and letters alike Armstrong nearly always signed himself 'Major'. The 'T.D.' in the cheque signature stands for 'Territorial Decoration'.

* * * * *

There is no doubt that Armstrong's years away from home during the 1914-18 War made him a changed man and he found great difficulty in settling back to the life of a small-town solicitor. Where most returning soldiers were warmly welcomed back to the bosom of their families, Armstrong found that his wife's attitude was even more domineering than when he had left and her behaviour was decidedly abnormal. In short, his homecoming was cold and without cheer.

Nor was this the only change, for Armstrong was soon to learn that the ageing Robert Griffiths had taken on a partner, Oswald Norman Martin, a young solicitor who had fought with the army in France and been invalided out of the service. As soon as he began to resume his law practice Armstrong felt the loss of his late partner. The carefree days of military service faded as he faced the uphill struggle of revitalizing his run-down business.

Old Mr Cheese was a country solicitor with a position of trust in the community which he had built up over years of dealing-with the financial and business secrets of many of the foremost families. He was a Hereford man who had lived most of his life in the area and was active in local politics. His identification with the lives and affairs of the local people was so complete that no newcomer could hope to emulate it.

People can be very fickle about their relationships with lawyer and doctor and for all Armstrong's acceptance in high places and the respect paid to him he remained an outsider. When it came to sharing confidences many of the local farmers preferred to go to men like Cheese and Griffiths whom they trusted implicitly as local men. In that respect Armstrong was a foreigner and consequently, now that he was alone, more business seemed to go to the rival firm where old Mr Griffiths was still at the helm. Moreover, Oswald Martin, Griffiths's new partner, was showing every sign of settling down well and the younger man's drive was giving the business a boost.

Armstrong became acutely embarrassed by Martin's success which occurred largely at the expense of his own. This hurt both his pride and his pocket. Martin concentrated a part of his work on solving income tax problems, thus providing a valuable service to the local farmers who badly needed advice on such matters. A booklet aimed at giving farmers assistance in the preparation of their income tax returns was written by Martin and sold locally. The publication was a huge success and the proprietor of the Hay general shop was so impressed that he displayed a placard in his window proclaiming 'Martin's *Farmers' Tax Book'*. This put Armstrong in a bad mood and he told the shopkeeper, 'Solicitors are not allowed to advertise, I will show him'. From that moment Martin was cast in the true role of rival.

Of course the two men had a professional relationship which was conducted with courtesy but there was nothing more, no real social aquaintance or friendship. Armstrong set great store by an adherence to manners and it was an important feature of his personality; rarely did he display any open animosity or bad grace. But while the two rivals conducted business from their offices in Broad Street, Armstrong was forced to take account of another problem nearer home—his wife's behaviour.

Katharine Armstrong was a plain woman, slightly built and of medium height. Her eyes tended to protrude giving her face a staring quality and she was sightless in the left eye as the result of a cycling accident before she was married. She was recognized as a pianist of some merit and was respected by her servants and neighbours for the way in which she ran her home. People in Hay still remember Major and Mrs Armstrong. Mr Eddie Williams recalled Armstrong walking to work, 'the typical army major, dapper and straight as a ramrod. He sometimes carried a swagger stick under his arm'. Beside him, Mrs Armstrong looked tall and gawky and they struck people as an ill-assorted couple. They were known as 'Mutt and Jeff' on account of the difference in height, and the less respectful giggled and turned away when they approached. But the physical disparity was not the only characteristic of the Armstrongs—there was also mental incompatibility. It became increasingly obvious to everyone who knew or met them that Katharine's urge to dominate her husband was reaching pathological proportions. She belittled him and held him up to public ridicule in ways which embarrassed those present but produced only acquiescence in the little man.

Mrs Armstrong was a strong opponent of alcohol in any

shape or form and hated smoking. She allowed her husband to smoke in only one room of the house and never out of doors. If he broke the rules and had a crafty pipe of tobacco while out alone, the merest chance that Katharine would appear on the scene caused him to hide the pipe away. Wine and spirits were vigorously denied him. At dinner parties Herbert's glass was never allowed to be filled. Katharine would shoo away the servant with the wine bottle with the curt command, 'No wine for the Major'. On rare occasions, if he had a cold for example, he might be permitted a glass of port. Otherwise it was strictly teetotal whether he liked it or not.

Armstrong was rebuked in front of the servants for being a few minutes late for a meal at his own table. How could he expect the servants to keep good time if the master was late, chastized Katharine. On another occasion, she dragged him away from a tennis match loudly declaring that he must come home as it was his bath night. Poor Herbert, racket at the droop, followed dumbly as he was bid.

Such restrictions imposed on anyone who had not led the most cloistered of lives would have been intolerable. But Armstrong accepted this tyranny without complaint and always behaved with perfect grace and consideration to his wife. At church he would fuss over the opening or closing of the window near their pew to ensure that she was not in a draught.

There were those in Hay who thought Mrs Armstrong a good, well-meaning woman but a bit hard on the Major; there were others who thought she was a perfect bitch. The most universal reaction to this unnatural domination was of sympathy for the little man who behaved so admirably. Most people thought them an odd but nevertheless affectionate couple.

Despite outward appearances it could hardly be expected that this situation would not create some kind of response. The immediate reaction it seems was for both parties to withdraw into themselves; Mrs Armstrong developed hypochondria to a marked degree and the Major sustained himself with the various public interests in which he commanded respect and authority. For both husband and wife, these reactions provided escape from a life completely lacking in domestic intimacy.

Mrs Armstrong soon deteriorated into a humourless eccentric who shunned physical contact; when walking along the pavements of Hay she would draw her coat close about her to avoid touching passers by. She had long been something of a hypochondriac, although those who were well disposed towards her said that she was delicate in health. Now she took to dosing herself with a variety of homeopathic medicines some of which were kept in a cabinet in her bedroom. The medicines were bought from Macsymon's Stores in Liverpool and the Major often ordered them for her by post. There were orders for Tincture *Lachesis*, 'not the smallest size (6½d) but the next size larger (9d)', for Tincture *Nux Vomica, Mercur Sol* Powder, *Aconitum Nap* Pillules and many others. Sometimes the need was so great that the medicines were ordered by telegram.

If Mrs Armstrong's escape from realism was aided by hypochondria, her husband's outlet was a passion for gardening, although he preferred to leave the real labour to his hired help. 'I have always had considerable trouble with weeds on the path of my vegetable garden', said the Major. He grew to loathe those weeds and got down to the serious business of exterminating them. From 1912 onwards he bought large quantities of weed-killing agents which he kept in various tins, jars and containers, including an old Cognac bottle. With these he waged war on the weeds which grew in the paths around Mayfield.

When the fit took him Armstrong, attired in breeches and trench boots, would set to work with his death-dealing chemicals, using either proprietary weed-killers or arsenical preparations made up to his own formula. 'I have dabbled in chemistry', he boasted to the local chemist when being offered advice. But he was fighting a losing battle as his long list of arsenic purchases over the years testifies. Nevertheless, he applied himself with neurotic energy and systematically treated single offending weeds with individual doses of weedicide from a special applicator.

This was Armstrong at his most fastidious but he also delighted in self-advertisement. An example of this was his design of an office seal for stamping documents. The duties of a Notary Public required such a seal and it was customary for the die to bear the words 'Notary Public' and the official's name. Armstrong took the unusual step of incorporating on his seal a motif depicting a mailed arm and hand. The 'Armstrong–strong arm' correlation is obvious but such flamboyance was unheard of in what was and still is a highly conservative profession.

Armstrong was an educated, well-read man and kept a good library at Mayfield. in fact, Oswald Martin was in the habit of borrowing books from him. But again he had to let the world know how clever he was. His letters and diaries frequently contained expressions in French, such as, 'très distraite', 'entre nous' and 'au contraire', in contexts which did not require them, though in a letter to a friend he described his French as 'a la Stratford atte Bow' like that of Chaucer's Prioress.

Herbert Rowse Armstrong made up for his small size by cultivating a social position which kept him in the forefront of local affairs. The Army, Church and Freemasons helped to consolidate his image as a prominent citizen, while his fussing over trivialities fed his vanity.

Despite the esteem in which he was held by the people of Hay, the Major was still a mouse in his own home. He appeared to accept his wife's domination, but the way she humiliated him must have hurt.

In the society of the 1920s, the husband was very definitely head of household and chief decision maker. He was assisted in this role by whatever degree of participation he deemed appropriate to his wife. At Mayfield the roles were reversed, and common knowledge of the fact brought the little Major a lot of sympathy.

It does not take much imagination to see the men of Hay discussing the unfortunate lot of their henpecked solicitor in the town's pubs and clubs. 'Poor old Armstrong. He can only smoke in one room of the house you know', or, 'His wife won't let him drink, not even at parties—"no wine for the Major" she says.' No doubt the feelings of sympathy were superseded by criticism and advice. That, too, can be imagined.

* * * * *

Mrs Armstrong first became ill in 1919. In May, she attended the Broad Street surgery of Dr Thomas Ernest Hincks complaining of pain in the right arm, particularly in the shoulder joint, and of a numb sensation in the fingers. She gave a history of rheumatism and the doctor diagnosed her complaint as brachial neuritis. Her physical condition was good and there was no evidence of heart disease.

This neuritis improved by July and apart from some bilious attacks in August Mrs Armstrong had no occasion to consult the doctor for several months. The following year, on 15th August, Major Armstrong asked Dr Hincks if he might have a sleeping draught for his wife who was restless and unable to sleep. Hincks saw Mrs Armstrong on the 18th and 20th August and on these occasions it was evident that her mental health had declined. She was suffering from delusions and her speech was affected. Hincks examined her and detected a mitral murmur of the heart; he also found albumen in the urine.

Major Armstrong was concerned about his wife and on the 21st he sent a telegram to Ida Bessie Friend, his wife's sister who lived at Teignmouth. She responded quickly and Armstrong met her at Hereford and took her back to Mayfield. They were joined there by Arthur Chevalier, an old family friend who had come down from Liverpool. Chevalier, a solicitor and executor of Mrs Armstrong's will, had been contacted by Armstrong two days previously. Armstrong told him about his wife's delusions and Chevalier '. . . formed the opinion that she ought to have attention. When I suggested she should go away from home, and that he should see Dr Hincks about it, Major Armstrong at once went with me to see Dr Hincks.'

Hincks was worried about Mrs Armstrong's mental condition and on the 22nd he decided to seek a second opinion. He telephoned Dr Frederick James Jayne, a general practitioner in neighbouring Talgarth, to discuss his patient and asked him to come and see her. Jayne went straight to Mayfield; Hincks had left by the time he arrived. He spent about twenty minutes talking to Major Armstrong and then examined his wife. Jayne thought, 'Mrs Armstrong was pale and thin and presented a very sad picture. She was very listless and seemed to take no interest in my conversation with

her. I had some difficulty in getting her to speak at all, and
when I did succeed I came to the conclusion that she was of
unsound mind.' Mrs Armstrong told the doctor that she lived
an un-Christian life, had been unkind to her children and had
defrauded tradespeople.

As Jayne was about to leave, Hincks returned to Mayfield
and together with Major Armstrong they discussed what was
to be done. The doctors agreed that Mrs Armstrong should be
certified as insane and sent for treatment to Barnwood, a
private asylum near Gloucester. Major Armstrong agreed with
this course of action after discussing it thoroughly with
Chevalier and Hincks.

It was not possible to certify Mrs Armstrong there and then
as neither doctor had the appropriate certificates with him.
Consequently, Dr Jayne returned to Talgarth and obtained
three Lunacy Certificates from Talgarth Mental Hospital.
He filled in and signed one certificate and sent it with the
other two forms to Dr Hincks by special messenger. The
procedure at that time for certifying a person as a lunatic
was that a reception order be given to the Superintendent of
the asylum. This order was obtained by the husband or
wife of the patient who signed a petition and accompanied
it with medical certificates signed by two doctors. One of
these signatures was normally that of the patient's regular
doctor, in this case Dr Hincks. He described Mrs Armstrong's
condition as melancholia with delusions and the only cause
he could adduce for it was the change of life; Jayne reached
much the same conclusion.

Armstrong's 'Petition for an order for reception of a private
patient . . . in the matter of Katharine Mary Armstrong, a
person alleged to be of unsound mind' was addressed to
Charles Tunnard Moore, a local magistrate. Armstrong simply
asked for his wife to be admitted to the asylum at Barnwood
and promised to visit her every six months.

The petition was accompanied by a 'Statement of particulars' and by a questionnaire containing twenty-three questions.
The most important of these, together with the replies given
by Armstrong, were as follows:

Q   What is the patient's natural temper and disposition,
      and favourite pursuit and tendency? Has she led an active

or sedentary life?

A   *Cheerful but anxious. Household duties and literary task.*

Q   Has she always been temperate and industrious?

A   *Yes. Total abstainer.*

Q   Has she at any time undergone any serious disappointment or reverse, pecuniary or otherwise?

A   *General strain in family care and household management during and since the war.*

Q   Before the patient manifested the symptoms of insanity, did she suffer from loss of sleep or appetite or exhibit any change in temper or disposition?

A   *Sleeplessness for ten days prior to reception and nervous excitement with slight irritability for some months prior.*

Q   What circumstances are supposed to have caused the mental disorder?

A   *Change of period of life.*

Q   In what manner has insanity shown itself?

A   *Delusions that she is being followed about; that she has neglected her family and husband and is liable to arrest.*

Q   Is the patient violent towards herself or others, and in what way? Or has she broken glass or furniture, torn clothes or bedding, or done mischief of any kind?

A   *No signs of violence: au contraire, apathy to surroundings and acute introspection.*

Q   Has she threatened or attempted self-destruction; if so, when, and by what means?

A   *No.*

Q   Is the patient's bodily health, good, bad or indifferent?

A   *Generally good but of livery tendency.*

Armstrong signed the completed petition, not missing the opportunity to add the little flourish, 'Major T.D.'. The magistrate duly added his signature to the order, and the papers which declared Mrs Armstrong a lunatic and asked for her to be admitted to an asylum were complete.

Dr Hincks had arranged for a car and driver to take the sick woman to Barnwood, but when he returned to Mayfield at mid-afternoon he found her physical condition had deteriorated. He was concerned about her fitness to travel. At that time her lips were blue, she had a pulse of 120 and complained of stomach pains. She had been vomiting but made light of this by telling Hincks she was subject to bilious attacks.

As the necessary arrangements had been made to admit Mrs Armstrong to Barnwood, Hincks thought the best course was to get her there as soon as possible. She was accompanied on the car journey by her husband and sister; Dr Hincks sat with the driver and took the precaution of putting a basin in the car. On reaching Barnwood, Hincks immediately consulted with Dr Arthur Allen Deykin Townsend, the Medical Superintendent, while Mrs Armstrong was admitted.

The new patient was examined by the asylum's Assistant Medical Officer, Dr Janet Smith, who made up all the notes concerning Mrs Armstrong. At the time of admission Dr Smith made the entry: '. . . She has rather a careworn and tired expression. Complexion is very pale and sallow; she looks ill physically and there is sordes around her mouth. Temperature on admission, 100°; pulse 120'. The doctor detected two heart murmurs and a urine sample was found to contain a small amount of albumen. Apart from the patient's mental condition, the response of the nervous system was normal. There was no family history of insanity but from her youth Mrs Armstrong had been the kind of person to worry over small matters. That did not prevent her from leading a normal, active life until her recent delusions. Mrs Armstrong spoke of neglecting her husband and family and of committing crimes for which she would be arrested. She had never been violent and had made no attempt at suicide.

The day following his wife's certification and admission to Barnwood, Major Armstrong wrote to Dr Townsend enclosing the agreement for her reception and a cheque for £81 18s. 0d. which represented one quarter's payment in advance.

The patient was sedated and given fluids, with the result that her temperature and pulse rate came down within two days. By the end of the month she was taking some solid food but was still weak and depressed. Dr Smith's report for 7th September noted, 'There is loss of power in hands and feet with wasting of the muscles'. The patient's limbs were massaged twice daily and a general tonic prescribed. There was little improvement during September and October and on 15th October Dr Townsend wrote to Major Armstrong: 'I am sorry we have come to the conclusion that Mrs Armstrong is suffering from neuritis which is involving both hands, feet and legs; this gives her feelings of discomfort and she has some loss of power and co-ordination. What the exact cause is it is difficult to say, it is probably toxaemic.' A few days later, Dr Soutar of Cheltenham was called in to examine Mrs Armstrong and his diagnosis that she was suffering from neuritis confirmed the opinion of the Barnwood physicians.

On 3rd November, Dr Smith reported, 'There is slight improvement both in mental and physical condition.' Two weeks later Mrs Armstrong was able to get out of bed for the first time in three months and to walk a few steps with help. Despite the fact that she continued to worry and fret, her progress continued and by 12th December she was able to walk unaided and her general health was much improved.

A possible cause for Mrs Armstrong's condition was suggested by the Major to be 'change of life' and this view was also put forward by Dr Jayne. It was certainly the case that when Mrs Armstrong was admitted to Barnwood she menstruated for the first time in nearly a year. This was probably due to the upset caused by her illness and then being taken from her familiar home surroundings and admitted to hospital. If Mrs Armstrong was experiencing the menopause with all the physiological and psychological adjustment that involved it might have exacerbated her already estranged relationship with her husband. Less congenial aspects of a woman's character, such as bad temper and bouts of depression, come to the fore at this time. In Katharine Armstrong's case, the menopause might have accounted for her shrew-like behaviour to her husband when he came home after four years' military service.

With her return to better health Mrs Armstrong began to take a serious interest in her affairs again. She wrote twice to Arthur Chevalier and on the 31st December sent a letter asking:

'A huge request. Will you, if at all possible, come and see me on urgent business tomorrow or Monday? I never showed you a document in which your name occurs.

Oh do come for love of my husband and children, I am
unworthy.
With kindest regards,
Yours sincerely,
K. M. Armstrong.
I improve, but do come without delay.'

The document referred to was Mrs Armstrong's will and
she took this up again with her sister Bessie. In a letter dated
11th January, she wrote, 'I forgot to ask where is my original
will, I think all executors ought to know. Will you tell Arthur?
Is it with yours?'

Mrs Armstrong had made a will, dated 17th January 1917,
in which she made bequests to the children and left £50 per
annum to her husband. She gave this will, for which Arthur
Chevalier was an executor, into the care of her sister, Bessie
Friend, keeping only an epitome among her private papers
at Mayfield .

But in August 1920, when Mrs Armstrong was taken ill and
sent to Barnwood, Bessie Friend learned that there was
another will. She spoke to Major Armstrong about it and
he said, 'Yes, that is all right, she had made another.' Bessie
thought this quite in order because Mrs Armstrong had
spoken to her about altering her will, saying, 'I do not
think I have left enough for my husband.'

Mrs Armstrong was also concerned about her release from
the asylum and now that she felt better quite naturally
wanted to get back to her husband and children. Major
Armstrong visited her about twice a month and she implored
him to seek her release.

In a letter to Arthur Chevalier on the 2nd January the
Major wrote 'As soon as I can persuade the MO [sic] that
she can be moved I shall have her back as I don't think she
will improve in the least where she is. When she finds she is
really back she will pick up as she is certainly physically
better. It is quite clear the loss of power was functional and
not organic—they had to call it neuritis for want of a better
name'. Mrs Armstrong left her sister in no doubt as to her
wishes when she wrote on the 17th, 'I would never have come
had I realised that I was losing my liberty . . . My dear old boy
says he will fetch me this week . . . I wish you would wire to
H. not to delay a day in fetching me: I am miserable and
aching to go home.'

On 11th January, Hincks wrote to Dr Townsend on the Major's behalf saying that he was glad to hear that Mrs Armstrong was improving both mentally and physically: 'From what Major Armstrong tells me she appears to have lost her delusions and to be normal mentally. Her principal worry seems to be her surroundings and her anxiety to get back home to start her household duties again.' Hincks suggested that Armstrong should call at Barnwood after taking his eldest child back to school at Bath and take his wife home with him. Two days before Hincks wrote this letter, Dr Smith had noted in her report on Mrs Armstrong, 'There is some improvement, but she is still depressed and accuses herself of having failed in her duty to her family.' But the doctor concluded that her 'general health has much improved. She walks without difficulty.'

Dr Townsend was surprised at this formal request for Mrs Armstrong's release and he wrote to Hincks, 'In my opinion she is not yet well mentally.' Nevertheless, taking into account the improvements which had taken place and in view of Mrs Armstrong's strongly expressed wish to return home, he suggested that she should be given 'leave of absence on trial for three months'. In the event that there was a relapse she could return quickly to Barnwood without recertification. Hincks passed on Dr Townsend's suggestion but Major Armstrong was not too happy about it. He wrote to Townsend on the 14th: 'After careful consideration I do not wish my wife to avail herself of this and prefer that she be released.' He went on to say in his letter that he thought his wife's delusions had absolutely ceased and he felt sure that she would benefit by returning home. He said that he would like to collect her on Saturday, 22nd January.

Dr Townsend remained firm in his view concerning Mrs Armstrong's fitness to be released and he told Armstrong that it would be impossible for him to discharge her as recovered. This seemed to settle the question of the terms of release and Mrs Armstrong duly went home to Mayfield. Townsend was not at Barnwood when she left but Armstrong later wrote the following letter to him, dated 24th January 1921.

Dear Dr Townsend,
 I was sorry not to have seen you on Saturday, but you

will be glad to hear that we had a comfortable journey and Mrs Armstrong is none the worse. I have been able to disabuse her mind of some absurd ideas and no doubt the others will also vanish. I fear from what she has told me, she has been rather a trying patient. Personally I am grateful to you for the care you took while she was there.

As to my last a/c, the treasurer has £81-18-0 which will have borne bank interest since 24th Aug. 1920. Will you ask the treasurer to put one against the other; there may be a little due from or to me, but he can adjust this.

Yours sincerely,
H. Rowse Armstrong

In his reply, Dr Townsend said that there was no accrued interest on the advanced deposit. He added, 'I shall hope that at a later date to hear that you are able to report that Mrs Armstrong is perfectly well.'

* * * * *

When Mrs Armstrong returned to Mayfield she could not walk very well but was naturally pleased to be home. The next day, Major Armstrong telephoned Muriel Gladys Kinsey, a local nurse, requesting her to come and look after his wife who he said was weak and not able to manage by herself. The nurse went to Mayfield in the mornings and evenings. She described Mrs Armstrong's physical condition as good—she was able to walk about the house and go upstairs, but thought her mental condition was weak.

Dr Hincks called at the house on the 25th January, not specifically to see Mrs Armstrong, but to attend the house-keeper, Emily Ellis Pearce. However, he was shown into the drawing room where he was greeted by Mrs Armstrong. He was a little apprehensive as he thought she might bear him some resentment for having certified her and sent her to Barnwood. But her greeting was friendly and the doctor 'noticed nothing wrong with her that day'.

Within a day or two of being home Mrs Armstrong asked Nurse Kinsey if 'it would be sufficient to kill anyone if they threw themselves through the attic window'. The nurse reported this to Major Armstrong and also to Dr Hincks and concluded that Mrs Armstrong needed constant attention from someone more experienced in mental nursing. Several months previously, when Mrs Armstrong first experienced delusions, Arthur Chevalier had warned Major Armstrong that in his opinion she might try to commit suicide. He advised Armstrong to take precautions, such as putting his razors away, and the maids were told to keep a watchful eye on Mrs Armstrong at all times.

Major Armstrong realized that his wife should have a resident nursing attendant and so on the 27th January he sent a telegram to Eva Allen, a professionally trained nurse who lived at Cardiff. Nurse Allen answered the call at once and arrived at Mayfield that same evening. She relieved Nurse Kinsey and took charge of Mrs Armstrong whom she found to be very frail. Up to that time Major and Mrs Armstrong slept in the same room, but in separate beds. With the arrival of Nurse Allen, a new regime came into being; the Major moved into another room across the passage, and the nurse slept in the same room as her patient. Mrs Armstrong took her meals in the dining room with the rest of the family and her appetite was good.

From the moment that Mrs Armstrong became ill there were unmistakable signs of the Major's growing mastery at Mayfield. During this early period of convalescence, Katharine went into Hay and visited the general shop there. The proprietor thought how much better she looked and said so to Armstrong himself when he was in the shop a few days later. The Major, far from being pleased, seemed to be annoyed by the shopkeeper's remarks and denied that his wife had been in Hay at all since returning from hospital. Mrs Armstrong was never seen in the town again.

There were other more subtle changes too and these were reflected in Armstrong's diary. In 1919, among references to items of clothing sent to the laundry and records of when petrol and potatoes were bought, the most interesting engagements were meetings of the Bible Society and the Parochial Church Council. But in 1921, when his wife was ill, the Major had more exciting entries to make. There were trips to London and notes such as, '6 Jan—Whitney dance' and '14 Jan - Bachelors dance, Hay'.

About the end of January, Mrs Armstrong complained to Emily Pearce about her legs, saying that she felt as if there were weights attached to her feet. She used a stick when she went into the garden and complained of loss of power in her hands and sometimes found it difficult to hold things such as a teapot. She was depressed at times and imagined that strange things were happening around the house. She actually came downstairs in the middle of the night on one occasion looking for people she thought she heard there.

Apart from such mental aberrations, her general condition was satisfactory and after a visit on 30th January, Dr Hincks 'found really nothing wrong with her'. Mrs Armstrong celebrated her forty-eighth birthday on 8th February and those closest to her believed that her health was improving. Possibly they were not the best judges of the situation. Certainly, Nurse Kinsey, when she paid a social call on 10th February, was surprised at Mrs Armstrong's appearance. She was wasted, her skin had discoloured and she complained of having severe pains and of vomiting. Muriel Kinsey thought 'she looked like a jaundice case'.

Dr Hincks called on the 11th and saw Mrs Armstrong in the drawing room. She told him about the return of 'those curious feelings' in her feet which she described as 'springs pressing her up from the ground'. Hincks recalled that Dr Townsend had spoken of this condition while Mrs Armstrong was at Barnwood. The asylum doctor regarded the condition as functional rather than organic, that is, due not to disease or physical damage but to mental causes. Hincks, therefore, tried to persuade Mrs Armstrong that she could walk and he took her arm in an attempt to walk her around the drawing room. Her efforts showed a high-stepping gait; she raised each foot high off the ground and hesitated a long time before banging it down. She was unable to walk despite the doctor's assistance.

Hincks then decided to give her a thorough examination and he called the nurse to help him get Mrs Armstrong upstairs and into bed. It did not take long to establish that the knee-jerk was totally absent and that there was no ankle clonus (reflex of the ankle joint). The grip of Mrs Armstrong's hand was also diminished and she told the doctor that she could no longer knit or play the piano. Dr Hincks left Mayfield

concerned for his patient but so puzzled by her symptoms
that he was unable to form a definite diagnosis.

That weekend Mrs Armstrong ate her Sunday lunch with
the rest of the family and dined off boiled leg of mutton and
vegetables with junket and preserved gooseberries for
dessert. About twenty minutes after the meal, she started
vomiting. She had complained to Nurse Allen on various
occasions about feeling sick but this was the first time that she
had actually vomited. She was put to bed at once, and as none
of the others who had taken lunch with her was ill it was
assumed that she had suffered a bilious attack. She was, after
all, known to have poor digestion and to be prone to
biliousness.

She was slightly better on the following day and sat in the
porch wrapped in an eiderdown and was provided with hot
water bottles by Emily Pearce. This hardly seemed a good
idea for an invalid in the month of February, and as Emily
Pearce put it, it was from that day that 'Mrs Armstrong's
health changed for the worse'. She became very ill, and the
household assumed, not without reason, that she had caught
a chill. She took to her room and did not come downstairs
again except on the shoulders of the undertakers.

Dr Hincks was called on the 16th February and it was
plain that Mrs Armstrong's condition was serious. Her skin
was discoloured, she complained of constant abdominal
pain and her pulse was running at 120. She could not keep
solid food down and subsisted on milk and Benger's Food.
The house revolved around her needs and Nurse Allen
worked around the clock, taking only short breaks when she
was relieved at the sickbed by either Emily Pearce or Major
Armstrong.

Katharine Armstrong had never been a strong woman but
she was now reduced to a shadow of her real self. Her husband
altered his routine in order to spend more time with her. He
left for his office later in the mornings and returned an hour
earlier. He also took lunch at home every day save Thursday,
which was market day, and always looked in on his wife. In
the evenings he sat at the bedside and occasionally read to
her.

Dr Hincks now called daily and on the 17th he gave Mrs
Armstrong an injection of morphia to alleviate her pain. He

said that she was 'very acutely ill', a conclusion that Nurse
Allen had already arrived at for she had little rest day or
night ministering to her patient. The sick woman was still
vomiting and was so weak that she could not use the bathroom. This already distressing state was added to on the 19th
when Mrs Armstrong had diarrhoea. She was frightfully thin,
too weak even to sit up in bed and her skin had become a
very dark, copper colour. The doctor warned Major Armstrong
that he did not think he could pull his wife through.

During the early hours of the 22nd, Nurse Allen noticed a
change for the worse in her patient and her experience told
her that the end was probably near. Mrs Armstrong said to
Eva Allen, 'Nurse, I am not going to die, am I, because I have
everything to live for?' At 8 a.m. the maid was sent to fetch
Major Armstrong; he hurried to his wife and they conversed
for a brief moment. Dr Hincks was telephoned and he arrived
at about 9 a.m. By that time Mrs Armstrong had lost
consciousness and the doctor told Armstrong there was
nothing more he could do and he did not think she would
last the day out. Dr Hincks left to return to his surgery and
Major Armstrong asked him for a lift into his office as he had
a lot of work on hand.

Mrs Armstrong died at about ten minutes past nine. Only
Nurse Allen and the maid were present. Eva Allen was upset
and cried, probably with relief that the poor woman's agonies
were ended. She telephoned Armstrong at his office and told
him that his wife had died. The Major went to see Hincks at
his surgery but the doctor was out on his rounds. He then
returned to Mayfield and on his way telegraphed to Bessie
Friend who came to the house at 1.30 p.m. Armstrong's
diary entry for the day read, '22 Feb—K died'.

Nurse Allen asked the young maid, Inez Rosser, to help
her lay out the body. They found some white stockings and
while they were dressing the corpse one of the legs twitched
and frightened the maid out of her wits. After completing this
unpleasant task they pulled the curtains over the house in the
customary mark of respect to the deceased. The first thing
Major Armstrong did on his return was to open them.

Later in the day Armstrong sent an obituary notice to
the *Morning Post* and discussed the funeral arrangements
with Dr Hincks. The doctor made out the death certificate.

20 Sun—2nd in Lent. Sun sets 5.21

Nurse & boys here for night

Confirmation—Bishop at 6.0

21 Mon

K. worse. Beaven Wills ?

1 Tin Petrol

22 Tues—O Full Moon 9.32 a.m.

K. died

23 Wed

3 pm Camp Council

24 Th *wrote Arthur*

Arthur Came

Mrs Seymour Came

25 Fri *K. funeral 3 pm Cusop*

Mr & Mrs Way Came

26 Sat *Mrs Seymour ↲*

Arthur ↑

Memo

Armstrong's diary entries for the week commencing 20th February 1921

He gave the immediate cause of death as gastritis but mentioned heart disease and nephritis as contributary factors.

The second night after the death, with the body lying in its coffin in Mayfield's main bedroom, Armstrong said to Inez Rosser, '.. I want you to come and hold a candle for me'. The girl lighted the way to the bedroom and stood by the coffin as the Major soaped his wife's fingers and removed her rings.

DEATHS.

ARMSTRONG.—On February 22nd, at Mayfield Hay, Katharine Mary, the dearly-beloved wife of Major H. Rowse Armstrong, T.D.

Announcement of Mrs Armstrong's death in the *Morning Post*.

So Katharine Armstrong died exactly a month after leaving Barnwood. Dr Townsend learned of her death through a newspaper obituary notice and was surprised that Major Armstrong had not the courtesy to tell him. But Townsend wrote to him offering his deepest sympathy and asking, 'I did not hear that Mrs Armstrong had been ill; was there any sudden development?' There was no answer to this letter.

The funeral was fixed for 3 p.m. on 25th February at Cusop Church. Humphrey Vines Webb, the Hay undertaker, carried out all the arrangements. The oak coffin was made in his workshop and he himself engraved the inscription on the nameplate; *Katharine Mary Armstrong, born Feb. 8th, 1873, died Feb. 22nd, 1921, aged 48.* The inside of the coffin was lined with wadding, and domett and wood shavings were put under the bottom covering. Webb and his son lifted Mrs Armstrong's body into the coffin and some newspaper was put under the head to raise it to the proper level. When the coffin was carried out of Mayfield's front door to the hearse, Major Armstrong was in a front window alcove discussing the question of fishing rights with a client. The entry in his diary for that day read, 'K's funeral 3 p.m. Cusop. Mr & Mrs Way came'.

The *Brecon & Radnor Express* carried an announcement of the Major's loss under the heading, 'Death of Mrs Armstrong—A Popular Hay Lady'. The paper reported that 'Mrs Armstrong had passed the whole of her married life at Hay and had always identified herself with Church work and especially with foreign missions. Since the autumn of last year she had suffered from a nervous and physical breakdown and although a partial recovery had taken place the end came very unexpectedly . . .'.

The Rector of Cusop, the Reverend C.M. Buchanan, officiated at the funeral and the Vicar of Hay, the Reverend J.J. de Winton, read the lesson. The small number of mourners consisted of the family, friends, business associates and neighbours. Despite the description of the late Mrs Armstrong as 'a popular lady', it became a matter for general comment that so few attended her funeral.

The card on Armstrong's wreath read *From Herbert and the Chicks.* Among the floral tributes were tokens of respect and sympathy from the Office, Dr and Mrs Hincks, Mrs R.T. and Trevor Griffiths and one from Miss Pearce (Nana), *In loving memory of her dear friend.*

On the Sunday following the funeral there was a memorial service at Cusop Church. With the exception of Inez Rosser, who stayed behind at Mayfield to prepare lunch, the whole household attended. While she was alone in the kitchen of the empty house, Inez heard footsteps coming down the passage towards her and she was terrified when she thought she heard Mrs Armstrong's voice. The unexpected visitor turned out to be Bessie Friend, the dead woman's sister, who had left the church service early. Miss Friend bore a strong physical resemblance to her sister and had a similar manner and voice.

During this time when friends and relatives were gathered at Mayfield, Armstrong spoke privately to Arthur Chevalier. He said, 'I thought I ought to tell you that my wife has made a fresh will in which she has left everything to me and appointed me sole executor.' Chevalier asked, 'When did she make it?' and Armstrong replied, 'In the Summer.'

2   Excuse Fingers

*. . . he has continually endeavoured to get me to his
house for tea again . . .*

Oswald Norman Martin

DR THOMAS ERNEST HINCKS, 'Dr Tom' to the locals,
had practised in Hay since 1898. His surgery was near the
clock-tower in Broad Street. He was a big man with a ruddy,
outdoor complexion and a black moustache. There were few
homes in the district which had not welcomed his reassuring
presence at one time or another. Mounted on horseback in
full cry to attend birth, sickness or death, Dr Tom was one
of the institutions of Hay.

Hincks was in every respect the country G.P. and his wide-
spread practice was a wealthy one. He liked hunting, salmon
fishing and horticulture and had the knack of putting all his
patients at their ease by his understanding of social as well as
medical problems.

During the 1914-18 war, Hincks served with the Royal
Army Medical Corps in France and the Middle East. Military
medicine was a world away from the farming accidents,
diphtheria and scarlet fever which were his usual lot as a
doctor. Hincks worked in a social setting where the doctor
was also a friend. He attended the sick not only at their
bedsides but also by chatting over their troubles at the farm-
yard gate or while out for a day's shooting.

The country G.P. may have lacked some of the lustre of
the town doctor but he had to be a master of all the medical
arts, acting as consultant and performing his own post-
mortems. He also had to be inventive. Hincks, for example,
when he bought a car had it fitted with a stretcher attachment enabling him to take patients quickly into hospital.
His car was known affectionately as 'Uncle Tom's Cabin'.

Doctor Hincks did have one distinct advantage over his
town counterpart—he could think over diagnostic problems
while riding across the countryside on visits to patients. For
one thing, the late Katharine Armstrong's illness continued
to perplex him—Tom Hincks was soon to enter the story

again.

* * * * *

Emily Pearce said that after his wife's death Major Armstrong was 'nervy and unable to work; a little later he went to the South of Italy'. Armstrong applied for a passport on 13th March and on the 18th he entered in his diary, 'Left Victoria 7.10; Dover to Calais, Paris night train'. He spent twelve days in Italy and then travelled on to Malta. By that time his nervousness seemed to have vaporized for his diary contained a stream of engagements.

1 April	*Rigoletto* with Susan
2	Joliffe to dine club
5	Lunch at Bridges 1.30 p.m.
	Dine with Symons 7.15
6	*La Traviata* with Miss B
7	10 a.m. Miss Buchanan
	8.30 Buchanans' dance
8	10 a.m. Miss Buchanan
	11 Miss McRae
9	Motor ride S. Pauls Bay. I and Miss B.
12	10 a.m. Miss B
15	'Billeted' with Miss B

Armstrong left Malta on the 19th April and returned to London travelling by way of Rome and Paris. It appeared that the Major had cut quite a dash while on holiday. Certainly his diary for that period revealed an entirely different tone from the previous year's entries on such mundane matters as weeding the rosebeds and noting his junior clerk's salary increase.

The day after returning to England, Armstrong noted in his diary on the 29th April, 'Stay Ford Cottage. Ask MG'. The mysterious 'MG' turned up again in the diary and later stayed at Mayfield. The following week 8th May, Armstrong wrote to Arthur Chevalier, 'My dear Arthur—Once more I am back—arrived home a week ago and I am glad to say am quite fit again. You wouldn't know me for the same person, and I can now face the future with a correct sense of proportion which I had temporarily lost'.

Major Armstrong's growing self-assertion during the time

that his wife was ill was completed after she died. He was indeed a different person—something of the merry widower in fact. He joined in many social activities, took dancing lessons, travelled, entertained at Mayfield and no doubt smoked and drank as the fancy took him. A contemporary remembered seeing Armstrong at the local half-crown 'hops' where he used to make passes at the local girls, mostly teenagers: 'Will you come down and have some refreshments with me?' he used to ask. It was thought odd that the highly respected Magistrates Clerk should behave in such a fashion and he was regarded as 'a bit of a dasher' with the girls.

It is likely that the Major's sexual life had been an early victim of his wife's unnatural domination over him, not to mention her dislike of physical contact. The insights gleaned from his soldiering days added to his natural appetite and ensured that he looked for and found female companions. He was also contemplating re-marrying.

Life was being very good to Armstrong at this time and after his Continental holiday he received the pleasant confirmation that he was to inherit his late wife's money. Probate of her will was granted to him on 30th May 1921—the net amount was £2278 3s. 0d.

* * * * *

Only one cloud lurked on the horizon and threatened to spoil Major Armstrong's new lease of life. His business rival, Oswald Martin, was doing very well at his expense.

Oswald Norman Martin was a native of Tewkesbury and completed his training as a solicitor in 1913 just before the outbreak of war. His first post was in London where he hoped to gain useful professional experience but his career was hardly begun before the war intervened. Martin joined the London Scottish Regiment and was sent to France where he saw a good deal of active service. He was wounded in the face at Bullecourt in August 1918 and was sent home to England with shrapnel wounds in the neck and jaw. He was in hospital at Plymouth for six months and was eventually demobilized in February 1919. Martin did not attain commissioned rank during his war service but remained a private for the whole time.

After demobilization, he contacted Mr Robert Griffiths in Hay concerning a partnership in his business. Griffiths who was in his sixties and suffered ill health, was looking for someone to help him in his busy legal practice. He sized up this quiet young man who had served his country and suffered partial facial paralysis as a result, and decided to give him three months' trial before admitting him as a full partner. The serious-minded Martin worked hard, winning the older man's confidence and eventually became a partner in July 1919.

During these early months of Martin's partnership with Griffiths, Armstrong was still in the army; he returned to Hay in the autumn of 1919. Martin was first introduced to Armstrong when the latter called at Griffiths's office to discuss a business matter. Two months later, Martin received an invitation to take tea with Major and Mrs Armstrong on a Saturday afternoon at Mayfield. It was not the most joyous occasion, for Armstrong seemed to be put out that Griffiths had taken on a partner, and Mrs Armstrong looked slightly askance at Martin's casual sports jacket and flannels. But all the pleasantries were observed and Martin stayed for a couple of hours conversing with his hosts.

In November, Mr Griffiths died and Martin conducted the business on his own, but with the prospect of Trevor Griffiths, the old man's son, joining him when he qualified. Martin and Armstrong met frequently in the course of business and it often happened that they acted for the respective partners in property sales. Their relationship on the professional level was cool and social contact was almost negligible.

In a sense their relationship was symbolically cast as one of opposition. They were the only two solicitors in a small town, so that there was a certain amount of competition for business; their offices were on opposite sides of the same street; to a very great extent each knew the other's business, whether private or otherwise; and finally their lives and personalities were completely different. Armstrong was an attention seeker with an unhappy home-life, Martin was reserved, quietly successful, with a modest house and car, happily married and content with family ties.

In June 1921, Oswald Martin married Constance Muriel Davies, the daughter of the local chemist, at Cusop Church. After their honeymoon, they went to live at Radnor View,

Cusop, but soon after moving in they changed the name of
the house to Bredon Hill. Major Armstrong sent the couple
a wedding gift of two salt-cellars and some spoons which
the Martins acknowledged in a letter bearing the new house
name. Armstrong was invited to one of the Martins' 'At
Homes' and he lingered on talking long after the other guests
had departed.

There undoubtedly existed a sort of veiled tension between
the two men and it was perhaps inevitable that they would
clash. The crisis point came with the projected sale of the
Velinnewydd Estate at Brecon. The property belonged to Mr
John Williams Vaughan who towards the end of 1919
decided to sell it. The estate was broken up into lots and
two of the principal purchasers, represented by Mr Lewis
Jones, a Brecon solicitor, paid a deposit of £500 to Major
Armstrong, the vendor's solicitor. Completion of the sale was
fixed for February 1920 but that date came and went without
the contract being finalized. Mr Lewis Jones pressed Armstrong repeatedly, asking why completion had been held up.
Armstrong spoke of difficulties having to be cleared away and
promised to see the thing through, but despite all representa-
tions the matter dragged on for over a year.

During July 1921, events took a decisive turn when Mr
Lewis James died unexpectedly in Brecon. The previous
day he had journeyed fruitlessly to Hay to try to persuade
Armstrong to complete the outstanding sale. It was at this
point that Oswald Martin, just recently married, entered the
scene, for in August he was asked by the intending purchasers
to act on their behalf. He wasted no time. On 6th August he
wrote to Armstrong asking him for a statement of the exact
position regarding the sale, and sought 'the reason why
completion had been delayed such an excessively long time'.
He followed his letter with a personal visit to Armstrong's
office two days later. Armstrong told him that there was
some slight difficulty which might delay completion for a
day or two but he did not say exactly what it was.

Martin, like the late Lewis Jones, made several representa-
tions to Armstrong but on each occasion came away empty
handed. He even sent Armstrong duplicate sets of documents
to save time. Not without good reason, the buyers were
running out of patience and they instructed Martin to give

notice to Armstrong that unless completion was settled on 20th October the contracts would be rescinded and demands made for repayment of the deposits together with costs and expenses. Before writing, Martin did the friendly thing and on 26th September he told Armstrong of his clients' instructions.

That same day Martin sent the draft conveyances to Armstrong by registered post with a letter giving formal notice that the buyers required completion by the 20th October or the return of the deposit money. A few days before this ultimatum was due, Armstrong told Martin that there still remained some difficulty. Whatever the difficulty was Armstrong kept it to himself and did not even discuss it with his own client. Mr Williams Vaughan had dealt with Armstrong for twelve years and was as anxious as the purchasers to complete this particular sale. He pressed Armstrong repeatedly about the delay but never obtained a satisfactory answer, or so he later claimed to the police.

The two buyers, determined to see through this long drawn-out business, called at Martin's office with the balance of the purchase money on the day appointed for completion. Martin telephoned Armstrong about midday asking him if he was ready to tie up the deal. The Major said that he was not and Martin replied that in accordance with his clients' instructions he would have to rescind both contracts. Armstrong then asked Martin as a personal favour to persuade his clients to give him a further week. Martin would not agree to this but did consent to Armstrong's request to talk to the two purchasers himself. This was a most strange occurrence in legal work of this kind. Nevertheless it was agreed, and Armstrong went over to Martin's office and spoke to the two purchasers. Martin was present as Armstrong, in a state of some distress, pleaded for a further week to complete. On Martin's advice the purchasers refused; they demanded the issue of notices withdrawing the contracts and requesting the return of their deposits. Martin carried out these wishes and the formal notices were sent by registered post, being delivered to Armstrong's office the following day, 21st October.

At the very moment when their relationship was at its most tense. Armstrong extended to Martin the first of a succession of invitations to tea. Would he take tea at Mayfield that afternoon? Martin said he could not manage it. What about Saturday then? No, that was not possible either. Well then, what about Sunday? No, unfortunately that was inconvenient too. This strange little game was ended when Martin said that he could manage Monday, although, in the event, he had to put if off until Wednesday, 26th October. The time was arranged for 5 p.m. and on Wednesday morning, Martin suggested that they should both drive up to Mayfield in his car. Armstrong declined, saying, 'No, I have something to do at the house so must go there before you.'

Martin was detained at his office for a few minutes and arrived at Mayfield at about 5.10 p.m. after driving the short distance from Hay. When he arrived, Armstrong was in the garden talking to his jobbing gardener, Robert McGeorge; they were discussing some work that was to be done. It was getting dusk as Martin joined his host and listened to the Major's plans for improving the house and garden. After ten minutes or so, they went into the house and on entering the drawing room, Armstrong told his housekeeper, Emily Pearce, that they would take tea. Martin sat in a chair near the window and Armstrong sat facing him.

Miss Pearce had been told the previous day that Mr Martin was coming to tea and she and the maid, Harriet Price, had made the necessary preparations. The table had been laid about 4.15. Plain scones with currants in them had been made by Emily Pearce in Mayfield's kitchen and she had also cut and buttered both plain and currant bread. The food was put on plates which in turn were placed on a three-tier cake stand. This was set in front of the oval table on which the crockery, milk and sugar had already been placed. There was no butter or jam on the table. All was now ready for the two men, except for making the tea. Major Armstrong was in the house while these preparations were being made and Emily Pearce asked him if the table would do as it had been laid. He said it would.

When Martin arrived and was seated in the drawing room, Emily Pearce told Harriet Price to make the tea. This she did and took it into the drawing room where she placed the best teapot and hot-water jug on the table in front of Major Armstrong who said, 'Thank you'.

Darkness was falling quickly as Armstrong poured Martin

a cup of tea and then handed him a buttered scone with the apology, 'Excuse fingers'. While Martin was eating the scone, Armstrong lit the gas-lamp in the room. Fumbling in the half-light, he dislodged the globe which fell to the floor and broke. Armstrong was also eating and he put a plate of buttered, currant bread on the table for his guest.

Martin thought that the reason for being asked to tea at Mayfield was to discuss business matters but Armstrong spoke of being lonely and not liking to have tea alone in the evening. Martin was fond of currant bread. He ate several slices and had a second cup of tea. They smoked, and conversation turned to office organization. No matters of importance, such as the repayment of deposits in the Velinnewydd sale, were discussed.

Before Martin left, the Reverend C.M. Buchanan, Rector of Cusop, called at the house and Armstrong went out of the room and spoke to him in his study. They conversed for about fifteen minutes and Armstrong saw him out. Shortly after that, at about 6.30, Martin took his leave. He said that he had arranged for his clerk to call at his house to finish off some work. Armstrong did not press him to stay and he left in his car. Within a few minutes Armstrong also left, telling Harriet Price, 'I am going down to the office and shall be back for supper'.

Martin arrived home a few minutes after 6.30, put the car away and went into the house. In answer to his wife's question about what he had eaten for tea Martin replied, 'Oh, some currant bread and butter, and scones.' He had expected to find his clerk waiting for him, but Alan Preen did not reach the house until 6.45. Preen apologized for being late and Martin said, 'It is quite all right, I have only just got in myself from Mr Armstrong's.'

Martin and his clerk started work straight away and at 7.30 Mrs Martin announced that supper was ready. Martin said, 'I feel sick, I do not think I can eat anything,' but his wife urged him to have something, saying, 'You will feel better after it.'

The Martins had their supper of hot jugged rabbit and cold coffee cream in another room; Preen carried on working. Martin had little appetite and he just picked at the meal. Within half an hour he had finished and rejoined his clerk.

Mrs Martin brought them both some coffee and Preen thought that his employer was irritable and looked somewhat yellow. Suddenly, without saying anything, Martin left the room and at about 8.45 Mrs Martin told Preen that there was no more work to be done that evening. The clerk collected up his papers and left.

The reason for Martin's abrupt departure was that he was feeling very sick and had hurried to the bathroom. He was not sick then but felt very ill; he came downstairs and lay on the settee. About 9.15 he again rushed to the bathroom and was violently sick. He vomited several times before going to bed and was sick at intervals throughout the night. The worst bouts of vomiting were accompanied by severe pain, but despite feeling very ill he noticed that the vomit was dark and foul smelling. He also felt shivery and his wife made up a hot water bottle and provided him with mouth washes.

Mrs Martin was worried about her husband and wanted to call the doctor. That would have meant sending the maid into Hay as they had no telephone. Martin said he would prefer to wait until the morning.

The early stages of the sickness produced between a quarter and a half pint of vomit on each occasion; it was dark reddish-brown in colour and Mrs Martin, who had served as a nurse during the war, was afraid the violent straining would cause a haemorrhage. Her natural good sense and nursing experience served her well; she kept her head and did everything possible to make her husband comfortable. As the night wore on, the sickness gradually abated, the vomit becoming lighter in colour although no less foul smelling. During the early hours of the morning, Martin had diarrhoea and noticed that his heart was beating at a very rapid rate.

At about 6 a.m. Mrs Martin telephoned Dr Hincks from a nearby house. She asked the doctor to come as soon as he could. He arrived at 9 a.m. and examined Martin. The sick man's temperature was normal, his tongue was clean; there was slight abdominal pain and his pulse rate was high at 120 (the normal pulse is 72 - 80). In answer to the doctor's questions, Martin said he had been perfectly well the previous day and had not eaten anything indigestible. He mentioned that he had taken tea in the early part of the evening with Major Armstrong. 'What did you have for tea?' asked Hincks.

'A currant bun and two cups of tea', replied Martin.

Dr Hincks assured Martin that his sickness was 'merely a bilious attack brought on by overwork and lack of exercise'. He told Mrs Martin that her husband was to have no food but could take some plain soda water with a little lemon. The doctor also gave Martin two tabloids of calomel and applied a mustard plaster to his stomach.

Later that morning, at about 9.45 a.m., even before going to his own office, Armstrong appeared at Martin's premises in Broad Street, 'Could I see Mr Martin?', he asked. Alan Preen, who had seen Armstrong come down the lane *en route* from Mayfield and come direct to Martin's office, told him that Martin had not yet arrived. The Major went out, but returned again at 11 a.m. and asked the same question. This time he was told that news had been received that 'Mr Martin was bad'. Forty-five minutes later, Armstrong again went across the street. This time he spoke to a junior clerk who had just returned to the office from the Martin home. In reply to questions, the girl said that Mr Martin had been up all night with a bilious attack.

Armstrong called again at 2 p.m. and 3.30 p.m., although on those occasions he had business to attend to in that he needed to see documents relating to a sale. While talking to Preen about Martin's illness, Armstrong said, 'It looks rather bad because he was up at my house to tea last night.' Preen and the other employees in Martin's office treated this as a joke and Armstrong joined in the laughter.

Dr Hincks had returned to his surgery after visiting Martin on Thursday morning satisfied that he had treated a case of severe bilious attack; he had taken as a jest a remark about poison made at the bedside by Mrs Martin. The doctor's mind was on other things when Major Armstrong appeared at the surgery door: 'You were up at Cusop early this morning and you visited my confrere. What's the matter with him?' 'Oh', replied Hincks, 'he's got a bilious attack.'

On Friday morning, Major Armstrong called on Martin at Bredon Hill. The maid showed him into the drawing room where he saw Mrs Martin. He said that he had called to ask how her husband was. Mrs Martin said, 'He is better, thank you'. Armstrong seemed somewhat surprised at this: 'Oh! Better? He is subject to these attacks, isn't he? Hasn't he had

jaundice?' Mrs Martin said that her husband had never had
jaundice and she went on to tell Armstrong of the violent
sickness and how they were unable to account for it.
Armstrong then changed the subject and told Mrs Martin,
'Your husband and I have several matters in hand together
just now and it is most inconvenient that he should be ill, but
tell him that everything that I can do to assist him I shall be
most pleased to do. I will treat his business as if it were my
own.' Mrs Martin thanked him for his offer of help and he
left.

Later that day, Alan Preen visited Armstrong's office on a
business matter and during the conversation Armstrong
mentioned Martin's health: 'I noticed he was looking bad as
he sat in the chair smoking after tea.'

* * * * *

The central figure in the family inquest on Oswald Martin's
illness was his father-in-law, John Fred Davies. He was a
dispensing chemist with a shop in High Town, Hay, and it is
probable that Constance Martin rushed out to see him with the
prescription left by Dr Hincks.

Davies was a shrewd, highly intelligent man with an
inquisitive streak in his nature. He had been in business in Hay
for forty years and rightly treated pharmacy as a professional calling. Despite the scientific knowledge and training
required for his job, the pharmacist was regarded as a trades-
man like the butcher or ironmonger, and Davies resented this
a little and was conscious of his lack of status compared with,
say, the solicitor or doctor. But one thing Davies had which
made him a professional was an alert, exacting and questioning
mind. On learning of his son-in-law's illness, several thoughts
began to form in his mind and his knowledge of poisons
caused him to read more than biliousness into Oswald's
symptoms. He decided to pay Dr Hincks a visit.

He found the doctor in his surgery that afternoon. He
asked him what was the matter with Martin. Hincks told
him it was a bilious attack. 'Are you sure of that, Doctor?'
asked Davies; 'Are you sure that he hasn't been poisoned? I
wanted to put you on your guard because it's always easy to
be wise after the event.'

This bluntly put question ruffled the doctor and he wanted to know why Davies had asked it. The chemist referred to Mayfield and added that 'He wouldn't trust him [Armstrong] a yard'. Davies went on to mention that he had made several sales of arsenic to Major Armstrong who had said that he wanted the stuff for killing weeds. Hincks obviously thought the chemist was dramatizing and repeated that Martin's illness appeared to be just biliousness. But he promised to keep in mind what Davies had said.

Later that evening when he had closed the shop, Davies visited Martin and observed his son-in-law's last attack of vomiting while he was there. He felt Oswald's heart beat which was very rapid, and he told him that he thought his symptoms were those of poisoning. Together, the two men went over the events of the past few days paying particular regard to the meals taken by Martin. The only food that he had not eaten with his wife and household had been tea taken with Major Armstrong shortly after 5 p.m. on 26th October. Four hours later, after supper with his wife and maid, Martin was violently ill. As Mrs Martin and her maid were quite well, suspicion in Davies's mind centred on the tea party at Major Armstrong's home, and he told his daughter and son-in-law so.

If his reasoning was correct, it occurred to Davies that another attempt might be made to administer poison. He disclosed this fear to the Martins and warned them about receiving gifts. The couple exchanged startled looks and told Davies about a box of chocolates which Oswald had received earlier the previous month.

* * * * *

On the morning of 20th September, the postman had called at Bredon Hill and delivered a small parcel. It was wrapped in ordinary brown paper and was addressed to O.N. Martin Esq., Bredon Hill, Cusop. Martin recalled the date because he and his wife had been invited to the Griffiths's tennis party. There was another reason for remembering too, because just three days previously he had written to Major Armstrong giving notice of completion in the sale of the Velinnewydd Estate.

When he took off the outer wrapping Martin found a one-pound box of Fuller's chocolates but there was nothing to indicate who had sent the gift. Neither Martin nor his wife was especially fond of chocolates so they put the anonymous gift to one side and thought little more about it.

The box of chocolates was once again opened that evening and the Martins ate one or two. The next time the chocolates were produced was on 8th October when Martin's two brothers and their wives came to stay for a weekend. Gilbert Charles and John Osborne Martin were in business together at Tewkesbury and when they came to Hay to see Oswald and Constance they stayed at Rosedaly, a nearby guest-house, as Bredon Hill was not large enough to accommodate them all.

The visitors drove down from Tewkesbury on the Saturday evening and arrived at Bredon Hill about 8.30 p.m. After the greetings were over they sat down to supper. Constance Martin had prepared fish cakes, beefsteak pudding and fruit salad with cream. They relaxed after the meal and exchanged news and gossip. Thinking her guests might like some confectionery, Constance took some of the chocolates from the Fuller's box and put them in a sweet-dish. Gilbert's wife, Dorothy, was tempted and ate at least one of the chocolates. No-one else ate any.

The party broke up at about 11 p.m. and the guests went to their lodgings at Rosedale. In the early hours of the morning, Dorothy Martin awoke and told her husband that she was feeling unwell. She got out of bed and went to the bathroom; she made several trips and after two or three bouts of diarrhoea she was sick. She noticed that the vomit was a pale, yellowish brown: she was only sick twice but the diarrhoea continued until the morning. She felt she had a high temperature and she was conscious that her heart was beating very fast. Her husband felt her pulse and said it was beating twice as fast as his own. Dorothy said, 'I never remember my heart beating at such a rate before'. Gilbert wanted to send for the doctor but his wife would not agree without having her temperature checked first.

She did not go to Bredon Hill for breakfast the next day, as arranged, but stayed in bed. Her husband told Oswald and Constance what had happened and asked if they had a thermometer. They did not have one so Oswald drove his brother to his father-in-law's shop in Hay where a thermometer was purchased. Constance went to see her sick sister-in-law, taking some soda-water and milk, and while she was there, the two men returned with the thermometer. Constance took Dorothy's temperature which was 99.5 degrees: there was nothing to worry about there and it was decided not to call the doctor.

Dorothy stayed in bed until after lunch and then felt well enough to join the others at Bredon Hill. The sickness had stopped by then but she had one or two attacks of diarrhoea and felt weak and exhausted. As everyone else was feeling well they came to the conclusion that Dorothy had caught a chill. On Mr Davies's advice, Gilbert decided not to drive Dorothy back to Tewkesbury on Sunday night as planned. They stayed over until Monday morning, by which time Dorothy was feeling a lot better, and they returned home by train. She subsequently made a complete recovery and everyone dismissed the incident as a disappointing weekend when Dorothy had caught a chill.

* * * * *

It is doubtful if any of those close to Oswald Martin's illness got much sleep that Thursday night. The patient himself, relieved that the acute distress had subsided, lay in bed next to his wife and went over with her the details of the tea party at Major Armstrong's home. He recalled Armstrong's repeated invitations to tea and his own refusals which eventually reached a point where he felt that to decline further would be rude. Constance Martin, for her part, thought about the future: if Armstrong had indeed tried to poison her husband, would he try again and where would it all end?

Market day was always a busy time for the local chemist, but this particular Thursday had been very tiring for John Davies. His concern for his son-in-law's illness and his suspicions regarding its cause taxed him late into the night. The more he thought about the matter the more his suspicions began to harden. He checked again on the symptoms of arsenical poisoning in a reference book, noting particularly that it could take fifteen or twenty days before arsenic was completely eliminated from the body through the kidneys. The best way then either to confirm or disprove his fears was to take a specimen of Oswald's urine for analysis. Davies also remembered advising his daughter to bury the remainder of the anonymous gift of chocolates. He decided now that he would ask her to give them to him instead.

The sinister significance of the chocolates preyed on the chemist's mind and early the following day he asked his wife to recover them if they had not already been disposed of. Fortunately, Constance still had the chocolates and Davies was able to examine them. He did not handle them but turned the top layer over with a pencil. He saw that at least two chocolates showed signs of having been tampered with: 'the ends looked as though they had been gouged out and I noticed minute particles of white powder adhering to them.'

Having satisfied himself that his suspicion had substance, Davies decided not to examine the chocolates further but to hand them over to Dr Hincks for proper analysis.

He saw Hincks on Sunday morning, 30th October, and asked him if he was sure that there was no suggestion of Martin's illness being attributed to poisoning. The doctor was still convinced that Martin had suffered a bilious attack, but after Davies had outlined his thoughts in detail, he consulted his reference books on arsenical poisoning.

A certain amount of professional rivalry existed between Hincks and Davies. In those days the chemist meted out treatment for many minor ailments and the doctor dispensed his own prescriptions. This arrangement brought about conflicts of interest from time to time and Davies did not altogether approve of the disparity which he thought existed between Hincks's treatment of his panel and private patients. Nevertheless, Hincks was willing to discuss the matter and the two men agreed that an analysis should be made of Martin's urine.

Davies took an empty Corbin quart bottle from his dispensary. He selected one which had previously contained hydrogen peroxide as that was a solution most unlikely to contain traces of arsenic. He washed it out thoroughly and took it up to his son-in-law's house on Sunday morning. Martin urinated directly into the bottle which was later sealed with a brand new cork by Dr Hincks. Hincks took charge of the bottle and Davies also gave him the box of chocolates which he had saved from destruction.

The doctor prescribed a bismuth mixture for Martin who was now recovering quickly. He came down for Sunday lunch and afterwards slept on the settee in the drawing room. He described that sleep as the best he had had since being taken ill.

Davies had agreed to pay the fee for the analysis and so on Monday morning, the 31st October, just over four days after the onset of Martin's illness, he and Hincks parcelled up the urine specimen and the box of chocolates and posted them to Clinical Research Association Ltd, the London Laboratory which carried out special analyses. The fate of Major Armstrong was thus wrapped up in this parcel with its unique contents.

* * * * *

With the despatch of the parcel the scene shifted away from Hay and into the world of officialdom. The package was received the following day by the Clinical Research Association. The letter which Hincks had sent with it, requesting specifically an analysis for arsenic, left no doubt in the minds of the technicians that this job might be a little out of the ordinary. The two specimens were numbered and the Research Association's Secretary wrote to Hincks the same day. He acknowledged receipt of the specimens but said,

. . . before undertaking an investigation of this nature we require a guarantee, either that we will not be called upon to give evidence in Court, or in the event of being so called upon, that in addition to the usual fee for examining the specimen, our expert will be paid £5 5s. 0d. for each day or part of a day of attendance at any Court out of London, together with first class travelling expenses and total accommodation, if necessary. If at any Court in London the fee will be £3 3s. 0d. for each day or part of a day of attendance.

Hincks received this reply on the 2nd November. The possibility of having to pay considerably more than just the

His Finest Hour! Herbert Rowse Armstrong, T.D., M.A.

(above) Mayfield —
home of the
Armstrong family

With his wife Katharine on
their wedding day

(above) Lieutenant,
Devon Volunteers

(above left) Adjutant

(right) Solicitor

(left) Freemason

Mayfield's study with bureau

The bedroom — scene of Mrs Armstrong's demise

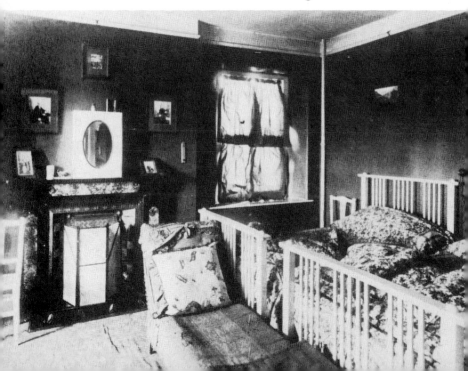

fee for analysis was an unexpected snag. While willing to
meet the normal fee, Davies did not feel inclined to accept
further commitment and neither did Dr Hincks. On the
same day the doctor wrote the following letter addressed to
the Secretary at the Home Office:

> A patient whom I was called in to attend was taken ill under
> somewhat suspicious circumstances. Symptoms suggesting
> possibly arsenical poisoning.
>   Subsequently, I took charge of a box of chocolates and
> sent them and a specimen of urine to the Clinical Research
> Association for analytical examination. Today I received
> the enclosed reply. As the case may prove to be one of
> extreme gravity involving further investigation and I am
> not prepared to guarantee the fees demanded, will you
> take the matter in hand or advise me what course to
> pursue?
>   I have written the Clinical Research Association to
> preserve the specimens intact and to hand them over to
> your representative if demanded.

The Home Office decided that the right course was to
refer the matter to the Chief Constable of the County asking
whether he thought the case required further investigation
with a view to possible criminal proceedings. So, a letter
was posted to the Chief Constable of Herefordshire on 3rd
November and his reaction was to send a police officer to
see Dr Hincks and take a statement. Hincks refused to co-
operate until the result of the analysis was known. The
doctor's response was duly relayed to the Home Office with
the additional information that the patient was recovering.

In noting the reply from the Chief Constable, one of the
Home Office officials dealing with the correspondence put
forward the following suggestion:

> Say to Dr Hincks that S of S [Secretary of State] finds
> that in the face of Dr Hincks's refusal to give information
> the Police have been unable to take any action.

It is clear from this rigid attitude that Dr Hincks's original
inquiry was in danger of foundering on bureaucratic rocks at
the Home Office. More than ten days had passed since the

doctor had first written, so on the 11th November he sent another letter to the Secretary of State asking if the analysis had yet taken place. He added that, 'In view of certain circumstances which have come to my knowledge I consider it essential that this should be done at once.'

Meanwhile, the file containing the first letter reached more sympathetic quarters and a minute was written pointing out that the doctor was simply seeking guidance:

> I rather sympathize with Dr Hincks. If the police were to gossip about the matter, it might ruin his practice. I think Mr Webster [Senior Official Analyst to the Home Office] might be asked to make the analysis (it would be covered by his retaining fee of £500).
> Say to Dr Hincks that if he will state the suspicious circumstances mentioned in his letter, which will be treated as confidential if no arsenic is found, S of S will probably be able to arrange for the analysis to be made.

This proposal of a definite course of action was dated 14th November. It can be seen how close Armstrong came to slipping through the net: but for the matter of the retaining fee paid to the Official Analyst it remains open to speculation that official inquiries would ever have started.

On the 15th November, a letter along the lines suggested was sent to Dr Hincks. He responded at once giving the details requested and politely complaining about the delays which had occurred. The file at the Home Office was minuted on the 17th with the terse comment, 'There is good ground here for suspicion'. Dr Hincks was asked to arrange for the specimens to be sent to Mr Webster at St Mary's Hospital, Paddington, requesting an analysis for arsenic.

It was two weeks before the results of the analysis were available. The waiting must have weighed heavily on Hincks for of those who believed Armstrong to be a poisoner he was the one who had committed his suspicions in writing; he was the one who had approached the authorities—it was his reputation that was at stake.

Mr Webster sent his report of the analysis to the Under Secretary of State at the Home Office on 3rd December.

I have examined the above articles [the urine sample and
the chocolates] and have to report as follows:

(1) Bottle: I have found arsenic in the urine in this
      bottle. I have estimated the arsenic and find it
      present in the amount of 1/33rd of a grain in the
      17½ ounces of urine.
(2) Box: Two of the chocolates in this box had the
      appearance of having been tampered with. A
      cylindrical hole nearly ½ inch long has apparently
      been bored and filled with a white powder, and
      an attempt made to conceal the white powder
      by covering with chocolate. This powder was found
      on analysis to be white arsenic (arsenious oxide).
      I have estimated the arsenic in one of the chocola-
      tes and find it present to the extent of slightly
      more than 2 grains (2.12 grains). Two grains of
      white arsenic have been known to cause death in
      an adult.

This report was acknowledged by Sir Ernley Blackwell,
Assistant Under Secretary at the Home Office, on the 5th
December. The official language no doubt concealed the
shock which the results of the analysis had produced.

Dear Mr Webster,
  I have to thank you for your Report upon the analysis
of a specimen of urine and chocolates which have been
submitted by Dr Hincks of Herefordshire.
  I am consulting the Director of Public Prosecutions
upon it.

Dr Hincks had still not been informed at this stage and he
was becoming more irritated by the delay as each day passed.
Apart from his own anxiety he was continually having to
answer Davies and Martin who were also pressing for news.
Martin was in a highly nervous state. Indeed, if their suspicions were correct, his life was in danger.
  To add to the tension, Armstrong made continuous invitations to Martin throughout November and December to
'come and have tea in the office.' In fact, Una Baker, the
teenage clerk who worked for Armstrong for six years, remembered that in November Miss Pearce called at the office and
left some cups, saucers, spoons and tea-plates together with

a teapot. Tea had never been made in the office before and she assumed that Major Armstrong had now decided to do so. After that, Armstrong began asking Martin to tea. The invitations were numerous, usually several a week, and a strange game of cat and mouse ensued. Armstrong would telephone to his fellow solicitor across the street, 'Would you care to come to tea tomorrow?' Martin would say that he was too busy or engaged with clients. Armstrong: 'Oh well, what about the next day then?' Martin: 'Sorry, I have to go to Hereford to meet some friends.' This was how the game was played; Armstrong always offered an alternative date when Martin declined and Martin was continually hard-pressed to find excuses without being rude.

When Armstrong thought he had secured Martin's agreement to come to tea on a particular day he would send Una Baker out to buy buttered scones from the Cafe Royal a few doors down from the office. Even when Martin did not come, the invitations did not stop. Each time the telephone rang Martin's heart skipped a beat—was it a client calling or was it Major Armstrong with another pressing invitation to tea? 'Martin, I've got some tea going, why don't you come over and join me?' 'Sorry, I've got to get some urgent letters in the post.' The invitations so outran Martin's ingenuity in thinking of plausible excuses, that he had to resort to taking tea early in his own office so that he could use that as a reason for declining Armstrong's request.

Worried by the long days of inactivity, Hincks wrote again to the Home Office on 6th December, asking for a copy of the analyst's report as soon as possible. The Home Office had not forgotten Hincks and on the 7th sent him a letter which omitted the report of the analysis but included an urgent summons.

....I am directed by the Secretary of State to say that, in view of the serious aspect which the case has now assumed, he would be glad if you would arrange to meet a representative of the Director of Public Prosecutions at the office of the Chief Constable of the County in Hereford.

The letter stressed the necessity for an early meeting and the urgency was underlined by a request for Hincks to reply by telegraph. And so the die was cast; after six weeks of waiting and wondering the three men of Hay—Hincks, Davies and Martin—now had the answer to their question. No doubt they all used that time to ponder the arguments for and against the view that a deliberate attempt had been made to poison Martin. Reflection might have led the others to weaken or strengthen their resolve but for Dr Hincks the longer he waited the firmer he became in his opinion that Major Armstrong had a case to answer.

In accordance with the Home Office request, Hincks met Mr H. Sefton Cohen, from the office of the Director of Public Prosecutions, at Hereford on 9th December. In the presence of the Chief Constable of Herefordshire, Captain E.S. Stanhope, and having read the analyst's report, the doctor made a lengthy statement giving full details of Oswald Martin's illness and his suspicions concerning Major Armstrong.

The doctor's words were loaded with urgency. '. . . Mr and Mrs Martin are becoming ill from strain, they are both convinced that Mr Armstrong will "do him in" sooner or later . . . I have attended Major Herbert Rowse Armstrong since his return from the war—in my opinion he is of abnormal mentality, very clever and well read; he has run after women, no particular woman that I know of, since she [Mrs Armstrong] was in the asylum, but I am informed has frequented village dances and pestered the girls there. He has three children, the eldest about fourteen; his late wife was rather inclined to keep a tight hand on him.'

In conclusion, Dr Hincks mentioned that Armstrong kept a revolver by his bedside and said, 'I think this man is a homicidal maniac and that if he gets to know that these questions are the subject of police or other investigation he may destroy himself, his children, Mr Martin and me.'

Hincks went back to Hay and no doubt quickly related the day's events to Davies and Martin. Mr Sefton Cohen returned to London to place the doctor's statement before the Director of Public Prosecutions, Sir Archibald Bodkin. On reading it, Sir Archibald immediately contacted Scotland Yard where the Assistant Commissioner for Crime, Mr F.T. Bigham, instructed the next detective officer on rota to take charge of the case. The conduct of the police inquiry thus fell to the lot of Chief Inspector Alfred Crutchett assisted by Sergeant

Walter Sharp.

Crutchett was a detective with nearly thirty years' experience in police work who had taught many junior officers the principles of criminal investigation. He was highly regarded by them and was thought of as Scotland Yard's 'schoolmaster'. His immediate superior, Superintendent F.P. Wensley, was later to say that Crutchett was, 'an officer in whose ability and discretion I had the highest confidence.' In view of the delicate nature of the work ahead, Crutchett's qualities were to prove of immense value.

* * * * *

The pace now quickened as Armstrong's destiny passed into the hands of the professionals. At noon on 10th December, Crutchett reported to the Director of Public Prosecutions. He was told to proceed to Hay under conditions of strictest secrecy and to begin inquiries into the suspected poisoning of Oswald Martin. Crutchett took a mid-afternoon train from Paddington and arrived in Hereford at 7.30; Sergeant Sharp arrived by a later train.

Crutchett's first stop was Hereford Police Station and then on to the office of the Chief Constable of the County. With the formalities of protocol over he drove across to Hay with Superintendent Lewis of the Herefordshire Constabulary. Their first visit in the market town was to the home of the chemist. John Davies gave the officers a detailed account of the story and their discussions went on late into the night. It was impressed upon Davies and his wife, Laura, that not the slightest hint of the police activities should reach the ears of the suspected man. There was little need for this as Davies had shown himself to be a man of discretion and judgement, and he co-operated fully with the detectives. The last act that night was to take down a written statement from him.

The chemist gave details of sales of arsenic which he had made to Major Armstrong and produced his Poison Book containing a record of the most recent sale together with Armstrong's signature. Like Hincks, Davies also ended on a note of urgency: 'My son-in-law is a temperate and clean living man, and enjoys good health, the only trouble being as a result of wounds. He is now apprehensive that Armstrong will endeavour to do him some harm.'

With this signed statement in his pocket, Crutchett left Hay at 1 a.m. and returned to Hereford. Pleased with the note on which the inquiry had begun, but feeling very tired, he suffered the irritation of being locked out of his hotel at Hereford and had to spend the night at the Police Station.

On the day following his arrival in Hay, Chief Inspector Crutchett, now accompanied by his Scotland Yard colleague, Sergeant Sharp, visited Oswald Martin. The interview took place in the British Camp Hotel at Malvern where Martin and his wife were spending a few days. The couple had felt in need of a break from the worries at Hay and not least from the attentions of Major Armstrong who daily pestered Martin to take tea with him.

Martin recounted the story of his illness which confirmed in every detail the versions given by Dr Hincks and John Davies. Bearing in mind the anxiety which Martin had been made to suffer, his statement was calm and balanced. He concluded with a remark which was to provide the police officers with a possible clue to the intentions of their quarry.

There is one point I forgot to mention in regard to Armstrong, and that was when I met him outside my office a short time after I had resumed work he asked me how I was and I said that I was getting quite fit. He then said: 'It seems a queer thing to say [or words to that effect] but you will be ill again soon, or have another attack soon.'

Mrs Martin went to the County Police Station at Hereford on 12th December and a statement was taken from her. Constance Martin had served in France as a VAD during the war and this nursing experience obviously served her well in looking after her husband during his illness. She gave a graphic description of his condition; Martin's retching was so frequent and so violent that his wife, half expecting a haemorrhage of the stomach, had examined the vomit for blood.

That same afternoon, Crutchett and Sharp went to Tewkesbury where they interviewed Martin's two brothers and took a statement from Dorothy Martin who had been ill after eating the chocolates. It was obviously important to try to trace the origin and sender of the mysterious box of chocolates, although there was not much to go on. The box of Fuller's chocolates had been wrapped in ordinary brown paper and was addressed to Martin in block letters. Unfortunately, this wrapping, which had no significance at the time, had become lost or destroyed. Constance Martin recalled that the postmark was imperfect and she did not think it was from Hay as it was too long; she thought the mark ended in 'ford'.

As a first step in the search Sergeant Sharp returned to London to find out how parcels were recorded by the Post Office. He discovered that the practice of keeping lists of ordinary parcels had been discontinued at the outbreak of war because of the work involved. Consequently, there was no way in which the sender could be traced.

The next move was to find out if possible where and by whom the chocolates had been bought. A police officer was sent to the Hammersmith factory of Fuller's Limited bearing the actual box and what remained of its contents. Fuller's Office and Business Manager, Horace Frogley, examined the box with great care. It was a 1 lb pack, retailing at six shillings, and the identifying number, 2451, stamped on the bottom of the box indicated that it had been packed on the 245th day (2nd September) of the year 1921. Unfortunately, Mr Frogley was not able to say where the particular box had been sent after leaving the factory, as no records of that sort were kept. A few days later Chief Inspector Crutchett travelled up to London and saw Mr Frogley himself. He showed the man from Fuller's three specimen chocolates and Mr Frogley identified them as 'Pistachio Noisette', 'Pine Cream' and 'Hard Nougat'. Despite drawing a blank in tracking down the sender of the chocolates, Crutchett no doubt could afford a smile at the thought of 'Arsenical Pistachio Noisette'!

The last possibility open to the police on this question was to examine the invoices of all Fuller's agents for Hereford and district regarding 1 lb boxes of chocolates supplied between 2nd September and the end of October. Nothing positive resulted from this, and local inquiries at Hay fared as badly. Neither the local postman nor stationmaster could recall handling any such parcel and the result of all these inquiries was that there was insufficient evidence to connect Major Armstrong with the purchase or posting of the particular box of chocolates.

But the net encircling Major Armstrong was now closing quickly. A copy of Mrs Armstrong's will, made on 8th July 1920, was obtained from Somerset House: she left everything to her husband. Crutchett also paid a visit to the Passport Office where he learned that Major Armstrong had applied for a passport on 13th March that year for the purpose of travelling on holiday to Europe. Mr Charles Tunnard Moore, a Justice of the Peace in Hay, had vouched for Armstrong as 'a fit and proper person to receive a passport'. Armstrong described himself on the application form as a Solicitor and Notary Public, aged 51.

The results of Crutchett's inquiries were now brought to-gether and carefully considered. There had obviously been good grounds for Dr Hincks's suspicion and the Director of Public Prosecutions decided on 23rd December to consult Sir William Willcox, Medical Adviser to the Home Office. When the Director telephoned, Sir William was engaged in the seasonal duty of sending off Christmas cards from his consulting rooms in Welbeck Street. He arranged to meet Sir Archibald the following day and when the case was outlined to him Willcox was immediately struck by the similarity with the Greenwood case in which, a year earlier, he had been an expert witness.

The two men met again on Boxing Day. Bodkin, who before his appointment as Director of Public Proescutions, had been one of the leading prosecuting counsel of the day, was sufficiently well-versed in medical matters to talk the same language as Willcox. He received Willcox's report on the case on 27th December and quickly resolved to order Major Armstrong's arrest.

* * * * *

On Saturday morning, 31st December, Crutchett and Sharp picked up Superintendent Weaver and drove to Hay where in Crutchett's own words they 'carefully carried out instruc-tions'. Major Armstrong later said he had not the remotest idea the police were coming.

With the Major behind bars, Oswald and Constance Martin probably got the best night's sleep they had had for several weeks. They were able to return to normal life in their own

home too, for after they learned that arsenic had been found
in Oswald's urine they did not sleep at Bredon Hill. Every
evening, after dark, they sought refuge with Constance's
parents at Prospect House opposite the clock tower in Hay.

No longer would Martin have to face the almost daily
ordeal of meeting Armstrong in Broad Street knowing that
he was a suspected poisoner. No longer would he have
to go through the mental contortion of finding an excuse
with which to decline the inevitable invitation to tea and yet
not give the game away. And, mercifully, he escaped
Armstrong's latest strategy which was an invitation to dinner
at Mayfield. Now the cat and mouse game was over.

The secret had been well kept by those in the know. The
only other person in Hay, apart from Hincks, the Daviesses
and the Martins who knew what was going on, was Trevor
Griffiths, Martin's future partner, who had been told in
confidence of the suspicions concerning Armstrong. On the
31st December 1921, young Griffiths made the diary entry:
'So ends the most exciting year of my life'.

On 1st January, Sir Archibald wrote an almost casual note
to Willcox: 'The man about whose case I consulted you last
week is in custody and I hear that "something has been found
in his house"—though I have no details as yet. Will you be
good enough to arrange with Dr Spilsbury and Mr Webster
to meet you at some convenient time before Dr S goes to
Hereford?'

News of Major Armstrong's arrest hit Hay like a bombshell.
Crutchett and Sharp had done their work well for no-one had
discerned the slightest hint of the activities of the police in the
town. After the event, of course, there were many stories
concerning the movements of the Scotland Yard men. It was
rumoured that Major Armstrong's office had been kept under
surveillance by detectives hidden in the town clock-tower.
Another version had it that the men were secreted in the
tower of the parish church. It was even suggested that
Sergeant Sharp disguised himself as a woman and obtained
a position as cook in a local house—presumably to be able
to observe Armstrong. There were many tales of detectives
spying from the bushes around Mayfield, and even peering
through the windows of the house. Miss May Lilwall, who
dined with a friend at Major Armstrong's home on the evening

of 23rd December, a few days before his arrest, said she saw a man peer through the window during dinner. She said nothing to the Major but mentioned it to her friend on the way home. In reality, of course, the police did none of these things for they simply could not afford to take the risk of alerting Armstrong to the fact that they were on his trail. Nor indeed was there any need to watch Armstrong.

After Armstrong had been arrested and confined in a cell at Hay Police Station, Crutchett and Sharp together with Superintendent Weaver and Sergeant Worthing, went to Mayfield where searches were made. A cupboard in the library revealed a paper packet labelled, 'Arsenic', and bearing the name and address of the Hay chemist. Two tins labelled 'Caustic Soda' were also found and these, together with over sixty bottles and medical containers, were taken away. The police also took charge of a revolver in a leather case with some ammunition, and various papers were taken from the bureau in the library.

In his report to Superintendent Wensley, Crutchett mentioned another interesting result of the searches at Mayfield: 'When searching Armstrong's bedroom there were two soiled "French letters" in the washstand drawer and three in the cupboard'. He added, '. . . that will give you some idea of the kind of man he is morally'. It was Crutchett's opinion that Armstrong had been intimate with one of his staff.

The detectives took statements from Armstrong's housekeeper, Emily Pearce, and his maid, Harriet Price. Miss Pearce, who was aged sixty-five, had served the Armstrongs for nine years. She said they were 'a devoted couple, and I never heard an angry word pass between them'. Both women remembered Mr Martin coming to tea with the Major, for they laid the table and prepared the tea and food. Neither had seen any arsenic or weed killer around the house, but Harriet Price recalled that her employer did a little weeding in the garden. In fact the weeds got the better of him and he had to call in a jobbing gardener to help.

The impact on Hay of the arrest of Major Armstrong was largely a feeling of incredulity. 'We were dumbfounded when he was arrested. He used to read the lessons in church'. This was the reaction of the undertaker's assistant, and it was typical. After all, Armstrong was a solicitor who had secured the trust of many people for whom he had transacted legal business and he was Clerk to the local magistrates, a position which gave him a say in correcting the misdemeanours of others. He was prominent in many aspects of the town's social and institutional life and while he was known to have been henpecked by his late wife, he was widely respected for his courtesy. Despite this general feeling about the man there were those whose confidence was not so easily obtained. One of these was Laura Davies, the chemist's wife, who spoke of Armstrong's callous behaviour at the time of his wife's death. She said that '*none* of the rumours I had heard about Mr Armstrong were to his credit'.

As he lay on his board bed in the cell at Hay Police Station, Armstrong may have thought about his impending appearance before the local magistrates. He, more than most, would know all about the legal procedures which would be set in motion.

It is quite likely too that his mind dwelled on the fate of another solicitor, Harold Greenwood, who had been arrested eighteen months earlier in Carmarthenshire on a poisoning charge. Perhaps there was comfort to be derived from the fact that Harold Greenwood had been tried and acquitted at Carmarthen Assizes.

* * * * *

Tucked away in the locked darkness of the sergeant's desk at Hay Police Station was the small bundle of items taken from Major Armstrong when he was arrested. These included three love letters signed 'Marion', a small folded piece of paper containing a white powder and a sheet of notepaper bearing a list of medical symptoms. These innocent looking scraps from a man's pockets were to acquire greater significance in the days which followed.

3   The Major holds Court

. . .I appreciate that the circumstances call for some explanation from me.

Herbert   Rowse   Armstrong

ON THE DAY that Armstrong was arrested, Sergeant Worthing made two trips to Mrs Williams's cafe in Lion Street. On both occasions he asked for 'some hefty sandwiches and a jug of tea'. 'What's on then, Sergeant?' asked Mrs Williams. 'You'll hear in due course', was the reply as the policeman returned to the station with the refreshments bought for Superintendent Weaver and the detective officers.

When the news of Major Armstrong's arrest did break, it flashed around Hay like wildfire: 'But he is our solicitor', gasped Miss Lilwall. Despite the sensational value of the news, the clerks in Oswald Martin's office only heard about it on Monday morning when the Major was due to appear in court. Percy Evans, the senior clerk, had to go to the police station on business and was staggered to learn the identity of the inmate of No.1 cell. He rushed back to the office and blurted out, 'It's Mr Armstrong—he's been arrested, he's in the cells.'

Some local residents refused to believe that Armstrong had been arrested at all. They believed that this story was mixed up with news of a big jewel robbery in London. Others linked it with the murder of Irene Wilkins at Bournemouth on the 22nd December 1921 and a few said the news was put about by Oswald Martin, 'out of spite'.

* * * * *

The courtroom of Hay, like the town itself, was small and compact. It lay behind the brick-built police station in Lion Street. A short corridor at the rear of the police station gave access to the cells, and a door at the end opened into the court. The room itself was no more than twenty-five feet square but it had a high ceiling and large windows. At one end were the familiar courtroom furnishings: the magistrate's bench with its painted wood-panelled front was raised up on a platform, behind it were shelves of legal books and below was an enclosure with a long table and wooden chairs for the Justices' Clerk and the solicitors. At the left of the entrance was the dock.

This tiny courtroom, eminently suitable for the ordinary police-court proceedings of a country town, was totally inadequate for hearing a charge of attempted murder brought against one of the town's most prominent citizens.

On the morning of Monday, 2nd January 1922, Major Armstrong appeared before the Bredwardine Magistrates at Hay. The court was crowded well beyond its capacity and there were seats only for the magistrates, the officials concerned in the case and the defendant's solicitor. The others who managed to gain admission had to stand. The scene was set for the Major to hold court.

The magistrates took their seats at 10.30 a.m. The Chairman was Mr Mortimer Bayliss and the three men sitting with him included Mr Charles Tunnard Moore, a neighbour of Major Armstrong. Mr T.A. Matthews, the Hereford solicitor, had hurried down to Hay the previous day in answer to Armstrong's request. Uneasily and with obvious distress, the magistrates waited for the prisoner to be brought from the cells.

There was dead silence as the court door opened and Major Armstrong walked in. He turned sharply to enter the narrow dock and bowed politely towards the Bench. All eyes were on the small, dapper man who stood rigidly to attention before the court. Armstrong was wearing riding breeches half-hidden beneath his army officer's British warm, a double-breasted coat with a deep fur collar; and he wore a red tie which seemed to accentuate the bright blue colour of his eyes. He showed no signs of anxiety as he stood before the magistrates, all of whom were known to him.

Poignancy was added to the opening procedures when the Chairman announced a temporary appointment to the office of Clerk to the court. This was a successor to Major Armstrong who normally held that office. Below the Bench, in the chair which the Major had occupied so many times, now sat eighty-two year-old Mr Cambridge Phillips.

Superintendent Albert Weaver rose from his seat and informed the magistrates that under instructions from the Public Prosecutor he was asking them to take only formal evidence of arrest that day and he requested that the prisoner be remanded in custody for a week. Mr Matthews raised no objection to a remand without formal evidence but the Chairman insisted that some evidence be produced to justify it.

The Superintendent then entered the witness-box and gave brief evidence of arrest: 'At 12.30 p.m. on Saturday last I saw the prisoner at his office in Broad Street, Hay. I told him I was about to arrest him on a very serious charge, and that as a police officer it was desirable that I should caution him that he need not say anything in answer to the charge, that I should take down anything he said in writing and that it may be given in evidence. I then said, "I now arrest you on a charge of attempting to murder one Oswald Norman Martin by administering poison to him, to wit arsenic, at Cusop on October 26th last". The prisoner replied, "I am quite innocent". That', concluded Weaver, 'is the only evidence I propose to offer today. I apply for a remand till this day week'. Weaver added ominously, 'There are other matters pending which Your Worships probably have in mind which I cannot mention in public now.'

Even as Weaver was speaking, men with shovels were already working in Cusop churchyard where a police constable was stationed to ensure that they would not be disturbed in the grim work they were about to undertake.

In the court there was some discussion concerning the time of the next hearing and Armstrong, seemingly oblivious of the fact that he was now the prisoner in the dock and not Clerk to the court, joined in. Leaning forward, he asked Mr Cambridge Phillips, 'What about the time of the court?' Mr Phillips mentioned that the following Monday was the Ordinary Petty Sessions day for Bredwardine and the two sittings would clash. Mr Matthews, on the other hand, saw no reason why both sittings should not be held. The Chairman agreed, and said that the ordinary court could sit at 10.30 and dispose of its business before 11 o'clock. He decided, therefore, that the case should be adjourned until the following Monday at 11 o'clock. Armstrong again interrupted saying, 'The court should be fixed at a time to coincide with the train service. It is a question of everyone getting here on time'. Superintendent Weaver consulted a time-table and remarked that 11 a.m. seemed convenient. With that point settled at last Mr Matthews said he did not propose to make an application for bail at this stage. After the depositions had been read, the policeman standing on duty at the entrance to the dock, nodded towards Armstrong who turned quickly towards the door and followed the constable out of court. Thus, within fifteen minutes, the first public act in the Armstrong drama was over.

* * * * *

Monday, 9th January 1922. The press scented that Hay was to be the centre of perhaps one of the biggest stories since the war and reporters descended on the little market town in their dozens. As much as £40 was being offered for photographs of Major Armstrong.

With public curiosity at its peak, the demand for admission to the tiny, seatless courtroom was insatiable. So eager were people to get into the room on that Monday morning that they besieged the entrance to the building and tried to force a way past the constables on duty. The police resorted to the use of staves to push the crowd back and restore order in time for the arrival of the officials and witnesses.

Major Armstrong, who had been transferred to Worcester Gaol after the first hearing, arrived by car from the railway station at 9.45 a.m. He was wearing his British warm with the fur collar turned up partially hiding his face. He stepped from the car and quickly followed Superintendent Weaver and a police constable into the building. Photographers who had taken up positions on the wall of an adjoining building took what pictures they could as the prisoner was escorted to the cells. Armstrong had left Worcester by an early train and while waiting for the Court to open he was given breakfast which had been bought for him at a nearby teashop.

Reporters and photographers were kept busy as various officials arrived at the court building; the stocky figure of Chief Inspector Crutchett was becoming well known, and the elderly Mr Cambridge Phillips exchanged good-humoured banter with the swarming pressmen: 'What, again?', he asked.

Among the last to arrive were Mr Matthews, the defending solicitor, accompanied by his chief clerk, and they were followed by Oswald and Constance Martin. In the courtroom Mr Gerald Paling, appearing in his first big case for the Director of Public Prosecutions, and Mr St John Micklethwait, barrister-at-law on the Oxford Circuit, prepared to put the prosecution's case.

Mr Micklethwait opened for the Crown and his speech lasted most of the morning. He drew attention to the painful duty that lay before the magistrates, but remarked that it was a duty of the greatest possible importance to the public owing to the gravity of the case. After warning the press about making grossly improper statements which could interfere with the course of justice, Mr Micklethwait told the court that the unusual nature of the case compelled him to speak at some length. But, before he could proceed, Mr Matthews interrupted requesting that all the witnesses should leave the court until they were required to give evidence. The Bench agreed and the witnesses left the room.

The charge was one of attempting to murder Oswald Norman Martin by the administration of arsenic. Before unfolding this remarkable story Mr Micklethwait thought it necessary to acquaint the court with details of the properties of arsenic.

Arsenic is a highly poisonous substance employed in a number of industrial processes and also widely used in pre- parations for killing weeds and destroying vermin. It was readily available to the public as white arsenious oxide which could be bought from the chemist for making up weed killer from a recipe. The only legal requirements were that the chemist should colour the white powder to distin- guish it from everyday substances such as flour and salt. The Poisons Act required that white arsenic be coloured by the addition of at least one-sixteenth its weight of charcoal or indigo. The only other stipulation was that all sales of arsenic should be entered by the chemist in his Poisons Book and be signed by the purchaser.

Now Mr Micklethwait turned his attention to the career of the accused man. He acknowledged the prominent position that Major Armstrong had built up by a combination of hard work, skill and personality. For a time this position was

unchallenged as the only other solicitor in the town was an
ailing old man. But then the ranks of the rival firm were
reinforced by the arrival of Oswald Norman Martin.

Rightly or wrongly, said the prosecutor, Martin formed
the opinion that the Major resented his coming to Hay. Mr
Micklethwait did not wish to make any suggestion on this
point but said he could well understand that Major Armstrong
should feel aggrieved. If there was any resentment between
the two men, the position Armstrong found himself in with
respect to the property sale for which Martin was pressing for
completion, might have further embittered him.

Mr Micklethwait then referred to what he called a date of
great importance, 11th January 1921—the day Major Armstrong bought a quarter of a pound of arsenic from the Hay
chemist. Before examining his witnesses, the prosecutor mentioned an occasion when Major Armstrong was being treated
by Dr Hincks for a certain disease, which he need not mention,
and a certain drug was being used. In the course of conversation, the Major asked the doctor, 'What is the drug you are
using?' The doctor replied, 'Arsenic.' Then Armstrong asked
what a fatal dose would be and the doctor answered, 'Three
grains,' 'Oh!', said Armstrong, 'One is sufficient, isn't it?'

Thus did the prosecutor prepare the way for his first
witness. It was 12.15 p.m. when Oswald Norman Martin,
looking pale and somewhat ill, entered the witness box. He
outlined his war career and early days as a solicitor in Hay.
Mr Micklethwait then questioned him about the arrival of
the box of chocolates at Bredon Hill.

'Was the box full of chocolates? Did you open it?'

'I opened it myself . . . there was a layer of white paper on
top of the box which was full of chocolates . . . there was a
"whitish" powder on the box.'

'Did you eat any?'

'We had some that evening, two or three, no more.'

'Any ill effects?'

'No . . .'

'What did you do with them?'

'They were put by.'

Continuing his evidence after the adjournment for lunch,
Martin told the court what happened when his brothers and
their wives visited Bredon Hill for supper on 8th October

1921.

Martin then gave an account of his dealings with Major Armstrong concerning the sale of the Velinnewydd Estate. Negotiations fell through on 21st October as Armstrong was unable to complete. Major Armstrong invited him to tea on 22nd but he declined; another invitation on the 24th he had to turn down for business reasons but a third on the 26th he finally accepted.

'When you went to Major Armstrong's house,' asked Micklethwait, 'were you in your usual health or feeling unwell or anything like that?'

'I was in my usual health.'

Martin went on to describe the violent sickness which he suffered at home about two and a half hours after leaving Mayfield.

'Have you ever in your life experienced an attack similar to this attack?'

'No, never.'

Mr Micklethwait directed his next questions to events which happened after Martin returned to work. The witness said he met Armstrong in the street about two weeks after going back to the office. Armstrong asked him how he was and said, 'It may seem a curious thing to say but you will have another attack soon.' Martin replied, 'I hope not.'

After that meeting came the stream of invitations to take tea with Armstrong. These continued into December at the time when Martin had proposed action against Armstrong regarding his failure to complete the property sale. Martin said, 'He asked me to tea at his office, and I did what I usually did, evaded the invitation, making the excuse that I was staying with my wife's parents . . .'

This first day of the hearing at Hay Police Court ran on into the hours of darkness and as the court was not fitted with electric lighting, oil lamps had to be brought in to illuminate the proceedings. In order to continue their note-taking, reporters bought candles at their own expense, no doubt being assured of recouping the cost from editors grateful for their newsworthy copy.

* * * * *

Tuesday, 10th January 1922. When the court re-assembled, the sun was shining so brilliantly that the blinds had to be drawn. Oswald Martin arrived carrying a couple of letter books under his arm; these he passed to Mr Micklethwait while making his way to the witness box. The prosecuting lawyer was joined by Mr Matthews and the two men retired briefly for consultation in a private room.

Armstrong had spent the night in a cell at Hay Police Station and was escorted to the dock by a constable; he bowed courteously to the Bench and stuffed into his pocket a bundle of papers which he had in his hand.

The two lawyers then came into the court, still conversing, and proceedings were about to start when the Chairman of the Magistrates realized that something was bothering the Acting Clerk: the elderly Mr Cambridge Phillips could be heard quite audibly muttering, 'Poor bloody crow'. Before Armstrong's case came on that morning, the court had heard a charge against a man who was alleged to have beaten a crow to death in a hedge. Phillips, a well-known bird lover, had expressed his disgust at the time but his indignation spilled over to the next case. The Chairman asked Phillips to keep his feelings to himself and the Acting Clerk eventually settled back into his seat, but not before he had uttered 'Poor bloody crow' again.

Mr Micklethwait told the court that he had copies of the letters which passed between Mr Martin and Major Armstrong and he asked to have them noted on the depositions. Martin formally identified them as correspondence relating to the sale of the Velinnewydd Estate.

Martin's cross-examination now began.

'Is it your impression', Mr Matthews asked, 'that Major Armstrong had a resentment at your coming to Hay?'

'That is my impression', replied Martin.

'And I gather obviously from what you say that you had the impression that he had a strong resentment?'

'I did not say a strong resentment.'

In his cross-examination, Mr Matthews asked questions about Martin's business life in Hay and his professional relationship with Armstrong. At this point Martin left the witness box and took a seat at a table in the well of the court as Mr Phillips complained of not being able to hear the witness's replies.

Martin said that he and Armstrong were friendly in their business relations and until October 1921 he had been in the habit of giving Armstrong a lift to work in his car. Mr Matthews asked,

'Up to October 1921, there was nothing to indicate that he was not perfectly friendly towards you and that you were not perfectly friendly towards him?'

'No, not perfectly friendly. I did not say that in the first place. I never admitted that there was any question of friendship apart from our business relations. I want you to understand, however, that there was no outward show of hostility.'

The defence went on to deal with the box of chocolates. Martin said that when he received the chocolates he was not suspicious but merely curious to know who had sent them.

'Your suggestion is', asked Mr Matthews, 'that Major Armstrong sent those chocolates?'

'It is not my suggestion at all,' retorted Martin.

'Do you, or do you not, suggest that Major Armstrong sent those chocolates?'

'I refuse to answer.'

'That will not do, Mr Martin'.

Mr Micklethwait intervened protesting that the question was not a fair one. The defence contended that it was, 'and', said Mr Matthews, 'I am going to have an answer to it, too'. The Chairman of the magistrates agreed that it was a fair question to ask and Mr Matthews put it to the witness again:

'Do you suggest that Major Armstrong sent you that box of chocolates?'

'I do not suggest it,' answered Martin.

The cross-examination continued with questions about the property deal. Martin said that Major Armstrong became very agitated over the settlement of the sale which led him to believe that it affected him personally, although he had no idea how. Mr Matthews pressed the witness on this point but Martin said he could suggest no other reason. 'I am not here to suggest anything', he said, 'but to say that his agitation was so great that it impressed me very greatly at the time and I could not account for it.'

This strong reply from Martin was a reminder to those present in the court of one of the many unusual features of the case: the prisoner, defender and principal witness were all solicitors.

Mr Matthews now directed his questions to the occasion of the tea party at Mayfield.

'Mr Armstrong only left you to speak to the Rector?', he asked.

'That is so', replied Martin.

'Do you remember particularly all the incidents connected with the tea?'

'Well, there were certain incidents which impressed themselves on my mind.'

'It is quite clear that the food was in the drawing room when you came in?'

'I remember seeing the three-tier cake stand on which, I believe, there were some bread and butter and some scones.'

'Can you remember what was on the top of the three-tier cake stand?'

'I remember there was a plate of scones'.

'How many?'

'I cannot tell.'

'There were more than one?'

'I recollect very indistinctly.'

'Your recollection is indistinct. This is a serious matter, Mr Martin.'

'Well you see, Mr Matthews, when you go out to tea you do not usually count the scones.'

Martin's recollection of the details of the tea party was somewhat hazy but he was quite clear that he did not tell Armstrong he was feeling 'off colour' when they smoked after tea.

When the court resumed after the lunch interval, there was some discussion about the date of the next hearing. Mr Micklethwait proposed an adjournment until the following Tuesday but Mr Matthews objected strongly saying that his client was in an extremely difficult position. His business was at a standstill and there were also domestic reasons for the case not being delayed.

Mr Micklethwait remarked that Major Armstrong had been arrested only ten days previously and inquiries were still being made of which he would have something to say later. Finally, Mr Matthews hinted at events to come when he reminded the

Bench, 'I am sure you will not lose sight of the fact that the case before Your Worships is the case you are dealing with. If there is another charge I am ready to meet it.'

Continuing cross-examination, Mr Matthews, went back to the tea party affair and asked Mr Martin about the buttered scone.

'You say that Mr Armstrong handed it to you himself?'

'Yes, it struck me as being a remarkable thing. He handed me the scone with his fingers and therefore it stuck in my memory.'

Mr Martin answered questions about what he had eaten for breakfast and lunch on that day, and again it was evident that his memory was not good. But, not surprisingly, the witness's recollection of his illness after the tea party was clear and concise, and Armstrong's efforts to get him to come to tea again were too recent for comfort.

Martin agreed that there was a fairly good library at Mayfield and that he had borrowed books right up to the time of Major Armstrong's arrest. He said that to have suddenly stopped doing so would have created suspicion.

Martin's cross-examination had lasted for nearly six hours but he still had to undergo a brief re-examination before stepping down from the witness stand. Since darkness was settling on the courtroom, there was a short adjournment while lamps and candles were lit. Then Mr Micklethwait asked a question which immediately brought a protesting Mr Matthews to his feet. The prosecutor referred to a defence question concerning the sender of the box of chocolates, but the Bench asked for it to be withdrawn. Mr Micklethwait then asked Martin, 'Do you know of any person other than Mr Armstrong who would be likely to send these chocolates?' Despite Mr Matthews's protestations, the magistrates allowed the question to be put. Martin replied that it was impossible for him to say who the sender was.

This piece of drama concluded Martin's evidence and the court rose for the day.

* * * * *

Wednesday, 11th January 1922. The hearing resumed at 11 a.m. and observers were quick to note that Mr Cambridge Phillips, who had been acting as Magistrates' Clerk, was not present. His place was taken by Mr W.H. Grout of Weobley. The reason given for Mr Phillips's absence was that he had been called away on business but the real reason was reflected in Chief Inspector Crutchett's progress report in which he said of Mr Phillips, 'He is not very swift with the pen. He is also rather defective in hearing.'

Mr Matthews was the first to speak in the day's proceedings and he asked that he might be given, on behalf of the prisoner, a list of everything that the police had taken from his client's house and office. Superintendent Weaver readily agreed to this but Mr Micklethwait pointed out that a number of the articles had been sent to London. It was decided that the list would be completed as soon as possible and Mr Micklethwait promised to give every assistance.

The day's first witness for the prosecution was then called. Mrs Dorothy Harriet Birch Martin, sister-in-law to Oswald Martin, stepped into the witness box and began to give evidence. Her voice was so low, however, that she was asked to leave the witness box and go to the well of the court so that she could be heard. She spoke of being violently sick all night after the supper party at Oswald's house.

'Did you have supper?' asked Mr Micklethwait.

'Yes', replied Dorothy Martin.

'After supper were some chocolates on the table?'

'Whilst dessert was on—that is to say, apples. There were apples, chocolates and other sweets on the table.'

'And did you have one or more of the chocolates?'

'Yes.'

'Do you recollect whether any other members of the party ate any of the chocolates?'

'To the best of my knowledge they did not.'

Dorothy Martin went on to describe the nature of her subsequent illness and a question about whether she and her husband had considered calling a doctor caused Mr Matthews to raise an objection. He said that it had been introduced solely to hurt the prisoner, to which Mr Micklethwait replied, 'I shall protect your interests, Mr Matthews.' The defence solicitor, so vigilant on Armstrong's behalf, retorted, 'I have not seen much protection yet.'

Gilbert Charles Martin followed his wife into the witness box and again the prosecution posed the question about bringing the doctor in. Mr Matthews immediately voiced his disapproval and a further brush between the lawyers ensued. When this row had subsided, the witness said that he did not call a doctor because his wife didn't wish him to.

The next witness was another member of the Martin family, Oswald's wife, Constance Muriel. She was stylishly dressed in a fur coat and blue hat and, unlike her sister-in-law, spoke up clearly. She described how the box of chocolates arrived, how Dorothy Martin became ill after eating some and related in detail her husband's illness after the tea party at Armstrong's house.

On the 28th October, Major Armstrong called at the Martin home and was shown into the drawing room. Constance told the court, 'He asked how my husband was. I said he was better and my impression was that Mr Armstrong seemed surprised.'

When cross-examining, Mr Matthews asked Constance Martin, 'Was it not a natural thing for Mr Armstrong to call and ask about your husband when he knew he was away from his work because of illness.?'

'I suppose it was,' replied the witness.

'I suppose it was your impression that he seemed surprised?'

'He gave me that impression by repeating the word "better".'

'The only thing that gave you the impression that he was surprised was that he repeated the word "better". There was no suggestion that he laughed or smiled?'

'No.'

Miss Emily Ellis Pearce, Major Armstrong's elderly housekeeper stared fixedly at her master when she took her place in the witness box. The prisoner did not return her gaze but averted his eyes throughout her evidence.

Mr Micklethwait asked the witness, 'Do you remember October. When Mr Martin came to tea?'

'I remember the tea, but I don't exactly remember when it was,' replied Miss Pearce.

'Do you remember what there was for tea?'

'I don't remember exactly: bread and butter, currant cake buttered—what we call "dough cake"—and scones.'

'Did you take them in?'

'I don't know. Sometimes I did, but I have quite forgotten.'

The prosecution was then switched to the question of Major Armstrong's use of arsenical weed killer.

'Have you ever seen any arsenic in the house?'

'No, I should not know it if I saw it.'

'In any conversation with Mr Armstrong did he call it arsenic?'

'I don't know; he may have called it weed killer.'

'What did he call it?'

'He did not call it anything, only to put down something to kill weeds.'

'Was the word arsenic ever used?'

'I don't know if it was.'

'What I am trying to get at is whether the word arsenic was ever used?'

'I don't remember if it was.'

When Miss Pearce completed her evidence and just before the court rose, Mr Micklethwait made a sensational announcement. Addressing the magistrates, he said, 'In my opening speech to you I told you that further inquiries were being made and that possibly further evidence would be brought forward in this case. I have now received certain information and it is this: When Mr Armstrong was arrested he was asked to hand over the contents of his pockets. Among the letters there was found a small packet and that packet contained a white powder. It now appears, and I shall be able to prove it in evidence before you when the time comes, that that packet which was in Mr Armstrong's pocket when he was arrested, contained a dose of white arsenic; and a fatal quantity.'

'A quantity of white arsenic,' exclaimed Mr Matthews.

'A quantity which would amount to a fatal dose,' Mr Micklethwait repeated to an incredulous courtroom. 'I have only heard this, of course, since my opening statement,' he continued, 'and as it will be, no doubt, a matter of very great importance when any question of bail comes to be considered, I thought it only fair to my learned friend that I should mention it today, and not keep it until tomorrow.'

The police, of course, had been delighted by this discovery and Crutchett wrote, 'It is very satisfactory to know that the contents of the small packet which was found on Armstrong is arsenic. It will help us immensely.'

The day ended with a further slightly sour exchange between prosecutor and defender. Referring to this latest revelation, Mr Matthews said, 'I draw my own deduction as to the object in mentioning it now.'

* * * * *

Thursday, 12th January 1922. There was an early surprise when the court re-assembled. Sir Archibald Bodkin, the Director of Public Prosecutions, entered the room, and recognizing the Chairman of the Magistrates as an old acquaintance, strode over to the bench and heartily shook hands with him.

The first witness of the day was Mrs Harriet Elizabeth Price, Major Armstrong's maid, who was examined by Mr Micklethwait. She told the court that she had been widowed the previous year and had then entered service at Mayfield where she worked with Miss Pearce, the only other servant. She said that generally she did the housework and Miss Pearce prepared the meals.

Mrs Price told the story of the tea party at Mayfield in her own words and was questioned by the prosecution about what happened when tea was finished.

'When you went into the room to clear away the things, do you remember seeing any scones which they left?'

'Yes.'

'Can you say how many there were?'

'Three.'

'Can you say whether there were any scones with currants in them or were they plain?'

'I cannot say.'

'What is your recollection of it?'

'I cannot say, because I don't know whether they were currant scones or not.'

'Were they buttered or   plain?'

'They were whole and not buttered.'

Mr Micklethwait repeated the words, 'they were whole' for the benefit of the Clerk to ensure that he included them in the depositions. Another row ensued when Mr Matthews protested that these words had not been used by the witness.

The prosecutor said he resented Mr Matthews's continual interruptions and claimed that the witness's reply had been heard by everyone. However, the matter was settled when Mrs Price repeated her answer—the scones were whole and not buttered. The scones left over from the party were put in a cake tin and eaten up some time later.

Mr Micklethwait then put some questions to the witness about the use of weed killer at Mayfield.

'Have you ever seen Mr Armstrong prepare weed killer for the garden?'

'No.'

'Or have you seen him weeding the paths?'

'No' . . .

'Your business as housemaid is to tidy up the house, bedrooms and so forth?'

'Yes.'

'Did you ever see any arsenic in the house?'

'I don't know what arsenic is.'

'And as far as you are aware you never saw it?'

'No.'

'Was the mention of arsenic made to you at any time by Mr Armstrong?

'No.'

Mr Matthews did not wish to cross-examine the witness so Mrs Price stepped down.

She was followed in the witness box by Mr John Hird, assistant to John Davies, the Hay chemist. He stated that Major Armstrong bought a quarter of a pound of arsenic in January of the previous year. Mr Davies's Poison Book was produced in court and the witness identified the prisoner's signature.

Hird said he asked Major Armstrong what the arsenic was for and was told it was for making weed killer. At that point Mr Davies had come forward and told Major Armstrong that he needed potash to dissolve the arsenic, but the prisoner replied that he had a private recipe. On Mr Davies's instructions, the witness tinted the arsenic with charcoal, according to normal practice, wrapped it in two papers and labelled it 'Poison'.

Mrs Laura Jessie Davies, the chemist's wife and Oswald Martin's mother-in-law, was called next. She said she did not

know Major Armstrong personally although he had called at
her house on one occasion to collect a subscription. On 27th
October, she went up to Bredon Hill and saw her son-in-law
in bed; he was very ill. Two days later, as a result of what her
husband had told her, Mrs Davies went back to Bredon Hill
and collected a box of chocolates from her daughter. 'At that
time,' she said significantly, 'certain communications had
been made to me.' Having examined the chocolates with a
magnifying glass she observed that one had been drilled and
another was chipped. After that, the box was put away in a
drawer of the writing desk.

Mrs Davies was succeeded in the witness box by her
husband John Fred, who said he was a practising chemist
with a business in Hay. Under Mr Micklethwait's questioning
he said he knew Major Armstrong and had sold him arsenic
on more than one occasion: he gave details of these sales.

27th July 1912	— 1 gallon of weed killer
23rd June 1913	— 3 gallons of weed killer
2nd May 1914	— ¼lb arsenic and 1 lb caustic soda
7th June 1919	— ½lb arsenic
4th May 1920	— 4 gallons of weed killer
4th August 1920	— 3 tins of powdered weed killer
11th January 192'	— ¼lb arsenic

Witness said the purchase on 11th January 1921 was the
one mentioned in his assistant's evidence and it was the last
occasion on which such a purchase was made by Major
Armstrong.

Referring to the purchase made on 7th June 1919, Mr
Micklethwait asked, 'Did you serve Mr Armstrong with the
arsenic yourself?'

'Yes,' replied Davies.

'What occurred when he came in for the arsenic?'

'. . . I asked him what he required it for, and he said it was
for weed killer. I told him that arsenic required some alkali
with which to make it soluble for the purpose of weed
killing. He said he had dabbled in chemistry and knew all
about it. I tried to serve him with weed killer, and he said he
preferred to make it himself . . . eventually he purchased half

a pound.'

The chemist went on to tell the court that the actual substance called 'arsenic' was arsenious oxide, arsenious acid and various other names, but it was generally known as 'white arsenic'. He added that the law required it to be coloured and he generally used charcoal for that purpose. So far as the sale on 11th January 1921 was concerned, his assistant did the actual selling. He was attending to other customers at the time but he recalled telling Hird not to forget the colouring.

The chemist was then cross-examined and Mr Matthews elicited from him that, considering the amount of ground which Major Armstrong owned, the purchases of weed killer and arsenic were 'not out of the common'.

Davies next described how the box of chocolates and urine specimen were sealed and sent away for analysis. The bottle used for the urine was of green glass with a concave bottom and had formerly contained hydrogen peroxide. He demonstrated in court how the cork had been tied down and the bottle sealed. The chemist also borrowed Superintendent Weaver's pocket-book pencil to show the size of the hole which he had seen in one of the chocolates.

The next witness was William Jay who had been a jobbing gardener at Mayfield. He had known Major Armstrong for fourteen years and had looked after his garden during the war. Jay was questioned at some length by Mr Micklethwait on the subject of weed killer and some of his answers produced laughter in what had otherwise been a very solemn hearing.

'Do you remember in 1920 buying some weed killer?'

'Yes'.

'Liquid weed killer?'

'I know I used some liquid weed killer'.

'Did you use it all up?'

'Yes, it was not much to use.'

'And did you have some tins of powder?'

'Yes, some time after.'

'Did you use all the tins?'

'No.'

'How much was left over?'

'Somewhere about half a tin. I think it was the smallest half.'

'When was it left over?'

'When I used it.'

Jay's reply to Mr Micklethwait's complaint that he had not given dates for those occasions when weed killer had been used produced further laughter in court. '. . .It is not a red-letter day in my life when I use weed killer,' retorted the gardener.

The last witness of the day was another jobbing gardener who had worked for Major Armstrong. Robert McGeorge said he had been at Mayfield since 8th October but the use of weed killer had not been discussed despite the fact that the garden was in a bad state.

On the morning of 26th October, between 9 and 10 a.m. McGeorge saw Major Armstrong at Mayfield and asked him about moving some trees. The Major promised to return to the house as early as he could in the afternoon to show where he wanted the trees re-planted. He did go back to Mayfield and McGeorge thought 'it might have been shortly after four o'clock' when he appeared in the garden.

'How long was he talking to you?' asked Mr Micklethwait.

'The best part of three-quarters of an hour, showing me what he wanted done.'

That concluded the day's evidence but once again there was a heated exchange between prosecutor and defender. Mr Micklethwait explained that he had scientific evidence to put before the court and he asked the Bench to remand the prisoner in custody for one week until the following Thursday. Mr Matthews objected to the remand and asked the magistrate to consider the individual in the case. 'After all,' he said, 'in the interests of the public he is the one individual you must consider. He was arrested on 31st December—I hope, at any rate, there were some materials to justify his arrest without a warrant—and therefore it is quite clear that a good number of witnesses were seen and their statements taken before that.'

He went on to say that he did not object to the first remand of eight days because he conceded that the prosecution needed time to compile their case. 'I do not know a private prosecutor,' he declared, 'who would dare to keep a lawyer in a busy practice in custody for so long, and I ask in the name of common justice that the case should proceed at the earliest possible moment. I ask that it should go on at least on Monday, and that it should proceed until the charge is removed.'

Mr Micklethwait said that the prosecution could not be ready by then. 'Here is a charge,' he said, 'one of the most serious crimes that can be committed. Although it is a charge of attempted murder, if one looks at it, it is really a charge of murder so far as the prisoner is concerned, because it was a mere accident that Mr Martin did not die.'

Not surprisingly, this brought a violent reaction from the defence, but Mr Micklethwait was unmoved in his contention that so grave a case could not be rushed.

As a compromise, Mr Matthews proposed to the Bench that the prisoner be remanded in custody at Hay instead of Worcester which would give him an opportunity to keep in touch with business matters. Superintendent Weaver now raised an objection on the grounds that the facilities at Hay were inadequate for both the prisoner and his custodians. In the end the magistrates decided to remand Major Armstrong in custody at Worcester Gaol until the following Thursday, 19th January.

* * * * *

While the revelations in court had startled people in Hay, there was still an air of disbelief that a locally respected man, an officer and a solicitor, could be guilty of the charge brought against him. Armstrong's demeanour in court was confident, even buoyant at times when he decided to give a helping hand. There was certainly no cowed acknowledgment of the charge on his part, or on the part of the great majority of onlookers when the Major was taken from the court to be returned to Worcester Gaol. Someone in the waiting room shouted, 'Three cheers for Mr Armstrong' and this was noisily taken up by the rest.

Despite this popular demonstration on the Major's behalf, there was a gathering feeling of expectancy—a feeling that further storm clouds were about to break above his head. The shadow of the late Mrs Armstrong had lain ominously over her husband while he held court in Hay. Now, not only the little market town, but the whole of England held its breath in anticipation of the following week's events.

Broad Street, Hay, where the two solicitors confronted each other

Mr and Mrs Davies and
John Rangecroft of the
Clinical Research Association

Davies's chemist
shop where Armstrong
bought his arsenic

The Police: Weaver, Paling, Sharp and Crutchett

The Doctors: Willcox, Spilsbury, Hincks and Webster

pilsbury and Hincks

Constance and Oswald
Martin

adame X at Hay

Madame X when young

Arriving for his trial

The women in the case — Nurse Kinsey, Miss Rosser,
Nurse Lloyd, Miss Pearce and Mrs Price

4   Exhumation of a Murder

I wondered if Armstrong had administered any of the arsenic to his wife and so caused her death, but I said nothing to anyone.

John F. Davies

THE HORRIFYING idea that Mrs Armstrong's death might not have been due to natural causes first came to Dr Hincks while he was riding in the hills on a call to a patient. He reined his horse in and rode back to his surgery at such a pace that the animal was in a lather of sweat. The doctor rushed into his consulting room and grabbed a book on toxicology. His fears were confirmed—the symptoms of Mrs Armstrong's illness closely resembled those of arsenical poisoning.

This revelation occurred at the end of October when Hincks was considering writing to the Home Office about his suspicions regarding Martin's illness. On Monday 2nd January, the same day that Major Armstrong made his first appearance before the magistrates, his wife's body was exhumed.

* * * * *

Chief Inspector Crutchett's inquiries in Hay concerning Oswald Martin's illness had led to a new line of investigation. Several people had expressed anxiety about the nature of Mrs Armstrong's death. John Davies was perturbed when he learned the precise details of the poor woman's symptoms and he formed an uneasy link in his mind between them and the arsenic bought in his shop by Major Armstrong. But Dr Hincks put more emphatically what others were reluctant to say, 'I had no suspicions at the time or *until the Sunday, 30th October 1921*, that she had been poisoned by arsenic—I think so now.'

Crutchett asked Dr Hincks if he would mind the police interviewing Dr Arthur Townsend, the medical superintendent at Barnwood, under whose care Mrs Armstrong had been placed before her final illness. Hincks raised no objection and told the police that he had already discussed the case with Townsend. A telegram was sent to Barnwood asking if Dr

Townsend would see a Scotland Yard officer the following day. The reply was affirmative and Crutchett and Sharp travelled immediately to Gloucester.

The detectives were given Mrs Armstrong's complete medical history from the time of her arrival at Barnwood until the day she was taken home by her husband. Dr Townsend also gave the officers correspondence between himself and Major Armstrong concerning Mrs Armstrong's admission and subsequent release.

The questions surrounding the circumstances of Mrs Armstrong's death were now thought sufficiently serious to warrant exhumation of the body. Consequently, with Major Armstrong arrested and held in custody, Chief Inspector Crutchett went to Leominster on the morning of Sunday, 1st January, to seek the necessary authority from Mr Southall, the North Herefordshire Coroner. An order sanctioning the exhumation was granted at once.

'Whereas application has been made to me Henry J. Southall for permission to exhume the body of the late Katharine Mary Armstrong from the grave in which it is interred in Cusop churchyard, the ground of such application being that medical examination is required for the purpose of justice: I do hereby, in virtue of powers vested in me by the 25th Section of the Act 20 and 21 Victoria, Chapter 81, grant my licence for the exhumation of the body of the said Katharine Mary Armstrong from the said grave.'

That same afternoon, Crutchett and Superintendent Weaver went to Cusop and spoke with the Rector. They explained the case to him and then made arrangements with the grave-digger for the disinterment. Digging began at 10.30 on Monday morning with P.C. Shakesheff of the Herefordshire Constabulary standing guard in the churchyard to prevent the public approaching the grave. The appearance of a steadily mounting pile of black earth, contrasting sharply with the fresh snow, caused rumour in Hay to reach a new pitch.

At midday, a number of reporters visited Cusop Churchyard where work at the graveside was still going on, but they were prevented from taking photographs inside the churchyard. Early in the afternoon the work was complete and the coffin was exposed and made ready for lifting. The time set for raising the coffin was 5 p.m. but this was postponed pending the arrival of officials from the Home Office. P.C. Shakesheff was joined in his cold vigil at the graveside by Sergeant Worthing. The policemen noticed that the coffin appeared to be in perfect condition despite its ten months underground: but it had lost a little of its polish.

Just before dusk there was a flurry of activity when police arrived at an empty, whitewashed house, called Church Cottage, which stood immediately across the road from the churchyard. They prepared it to receive the disinterred coffin by boarding up the windows to prevent anyone gaining a view of the interior. As darkness fell, the sexton took a hurricane lamp and a hand-bier to the edge of the grave. Those watching from beyond the churchyard walls were treated to an eerie spectacle: the faint light from the lamp just illuminated the open grave and threw into prominence the nearby marble headstones. Occasionally the dim figures of the police officers could be seen as they moved about to keep warm and the faint sound of their subdued voices floated ghost-like across the churchyard.

At 6.45 p.m. a car arrived at the scene. In addition to Crutchett and Weaver, it carried Dr Bernard Henry Spilsbury, the Home Office forensic expert. Without delay the three men, together with other officials, walked to the graveside. An assistant went down into the grave and passed ropes under the coffin: it was then slowly raised by the sexton and undertaker. When it was clear the coffin was lifted up and placed on the hand-bier.

Before the coffin could be moved from the churchyard it was necessary for the undertaker to identify it. The earth obscuring the nameplate was brushed away and proper identification was made by Humphrey Vines Webb, the undertaker. The coffin was then wheeled from the graveside and borne along the pathway to Church Cottage. The handful of people watching saw an assistant descend into the grave itself and scoop up samples of the earth on which the coffin had lain and put them into bottles.

When the party carrying the coffin reached Church Cottage the crowd reverently bared their heads but the reporters soon pressed around and photographs were taken. The party pushed through and disappeared into the house; a group of officials followed and the door was shut. Only a short time elapsed before the officials, Dr Spilsbury among them, emerged from the house and drove off. The door of the house was locked and a solitary policeman remained on guard.

The following day at about 10 a.m. the principal officials returned and Humphrey Webb, who had conducted Mrs Armstrong's funeral nearly a year before, unscrewed the coffin lid. The face of the corpse was covered with a handkerchief, the trunk and limbs were covered with the coffin lining and a towel lay over the legs and feet. When these coverings were removed the body was found to be clothed in a nightdress and stockings which had partly rotted.

Webb identified the body as that of Katharine Armstrong on account of the prominent teeth and the long plaits of dark hair tied with light-coloured ribbon which lay on either shoulder. Dr Hincks corroborated the identification. The exposed parts of the body showed advanced decomposition; the soft tissue had shrunk and the skin had been destroyed on parts of the hands and feet exposing the tendons and some of the joints. The soft tissue had gone from the lower part of the nose and the eyeballs had collapsed.

The post-mortem was carried out by Dr Spilsbury, assisted by Dr Hincks and Dr William Ainslie, a Hereford practitioner who represented Major Armstrong. The conditions in which the doctors worked were very poor; the lighting was deficient, ventilation and space were restricted and there were no facilities for washing. The body was removed from the oak coffin and placed on a trestle table from which the liquid products of putrefaction dripped on to the floor. Such conditions were hardly conducive to accurate observation and reasonable judgement, although Spilsbury was quite used to the inadequate provisions usually made for post-mortems of this kind.

Among the spectators outside the cottage was a seventeen-year-old lad from the town. He was watching the various comings and goings when Dr Hincks appeared at the door of the house and asked him to go into Hay and fetch a bottle of whisky. When the lad returned from his errand he handed the bottle over to Hincks and managed to satisfy his curiosity by sneaking a glimpse of what was happening inside the house. He saw Mrs Armstrong's body and said afterwards, 'I recognized her. She had two long plaits of hair hanging down over her

chest and a bow of pink ribbon on the end of each. I couldn't
sleep for a fortnight.'

The doctors would have been justified in taking a pull from
the whisky bottle in order to fortify themselves for their
gruesome task. In doing so they would have been following a
practice prescribed in a contemporary textbook on forensic
medicine which advised: 'There is seldom any risk to health
in removing a single body, yet certain precautions are necessary; thus it is as well to take a dram, and also to stand on the
windward side of the corpse. No post-mortem should ever be
conducted on an empty stomach.'

Spilsbury examined each organ and part of the body in
turn, noting its condition and putting specimens into jars for
subsequent investigation. Starting with the head, he found
that the hair readily came away and the right plait was
immediately removed and placed in a bottle. The scalp and
brain were well preserved and normal; the brain itself was a
soft, greenish mass and despite the offensive smell of
decomposition, the familiar convolutions were clearly distin-
guishable. There was no evidence of disease but a portion of
the brain was put into one of the pathologist's jars.

Next, Spilsbury opened the chest cavity to reveal the heart
and lungs. The heart was slightly reduced in size and there
was some thickening of the mitral valve and slight disease of
the aorta. The pleural cavities of the lungs contained fluid
some of which was taken as a sample. Although the lungs
were small no disease was detected.

The pathologist examined the other organs in the chest and
then gave his attention to the abdomen. The liver and both
kidneys were reserved for analysis. The stomach was normal
in size but contained a small amount of fluid which was put
into a bottle. Fluid was also found in parts of both the small
and large intestines.

When the examination was completed, the remaining
organs were replaced in the body which was then restored
and replaced in the coffin. Spilsbury observed that, 'the
body of Mrs Armstrong was in an unusually well-preserved
condition . . . The external appearance was that of a body
which had shrunken from loss of fluid and which was under-
going mummification rather than that of a body in which
putrefaction was taking place in the normal manner.'

One of Spilsbury's cards recording the exhumation of Mrs Armstrong.
Note the error—it was Cusop churchyard, not Hay.

The doctors and others present at the post-mortem emerged
from the house and were grateful to breathe in some clean
air; Humphrey Webb was sick and Weaver, Crutchett and
Sharp lit cigarettes while the crowd cheered them. Spilsbury,
carrying his specimen bottles, was driven away to Hay in
order to make a speedy return to London. His departure
signalled the completion of this grim work and all that
remained was for Webb to close the coffin the following day.

The only statement made at the time of the post-mortem
was by Dr Ainslie who was interviewed by a reporter from the
Hereford Times. He said that the body had been opened and
there was nothing inconsistent with the death certificate
which had been issued by Dr Hincks. He added that Dr
Spilsbury had returned to London during the afternoon carrying with him the internal organs. Various tests would be made
on these which would probably take several days.

* * * * *

The inquest on the exhumed body of Mrs Armstrong was

opened on the evening of Wednesday, 4th January. It took place at Cusop Elementary School where the school desks had been rearranged to accommodate the Coroner's Court. It was a bitterly cold evening and snow clung to the distant Black Mountains. The weather merely added to the chilling task which awaited the Coroner's jury. In the school playground, reporters gathered to await the arrival of the Coroner. Behind them lay the tiny churchyard with its centuries old yew trees, and a black scar in the snow marked the opened grave and was a reminder of the business in hand.

Henry Southall, the North Herefordshire Coroner, arrived by car at 4.50 p.m. in the company of Superintendent Weaver. They entered the school building and were followed shortly afterwards by the now familiar figures of Crutchett and Sharp who were driven up in another car. They found themselves in the cold, gloomy interior of the little schoolroom where oil lamps cast great dancing shadows on the walls.

The names of the jury were called and Mr Rees Williams was elected foreman. The twelve men now faced the duty of viewing the body and, led by Superintendent Weaver, they walked through falling snow to Church Cottage, some hundred yards away. The room containing the coffin presented a macabre scene. The room itself with its bare, damp walls and hollow-sounding floor boards was even more bleak than the schoolroom. Sergeant Worthing stood at the head of the coffin holding a candle and under its flickering light, the jurymen filed past, heads bared in respect, grimly taking in the almost unrecognizable features of the corpse.

With this unpleasant duty over, the jury returned to the schoolroom where the Coroner addressed them on their responsibilities. He urged them to listen without prejudice to the evidence and not to discuss the matter with friends or relatives. He also told them that parts of the body had been sent to London for expert examination and that a report of this would be essential to the progress of the inquest. The Coroner then adjourned the proceedings until Tuesday, 24th January.

The coffin containing the body of Katharine Armstrong was lowered for the second time into its last resting place in Cusop churchyard on Thursday, 5th January 1922 at 11 a.m. Apart from the grave-digger and sexton, those in attendance were Superintendent Weaver, the Reverend Buchanan and a representative of the *Hereford Times*.

* * * * *

Dr Spilsbury's post-mortem examination of Katharine Armstrong's body revealed a degree of preservation that was unusual after ten months' burial. In his report Spilsbury said 'this was especially noticeable in the liver, kidneys, stomach, intestines and uterus.' His examination revealed 'no natural disease which would account for the severe vomiting and diarrhoea which formed the most prominent symptoms of Mrs Armstrong's last illness.' Examination of the large intestine showed that it was quite empty and Spilsbury commented: 'That pointed to some irritant condition during life which had brought about an unusual emptying of the intestines as the result of diarrhoea.'

Spilsbury had handed over the specimens which he had taken at the post-mortem to John Webster, the Senior Home Office Analyst. There were fourteen jars containing samples taken from every major organ and tissue in the exhumed body. Two further jars contained sawdust and shavings taken from the bottom of the coffin and the sample of soil collected from the grave at the time. Analysis showed the presence of arsenic in every organ and in bone, muscle, skin, hair and finger nails. The total amount of arsenic found in the body was 208 milligrams; the liver alone contained 138 milligrams, or 2 grains, the equivalent of a fatal dose.

Katharine Armstrong's body was riddled with arsenic ten months after her death and even the wood shavings in the coffin had absorbed the poison as the body decomposed. This dramatic result of the exhumation was to cause a new charge to be brought against Major Armstrong who was on remand in Worcester Goal.

* * * * *

Rex v. Armstrong.

(*2 Mrs Armstrong (dec.^d)

Distribution of Arsenic

	milligrams
Stomach	2·5
Stomach Contents	2·0
Jejunum & Contents	1·6
Ileum & Contents	9·1
Caecum, Ascending } Colon & Contents }	37·6
Liver	**138·0**
Spleen	1·0
Kidneys	13·2
Left Lung	0·5
Heart	0·6
Fluid from Pleural Cavities	0·9
Portion of Brain (14 gs)	0·1
Bone from left Femur (4 gs)	0·01
Skin from left Thigh (3¼ gs)	0·25
Muscle (Back of left Thigh) 3½ gs.	0·21
Hair from Head (3¾ gs)	0·54
Finger Nails	0·06
Toe Nails	0·03
Total	208·2

Senior Home Office analyst John Webster's report on specimens taken from Mrs Armstrong's body.

One of the features of the police-court proceedings at Hay was that it became a long, drawn-out affair. The whole hearing lasted only eleven days but spanned a period of six weeks by virtue of various remands and adjournments. The exhumation of Katharine Armstrong's body and the sub-sequent Coroner's Inquest ran parallel with the hearing at Hay. The police court proceedings depended on the progress of the Coroner's Inquest and several adjournments were brought about by the need to wait for expert evidence.

Since the adjournment at Hay on 12th January, Armstrong had languished in Worcester Gaol and no doubt his trained solicitor's mind analysed again and again the charge which he had faced in court the previous week. He must also have taken note of Superintendent Weaver's portentous remark during his first appearance before the magistrates about 'other matters pending'. Armstrong knew only too well the significance of that remark and realized the very real possibility of another charge being brought against him.

Such fears as he may have entertained were justified when he re-appeared before the Hay magistrates on 19th January. He was brought to Hereford by train and thence escorted to Hay Police Court by Superintendent Weaver and P.C. Shakesheff. There, in the cells, before the court opened, he knew the worst. Albert Weaver, who had known Armstrong for eleven years and considered him 'a most affable man', formally charged the prisoner with murdering his wife. The charge read: 'that he did feloniously and wilfully and with malice aforethought kill and murder one Katharine Mary Armstrong on 22nd February 1921 at Cusop in the County of Hereford by poisoning her with arsenic.' Weaver cautioned the prisoner and Armstrong replied, 'I repeat what I said before, I am absolutely innocent.'

Mr Mortimer Bayliss presided over the same Bench of Magistrates that had officiated the previous week and seated with them was Captain E.S. Stanhope, Chief Constable of Herefordshire. The octogenarian Mr Cambridge Phillips acted as Magistrates' Clerk, but the depositions were written out by Mr W.H. Grout, the Deputy Clerk of the Weobley Petty Sessional Division. The legal representatives for the two sides were the same as before: Mr T.A. Matthews, who had spared no effort in preparing his defence, represented the prisoner, and Mr St John Micklethwait appeared for the Director of Public Prosecutions.

Mr Micklethwait addressed the court. His quiet voice barely reached the extremities of the tiny courtroom but his opening sentence electrified the already tense assembly.

'It now becomes my duty,' he said, 'to prefer against the prisoner, Major Armstrong, another charge of a more grave and more serious character even than the charge of attempting to murder Mr Martin. The prisoner is now charged with the wilful murder of his wife by poisoning her with arsenic. . .' The rest of his words were almost lost in the din made by reporters rushing from the court room to phone the news in to their papers. The *Hereford Times*, which devoted thousands of words to the progress of the case, quickly had a special edition on the streets; it sold in record numbers.

Unperturbed by the noise, Mr Micklethwait told the court about the Coroner's order for the exhumation of Mrs Armstrong's body and said that certain organs taken for analysis had been found to contain 'a quantity of arsenic amounting to not less than three and one fifth grains.' He said that there was no question or doubt, that Mrs Armstrong's death was due to arsenical poisoning. He proposed to show that there was a *prima facie* case against the husband of administering poison.

Mr Micklethwait gave a detailed account of events since Mrs Armstrong first consulted Dr Hincks in 1919 when she was suffering from neuritis and rheumatism. 'Dr Hincks will tell you', he said, 'that though she was not a robust woman, she was physically perfectly sound, and so far as her mind was concerned she was an intelligent, strong-minded woman, level-headed and her sister will tell you she was a good business woman.'

During the time that Mrs Armstrong was at the asylum at Barnwood, her husband showed himself to be considerate, visiting her from time to time and in January requesting that his wife should be allowed home. But it was also the case that on the very day Major Armstrong wrote to the asylum authorities requesting his wife's release he visited the chemist at Hay and bought a quarter of a pound of arsenic.

Major Armstrong was so anxious to get his wife home that he was prepared to go against the opinion of the asylum's doctors. Mrs Armstrong could not be sent home as cured, which was what her husband wanted, because she was clearly not well. The asylum's Medical Superintendent thought it wise only to let her home on three month's probation so that she could still receive a certain amount of medical supervision and be brought back quickly if her condition deteriorated. Major Armstrong objected to this arrangement and told the asylum that he wished his wife to be released immediately, saying that he would take full responsibility.

Mr Micklethwait asked the court why Major Armstrong was so concerned to have his wife back home since it was perfectly clear that she was still suffering from delusions. He referred to the occasion when Armstrong had asked Dr Hincks how much arsenic was a fatal dose and said, '. . .he was suffering from a certain disease which was a venereal disease, and I shall be in a position to show you that Mr Armstrong contracted that disease while his wife was at the asylum, and when this request was made for the wife to return home, he was not merely suffering from it, but was being actually treated for it and realized his condition perfectly. Why should a man in the state Mr Armstrong was at that time be so anxious to have her back unless there was some ulterior motive?'

Mrs Armstrong's last illness was described and Mr Micklethwait said, 'The case for the Crown is that Major Armstrong was slowly and surely administering poison to her. He was doing it every day. He was there with her alone and it was quite clear that he had ample opportunities.' During this opening speech by the prosecution, Major Armstrong sat in the dock, showing no emotion whatever. Sometimes, he appeared lost in thought with downcast eyes, and on other occasions he followed the proceedings closely.

Mr Micklethwait pressed his case unremittingly. He spoke of the nurse's surprise at the lack of feeling on Major Armstrong's part when, although it was obvious his wife was close to death, he chose to go in to his office at Hay. The court was told how a death certificate was issued by Dr Hincks, giving gastritis and nephritis as the cause of death; how the funeral took place and how a week or so later Armstrong went to the doctor in a highly nervous condition. Shortly afterwards, the widower left for a holiday in Italy and entries in his diary, mentioning various women's names, gave an indication of how he spent his time. Moreover, within twenty-four hours of his return from the continent, Armstrong was discussing marriage with a woman in Bournemouth.

At this point, Mr Micklethwait returned to other events which he said, 'throw light upon Mr Armstrong's anxiety to get his wife out of the asylum and to bring her back to him.' Mrs Armstrong's background was outlined and it was stated that she had inherited a certain amount of property on her mother's death and had also received stocks and shares during her mother's lifetime. When Mrs Armstrong died her husband produced a will dated 8th July 1920 in which everything was left to him: this document was drawn up in his handwriting. The date was important said Mr Micklethwait because if Mrs Armstrong's mind was so deranged on 15th August 1920 it was somewhat suspicious to find her making a will in July.

The will was witnessed by Miss Pearce and Miss Candy, both servants at Mayfield, and it purported to revoke all previous wills. The court was reminded that under the Law of Intestacy, when a married woman died without making a will, the whole of her property went to the husband. But Mrs Armstrong had made an earlier will, dated 17th January 1917, which she had given to her sister, Bessie Friend, for safe-keeping. This will was written in her own hand and in it she made various small bequests but gave her husband no interest whatever in the capital which was to be divided equally among the three children.

Bessie Friend remembered her sister saying in September 1919 that she was not satisfied with the will since she did not think it left sufficient for her husband. However, while she was in the asylum Mrs Armstrong had written to Bessie telling her clearly that the will in her safe-keeping was the last will.

The new will was written in Major Armstrong's handwriting and no-one could know better than a solicitor that the witnesses must see such a document signed and then sign it themselves in each other's presence. This practice had not been observed in this instance and one of the witnesses was not even aware that the paper to which she put her signature was a will. 'If that evidence is true', said Mr Micklethwait, 'the witnessing clause is a lie and no-one knew it better than Mr Armstrong. If that is so, that will is not worth the paper it is written on. By that will, Mr Armstrong was not only defrauding his wife but robbing his own children as well.'

There followed a legal wrangle when the prosecution asked that the evidence on the lesser charge of attempted murder against Mr Martin also be heard as it was material to the capital charge. Mr Micklethwait wanted to have the depositions on record in case any of the witnesses died before giving evidence at an assize court. But this evidence could only be read if it was made to apply to both charges. The Bench agreed that this could be done.

Mr Matthews, defending Major Armstrong, said that he would say nothing at that point regarding the charge which had been outlined. But he complained about not having been allowed to see the documents taken from his client at the time of arrest. It seemed that there were no longer any difficulties preventing the defence from seeing these papers and, with that matter cleared up, the witnesses were called.

The first was John Arthur Rangecroft, a senior laboratory attendant at the Clinical Research Association, who confirmed the receipt of the specimens sent by Dr Hincks. Next, was a bright, smiling youth of sixteen, William George Grant, a district messenger, who was obviously enjoying his moment of fame. In a clear voice that could be heard throughout the court he stated that he collected two parcels from the Clinical Research Association and took them to Mr Webster at St Mary's Hospital, Paddington.

The last witness before lunch was Una Mary Baker who told the court that she had been employed as a clerk by Major Armstrong for two years. She remembered that her employer started making tea at the office in November and she heard Major Armstrong invite Mr Martin to tea. Miss Pearce had brought butter to the office from Mayfield and Una spoke of being sent out to buy scones and buns. She never saw a packet of powder in her employer's possession; she was aware that probate had been obtained for Mrs Armstrong's will.

The examination of these witnesses proved something of an anticlimax after the excitement caused earlier by Mr Micklethwait's opening remarks. Interest was rekindled after lunch, however, when Mr Micklethwait referred again to the disease from which Major Armstrong was suffering. He wished to point out that this information originated from

Dr Hincks but he thought it only fair to emphasize that the information had been given only after the doctor had made a strenuous protest. Dr Hincks had raised the question of privilege and said he would do so again when called to give evidence. Mr Micklethwait said that if he did the prosecution would ask the Bench to overrule it. The Chairman of the Magistrates remarked that a case on that point had recently been decided by the Court of Criminal Appeal.

The first witness after lunch was Alan Preen, Mr Martin's clerk, who had been at Martin's house on the evening that the solicitor was taken ill. He described what happened and told the court about Major Armstrong's visits to Mr Martin's office on the following day.

Interest again quickened when Chief Inspector Alfred Crutchett of Scotland Yard entered the witness box. The detective related the circumstances of Major Armstrong's arrest with particular reference to the prisoner's attempt to search through the articles taken from his pockets. In answer to Mr Matthews, Crutchett agreed that on the day of arrest he and his two colleagues went straight upstairs to Armstrong's office without giving their names. He also agreed that Armstrong volunteered without a moment's hesitation to give them every assistance, as indeed did the staff. He added that at Mayfield, Miss Pearce and Mrs Price also afforded them every possible assistance.

Throughout the day, and also at the previous hearing there had been a number of skirmishes between prosecutor and defender and another occurred concerning additional evidence given by Miss Pearce. Mr Matthews thought that any further statement made to the police by Miss Pearce should have been taken in the presence of a representative of the defence. Miss Pearce was an elderly lady and he resented Crutchett's telling him that every facility to see her had been withdrawn.

It was now 4.30 in the afternoon and darkness descended quickly on the court room. Superintendent Weaver said that the police had been trying to get in touch with the Coroner since the inquest had been adjourned until the following Tuesday. But he had been unable to get through; 'I am afraid the press have commandeered the telephone lines,' he added apologetically. It was agreed that in the unlikely event of the

Coroner wishing to proceed with the inquest, a remand
would be granted until the inquest was over. Eventually it
was decided that the court stood adjourned until 10.30 a.m.
the following Tuesday, depending on the Coroner's decision
concerning the inquest.

For Major Armstrong that meant a return to Worcester
Gaol for another four days—a few more days for reflection
and analysis. He must have realized how much he had underrated the local people or perhaps the extent to which he had
overrated his own power and ability. What he had to face
now, in view of the new charge against him, was a minute
dissection of every aspect of his behaviour and activity. He
may even have felt grudging admiration for the way in which
the police had built up their case.

* * * * *

Tuesday, 24th January 1922. The court re-assembled at Hay.
Reporters were quick to note that neither Mr Cambridge
Phillips nor Mr Grout was present. In their places were Mr
F.R. James of Hereford with J.R. Gransmore as his assistant.
The central figure of the drama came as usual by train to
Hereford and then to Hay by car. He looked towards the
ever present newspaper representatives, as he was escorted
by Superintendent Weaver along the narrow path leading to
the court entrance. 'What? Haven't you had enough yet?', he
said cheerily to the photographers as he disappeared into the
building.

When he entered the dock Armstrong showed no sign of
the ordeal which he was enduring and he bowed politely to
the Bench and then again to someone across the room. His
dapper figure was clad in his customary British warm and on
this occasion he wore a black and white regimental tie.

There was a slight hold-up before witnesses were called.
Mr Matthews arrived fifteen minutes late and explained that
he had been detained in discussions with the Coroner about
the inquest. He requested a few more minutes in order to
talk with Mr Micklethwait. During the delay, Armstrong
smiled and chatted freely with Mr Chivers, his solicitor's
managing clerk. Perhaps he was feeling pleased at having had
returned at least one of his personal possessions: on the little

finger of his right hand he was wearing his plain gold ring.

The first witness of the day was a lady dressed in deep mourning. She was wearing a long black astrakhan coat, a black straw hat and a white muff. She answered Mr Micklethwait's questions in a clear, pleasant voice and told the court that she was Miss Ida Bessie Friend, sister to Mrs Armstrong. She described the journey to the asylum at Barnwood when her sister was sick in the car and she said that was the last time she saw her alive. Miss Friend produced the will which Mrs Armstrong had made in 1917 and Mr Micklethwait referred to bequests to Miss Pearce and to Major Armstrong. She confirmed that the original copy of the will which was in her sister's handwriting was in her care but said that a draft had been given to Major Armstrong.

Another argument ensued when Mr Matthews objected to a question put to Miss Friend asking if her sister had ever referred to the will. The Chairman of the Magistrates said he could not see how any statement made by Mrs Armstrong could be admitted in evidence if Major Armstrong was not present at the time. Mr Micklethwait quoted the ruling of Mr Justice Coleridge in his contention that such secondary evidence was admissible. He wanted to show evidence of a declaration intimating that the intention of the testatrix was that that will should remain continually her will. The Bench considered that the evidence could not be admitted. Mr Micklethwait, however, said he would re-introduce it at a later stage.

Miss Friend agreed that she knew of another will because, after her sister had gone to the asylum, Major Armstrong had told her that a further will had been executed. When Mr Matthews cross-examined the witness, the court heard that for many years the late Mrs Armstrong had been a strong believer in homeopathic medicine and was in the habit of treating herself with these preparations. Miss Friend gave the names of some of these medicines as *nux vomica, mercurius, magnesia* and *arsenicum* and said that they were usually bought from a firm in Liverpool. She could not remember the name of the firm but said that apart from Mrs Armstrong other members of the household also took homeopathic medicines.

Bessie Friend was followed in the witness box by Miss

Augusta Gertrude Hutchins who lived at Torquay and had once been nurse-companion to Mrs Armstrong. She identified her own signature as witness to the 1917 will and said that her employer seemed to be very familiar with drawing up wills and was in her opinion an intelligent woman. She had not seen either of the Armstrongs for two years.

Many of these present in the court were probably thinking about lunch when the last witness of the morning was called. This was Humphrey Vines Webb, the Hay undertaker, whose description of the arrangements made for Mrs Armstrong's funeral and details of the exhumation and re-interment no doubt spoiled a few appetites

After lunch, Henry John Hammonds, Chief Clerk of the Probate Registry at Hereford, produced Mrs Armstrong's will, dated 8th July 1920, and stated that probate had been granted on 30th March 1921. The gross value of the estate was £2419 18s. and the nett value, £2278 3s. Mr Hammonds declined to allow the Clerk of the Court to retain the original will, saying that he must take it back to Hereford. Asked by the Chairman of the Bench whether he was going back by car or train, he answered, 'I am here for the day'. This reply caused considerable laughter and Major Armstrong joined in.

Mrs Lily Evans, the next witness, told the court that she had been chief domestic servant to Mrs Armstrong and said that the signature, 'Lily Candy', on the will was hers. It was her maiden name. She said that Major Armstrong had asked her to sign the document. Neither Mrs Armstrong nor Miss Pearce was present and she did not know the paper was a will, she thought it might be something to do with her insurance. Mr Matthews strongly objected to the line of questioning which evinced these answers and they were deleted from the record.

Under cross-examination by Mr Matthews, Lily Evans said she had only signed one document for the Major and never one for Mrs Armstrong. Miss Pearce never asked her to go to see Mrs Armstrong in the drawing-room for the purpose of signing a paper.

Still on the subject of the will, Mr Micklethwait submitted that he had now shown justification for asking Miss Friend a question about the declaration made to her in respect of an earlier will. 'The evidence I want to put before you is this', he said, 'that there was in fact a valid will which Miss Friend had in her possession at the time, a will which will make it clear that Mrs Armstrong adhered to and regarded as her valid will.' Mr Matthews rose to his feet immediately. 'That was the very point we had this morning. I do not think it should be referred to again.' Turning to the Bench, he continued, 'He is telling you the evidence he proposes to call.'

This caused considerable discussion among the members of the Bench and the Chairman pointed out that what the prosecution wished to show was that the second will was invalid. He added that Mr Micklethwait seemed to want to produce evidence which was not necessary in the case at this time. Mr Matthews agreed that seeking to establish the second will as a bogus document not made by Mrs Armstrong would be material evidence if he were defending a suit as to the validity of the will, but in the present case it was hearsay evidence. In any case he said that he would be bound by the Chairman's ruling. The Bench withdrew for private consideration of this delicate point and when they re-appeared ruled not to admit the evidence. Mr Matthews worked very hard on his client's behalf and Major Armstrong must have felt much encouraged.

While the magistrates were absent from court, an incident occurred which evoked considerable criticism. Dr W. Black Jones, the magistrate for Breconshire and Radnorshire, who had a seat behind the magistrates' desk, took a photograph of the prisoner in the dock. Members of the public present in the crowded courtroom expressed resentment at the incident, since on the previous day press photographers had not been allowed to use their cameras inside the court and indeed one of them was turned out for attempting to take pictures.

Once the reaction to this incident had died down, the next witness was called. Miss Eva Allen told the court she was a certified nurse and had attended Mrs Armstrong during her last illness and up to the time that she died. She briefly described the decline in Mrs Armstrong's health and in cross-examination by Mr Matthews she agreed that from the start the patient was suffering from delusions and was known to be taking homeopathic pills. For the last week Mrs Armstrong took no solid food. During the evenings, Major Armstrong would read to his wife; in reply to Mr Matthews's questioning

Nurse Allen agreed that the Armstrongs were on very affectionate terms and were most happy.

Mr Micklethwait, seemingly defeated in the matter of introducing evidence concerning Mrs Armstrong's will, refused to let the matter pass and caused the sensation of the day by raising it yet again. He announced that on the basis of certain information which he had just received he wished to recall two witnesses, Miss Friend and Miss Hutchins, who were familiar with the late Mrs Armstrong's handwriting. He explained that Miss Friend said she had been shown a document, the will of 8th July, and gave it as her opinion that the signature was not that of her sister. The will had been shown to her outside the court by Mr Gerald Paling, a solicitor on the staff of the Director of Public Prosecutions. Miss Hutchins also said that the signature did not seem to her to be that of Mrs Armstrong.

Mr Micklethwait told the witness he wished to be certain that she had not seen the will before, adding, 'I only want to be sure because Mr Matthews contradicts me whenever I say anything.' In spite of all Matthews's protestations, the prosecution had succeeded in presenting the evidence on the signature of the will. Mr Micklethwait had judged his moment well, for daylight was fading quickly and as there was no electric lighting in the court there was only time to hear one more witness. That was Superintendent Weaver who gave evidence about the arrest and subsequent charging of the prisoner.

* * * * *

Wednesday, 25th January 1922. The day's proceedings were taken up almost entirely with the medical evidence. The prisoner, his usual courteous self, was brought in from No. 1 cell and on entering the dock bowed towards the magistrates.

Dr Arthur Allen Deykin Townsend, Medical Superintendent of Barnwood House Hospital for Mental Disorders, told how Mrs Armstrong was received into his care in August 1920. He described her mental and physical state at that time and said he diagnosed the case as one of neuritis followed by functional paresis. The patient improved while at Barnwood although her return to better health was more physical than mental.

Dr Townsend then described Major Armstrong's request for his wife to be discharged. He said that Mrs Armstrong's strong desire to return home stemmed in part from her delusions and her wish to make amends for what she considered to be her utter selfishness towards her husband and children. The doctor said he could not discharge her as recovered, although she was steadily improving, but in any event Major Armstrong called to take her home the following January. He received a note from Major Armstrong saying that his wife had a comfortable journey home and was no worse. He heard nothing further until he read of Mrs Armstrong's death in a newspaper.

Dr Townsend agreed with Mr Matthews that Major Armstrong was naturally concerned about his wife and further agreed, after considerable thought, that there was no undue hurry on Armstrong's part to get his wife home.

Three more witnesses appeared before lunch to clear the way for Dr Hincks, whose evidence was due in the afternoon. Miss Muriel Gladys Kinsey, a young woman dressed in nursing uniform, told the court that she had attended Mrs Armstrong for four days and left because she thought the patient needed more supervision and because she feared a suicide attempt. Next came Mrs Lucy Alice Lloyd, the Hay District Nurse, who stood in for Nurse Allen for one night at Mayfield. She said that Mrs Armstrong had vomited during the night. Finally, Sergeant Worthing described how he found a quantity of powdered and liquid weed killer in the outbuildings at Mayfield.

Dr Hincks was called immediately after lunch. His tall figure and ruddy countenance framed with greying hair and moustache gave his appearance in the witness box an aura of authority. The doctor was dressed in a fur-lined motoring coat and carried under his arm several large reference books. Mr Micklethwait asked him about his professional qualifications and after giving these Hincks found the atmosphere in the courtroom sufficiently oppressive to warrant the removal of his heavy coat.

He related how he had been consulted by Mrs Armstrong in his capacity as her family doctor in 1919 and 1920 and described how, with Dr Jayne, he had decided in August 1920 that she should go to the asylum at Barnwood. The following January, Major Armstrong asked him to talk to the asylum authorities about his wife's release and then took considerable exception to the condition that she only came home on leave. Dr Hincks saw her when she returned home and again on two visits in February when she complained about the feelings in her feet which felt like springs pressing her up from the ground. 'She had,' said Hincks, 'what we know as the "high-stepping gait".' He went on to describe in detail Mrs Armstrong's final illness and death.

'You prepared the death certificate? ' asked Mr Micklethwait.

'Yes.'

'What did you certify as the causes of death?'

'That it was due to gastritis, nephritis and heart disease. That would be the order, gastritis being the most recent.'

'At the time you gave that certificate you formed the opinion that those were the causes of death?'

'I formed the opinion at that time that death was due to those causes.'

'Having regard to all the circumstances is your opinion still the same?'

'My opinion,' said Dr Hincks, speaking slowly and emphatically, 'having regard to all the circumstances is that death was due to chronic arsenical poisoning.'

Mr Micklethwait then turned to what he called 'the next episode'—that of Mr Martin's illness. Dr Hincks said at first he formed the opinion that the patient was suffering from a bilious attack brought on by overwork and lack of exercise, and he prescribed a mixture. On the Sunday morning, however, after a talk with Mr John Davies he went more carefully into the symptoms. He described sending to the Clinical Research Association the bottle containing a sample of Martin's urine together with the chocolates. As a result of the reply received from the Association he wrote a letter to the Home Office. Dr Hincks said he remembered seeing Major Armstrong when he came to his surgery and inquired after Martin's health.

Having received an affirmative answer from the doctor on the question of whether he was attending Major Armstrong in November or December 1920, Mr Micklethwait gave notice of taking this line of inquiry further. He said to Dr Hincks, 'I am going to put a question to you. Don't answer it for a moment. I am going to ask you what you were attending him for.'

While Hincks was contemplating his reply, Mr Micklethwait turned to the Bench and explained that the witness had intimated he would object to the question on the grounds that a physician should not divulge details of his consultations with patients. While the doctor claimed that privilege, there were authorities to justify the prosecution's contention that it could be overruled. The argument was based mainly on a dictum of Mr Justice McCardie who held that in a court of justice there were even higher considerations than the privilege of a medical man.

The Chairman of the Magistrates declared that he was familiar with those rulings and said that the question should be answered. Mr Matthews was asked if he had any objection and he replied that it did not concern him; it was a matter between the doctor and the court. Dr Hincks then answered the question, saying that he was treating Major Armstrong with a medicine which contained arsenic. Mr Micklethwait was not satisfied with this, and said, 'what I want to get at is this. On 11th January 1921, was Major Armstrong suffering from syphilis?' Reluctantly, Hincks replied simply, 'He was.'

The doctor went on to say that when he was giving his patient an injection some discussion arose as to the nature of the drug being used. Armstrong inquired if it contained arsenic and on being told that it did asked what a fatal dose was. Hincks replied, 'Two or three grains', and Armstrong said, 'Would not one be sufficient?' Hincks told the court that he was flabbergasted for the moment and then added that Armstrong seemed to know more about it than he did. In reply to a question regarding Martin's illness, Hincks said that he had now formed an opinion that the symptoms were caused by Martin's taking what could have been a fatal dose of arsenic on Wednesday, 26th October.

This concluded the doctor's evidence-in-chief and, as Mr Matthews preferred to reserve his cross-examination, two more police witnesses were heard before the court adjourned. Sergeant Williams, the desk sergeant at Hay Police Station, described how he had taken charge of the brown paper parcel containing the items taken from the prisoner's pockets; and Detective Sergeant Sharp of Scotland Yard identified the diaries found on the prisoner as being in Armstrong's hand-writing and said that an inventory was made of all the articles taken from the prisoner, and from his home and office.

Since Mr Micklethwait was due to appear at the Assizes the following day, the court was adjourned until Friday of the following week. Once again Armstrong had to go back to Worcester Gaol to suffer another delay. He knew that the embarrassing disclosures made about him in court would soon be bandied about in Hay both in the drawing room and at the street corner. The proud reputation he had made for himself in the local community was slowly but surely dis-integrating in court; the name of Major Armstrong would now be cause for crude jest in the public houses.

* * * * *

Friday, 3rd February 1922. The strain on Armstrong was beginning to tell for when the court re-assembled, he lacked his customary well-groomed appearance and his hair was untidy.

Before Dr Hincks re-entered the witness box to be cross-examined, the Chairman of the Bench expressed his disapproval of the previous week's incident in court when an attempt had been made to take a photograph. He said that the offender, Dr Black Jones, was not a member of the Hay Bench, and indeed not of the Herefordshire Magistracy at all. The Bench was extremely displeased by the occurrence and considered that Dr Black Jones showed a great lack of taste.

Mr Matthews then directed his questions to Dr Hincks who said that he had not always attended Major Armstrong and his family while they were at Hay; he believed that another doctor had attended Mrs Armstrong for a time. Concerning his prescriptions, the doctor said exact entries were made in his book at the time of issue, but he very rarely entered the symptoms of his patients.

'May I take it', asked Mr Matthews, 'that in the case of Mrs Armstrong and the family there is no note in your book of the symptoms?'

'No, simply a certification.'

'The same thing would apply as far as Mr Martin is concerned I suppose?'

'The same thing would apply exactly.'

'So that the symptoms you have given us have been given from memory?'

'The symptoms I have given are from memory, and', added Hincks quickly, 'I should say aided by my prescriptions'.

Later, Dr Hincks said that he was wrong in giving that answer because he had an entry about Mrs Armstrong's illness, which was neuritis. He agreed with Mr Matthews that on 15th August it was Major Armstrong who was concerned about his wife and asked for a sleeping draught.

The doctor had difficulty in recalling what actually took place when he discussed with Armstrong and Arthur Chevalier whether Mrs Armstrong should go to the asylum. His impression was that Major Armstrong placed the matter entirely in his hands. He did not agree that Armstrong left the decision about Mrs Armstrong's return from the asylum entirely to him. He said he advised the prisoner that he should be guided by the Medical Officer at the asylum. When Mrs Armstrong returned home in January, Major Armstrong discussed with him the desirability of having a nurse in the house. There was no doubt that she was suffering from delusions and he made arrangements for a full-time nurse to be in attendance; Major Armstrong raised no objection.

Dr Hincks said that until 16th February he had been treating Mrs Armstrong for biliousness, but then considered that she was suffering from acute gastritis. After his wife's death Major Armstrong consulted the doctor about his own health and Hincks decided that he was suffering from strain. Armstrong asked him, 'Don't you think it would be a good thing for me to get away for a change?' The doctor agreed that it would.

So far as Martin was concerned, the doctor agreed that his estimation of the patient's pulse rate of 120 to 130 on 27th October was from memory. 'I think, Doctor,' said Mr Matthews, 'that certain suggestions were made to you immediately after Mr Martin was taken ill?' The doctor confirmed that this was so and said that it was Mr Davies, the chemist, who had suggested that Martin had been poisoned by Armstrong. The term used was 'foul play'.

Hincks had been in the witness box for an hour when Mr Micklethwait asked permission to interpose a witness who wished to leave early. Mr Matthews said that his legal colleague had been good enough to tell him about this witness. She was a lady who had requested permission of the Bench to have her name and address withheld. Mr Matthews added, 'As far as the defence is concerned it does not matter to me in the slightest, but I feel we ought to have regard to her wishes, and I believe Mr Micklethwait feels the same.'

The magistrates agreed and the Chairman asked the press representatives to make a note of the request and not to give details of the witness or publish any photographs of her. On this understanding the witness entered the court to a subdued buzz of excitement. She was middle-aged, wearing a mole-coloured coat with a matching motoring veil which obscured her pale face. It did not go unnoticed that the prisoner in the dock lowered his head and made no attempt to meet her eyes.

Madame X, as this witness was referred to by the press, told the court that she was a widow who resided with her mother. She had met Major Armstrong in August 1915 and was aware that he was a married man. She met him in London in July 1920 when they went to the theatre, and she did not see him again until the Spring of the following year. Later, in October, she visited Hay and stayed one night at Armstrong's home. Armstrong told her that if at any time she wanted a home, there was one for her at Mayfield. She was never officially engaged to him but Armstrong thought the first person to be told when they decided to become engaged should be her mother, and his own children some time in the future.

When cross-examined, Madame X said the friendship had been an entirely ordinary one throughout, and the prisoner had never attempted to disguise the fact that he was a married man with three children. It was in fact quite obvious that he was on affectionate terms with his family. Mr Micklethwait came back for one final question to which the witness replied that she could not explain the entry in Major Armstrong's diary which read, 'Stay Ford Cottage. Ask MG'.

Her examination complete, the veiled woman hurried from the courtroom, accompanied by her elderly mother. She quickly entered a large, closed car with drawn blinds which was waiting close to the door of the police court. The car drove away before the waiting crowd had a chance to see this mysterious witness.

After Madame X's evidence the court settled down again and Dr Hincks went back into the witness box to be cross-examined. The doctor was a key witness whose actions had been instrumental in causing both Armstrong's arrest and the subsequent gathering of all those present in the police court. This important witness was not without blemish, however, and Mr Matthews was quick to establish that the symptoms of Mrs Armstrong's illness which Dr Hincks had described earlier had been given from memory. Hincks had not taken her blood pressure, for at the outset he thought she was suffering from acute gastritis as there were no obvious indications to suggest otherwise.

Dr Hincks agreed that Major Armstrong was in a highly nervous state and heartily approved a suggestion that a holiday would do the widower good. Mr Matthews then asked him when he first informed the prosecution that Armstrong was suffering from syphilis. Hincks replied, 'I never made a communication until I was here. I have communicated the fact that I have treated him, but I had not given the name of the disease until I went into the witness box.'

'To whom did you disclose your books in the first place?'

'I produced my books in response to a letter from the Director of Public Prosecutions on 9th December 1921.'

Referring to the injection of arsenic which he gave Armstrong, the doctor said it was not given in the leg but in a vein in the arm. 'Did part of the conversation turn on the question of the injection?' asked Mr Matthews. 'Yes. Armstrong asked me how much arsenic I was giving him, and I said "I don't know".' Mr Matthews expressed considerable surprise at this answer but Dr Hincks repeated that he did not know, adding that the amount of arsenic in the injection was known only to the manufacturers.

Hincks had been in the witness box over an hour but before he stepped down he clarified for the Bench what he meant by the words 'chronic arsenical poisoning'. 'I have reviewed the whole case from start to finish. I have seen the report of Mrs Armstrong's history while in the mental institution at Gloucester and in my opinion I am perfectly convinced that she was suffering from arsenical poisoning the day I took her to Gloucester.' He added that he thought she had a remission of the symptoms during her stay at the institution because she became better and recovered the ability to walk. 'Shortly after her return to Cusop', he continued, 'she had a recurrence of her nerve symptoms, which I now attributed to a fairly large dose of arsenic—not enough to destroy life. Her fatal illness terminated with acute gastritis, which I attribute to arsenic, which must have been taken into the system in large quantities somewhere about the 16th. In chronic arsenical poison cases you sometimes find arsenic in the hair and nails.'

Dr Hincks was followed in the witness box by Arthur Chevalier, a solicitor and an old friend of Major and Mrs Armstrong. He gave evidence after lunch to a packed court and said that he had known the Armstrongs intimately for many years and had been in the habit of visiting them regularly until both he and Armstrong joined up at the beginning of the war. He went down to Mayfield at the pressing request of the Major before Mrs Armstrong was taken to the asylum: he found her considerably changed in her appearance and looking very ill.

Chevalier said that after discussing the matter with Dr Hincks it was agreed that Mrs Armstrong should go to a mental home. Major Armstrong consented reluctantly after Chevalier told him that he could not possibly have his wife properly nursed at home without considerable expense and housekeeping difficulties.

The witness did not recall Armstrong's mentioning a new will to him and the next time he heard from the family was after Mrs Armstrong's return from the asylum. Armstrong said he thought his wife would be better at home and spoke of how he had been longing to have her back. Chevalier attended the funeral and on the following day Armstrong referred to the will, saying that a fresh one had been made in the summer, which left everything to him as the sole executor. He took care to point out that although all the money was left to him he intended to use if for the benefit of the children.

The defence had no further questions so the court rose until the following Thursday.

* * * * *

Thursday, 9th February 1922. The prisoner was delayed on his journey from Worcester Gaol for the next sitting of the court when, on the road from Hereford to Hay, the car in which he was travelling had a puncture. The incident occurred uncomfortably close to home for Armstrong and while the wheel was being changed he sat as far back in the rear of the car as was possible to avoid being seen by passers-by. The party made up the lost time and reached Hay in good time for the sitting at 11 a.m.

Mr Micklethwait told the court that at the termination of the day's proceedings it would be necessary to ask for an adjournment of a week. That was the earliest date by which the scientific witnesses could attend, he explained. Mr Matthews, irritated by the constant delays and adjournments, pointed out that the Coroner's Inquest was due to take place then, adding somewhat sarcastically that he could not be in two places at once. Asked whether the Coroner would adjourn the inquest, Mr Matthews replied that he did not know as the Coroner 'is a law unto himself. He can adjourn at any time.' After due consideration, the Bench decided to fix the next hearing for Friday 17th February. Then came the day's witnesses, of whom several had given evidence previously.

Mrs Dorothy Martin was recalled and she confirmed her earlier evidence: that after eating one of the allegedly poisoned chocolates she felt sick and had a hot, burning sensation in her stomach. She was followed by Mrs Harriet Price, the former housemaid at Mayfield, who had also given evidence earlier. She said she now remembered that Miss Pearce had made the scones for the tea-party with Mr Martin and that there were currants in them. She gave additional evidence regarding the settlement of her claim for compensation which the prisoner had handled for her. Her husband, a farm labourer, had been killed in an accident in March 1921. Mrs Price had been awarded £225, a sum which was administered by Major Armstrong, and her mother-in-law £75. Mrs Price had received only £17 and Major Armstrong said that he would invest the remainder for her. But she had never received any further amount or any interest.

Mr Matthews cross-examined the witness and told her that he was the solicitor acting for her mother-in-law. He put it to

Mrs Price that she had never asked Major Armstrong to give her the full amount of the accident award and she agreed.

Miss Emily Pearce, the Armstrongs' faithful old housekeeper, was recalled and she made her faltering way to the witness box to have her evidence read over to her. She told Mr Micklethwait that she had been away on holiday when her mistress went to the asylum and that when Mrs Armstrong came back in January she was very weak and could just get up and down the stairs. On 14th February Mrs Armstrong stayed in the garden and a day or so afterwards she had taken cold.

In answer to a question by Mr Micklethwait concerning Mrs Armstrong's last illness, Miss Pearce said that her mistress was 'up and down in bed. . .'. Mr Micklethwait quickly went on to his next question but Mr Matthews sprang to his feet in protest. 'Let us have her last answer down first,' he demanded. 'She said Mrs Armstrong was up and down in bed.' The Magistrates' Clerk replied that he had not got it down. Mr Matthews retorted emphatically that the witness had said it and he wanted it taken down. The Clerk told him that he was going to take it from the witness and not from Mr Matthews.

After a further exchange, peace was restored, but only temporarily. Miss Pearce, somewhat flustered by these antics, confirmed that Mrs Armstrong did not stay in bed all the time: she got up on some days. Mr Matthews then suggested that Miss Pearce had become hostile to the prosecution to which Mr Micklethwait replied that the witness had been in Mr Matthews's charge since she had given evidence at the previous hearing. This remark created a further angry exchange and the prisoner's solicitor said angrily. 'It is most improper. I have never heard such a thing in my life! Since this charge was formulated the witness has been in the custody of Chief Inspector Crutchett.'

The Chairman of the Magistrates once again lowered the temperature of the exchange between prosecutor and defender and Mr Micklethwait resumed his examination of the witness. After answering questions about meals at Mayfield, Miss Pearce was asked whether Mrs Armstrong at any time said or did anything to suggest that she was likely to commit suicide. 'Once', said Miss Pearce, 'a day or two after she came back from the Home she went upstairs to the attic and said, "Would anyone break their back if they fell out of the window?", and I said, "Yes".'

'Then you agree with me,' said Mr Micklethwait, 'that she never expressed any desire to kill herself?' Miss Pearce replied, 'She did not say that, but she told me that when she was at the Home she had tried to get out of the window but she did not say she had tried to kill herself.'

Once again Mr Matthews was on his feet, exclaiming, 'I think I ought to stop this, I have not done so until now'. His opponent cut in, remarking in a highly sarcastic voice, how very good of him it was and continuing unperturbed to question the witness.

Mr Matthews was eventually placated and a fresh witness was called. A young girl of nineteen wearing a long, black coat and a brightly coloured hat entered the witness box. She was Miss Inez Elsie Rosser, a new witness, who told the court that she had been a housemaid at Mayfield from December 1920 until June 1921. She remembered Mrs Armstrong coming back from the asylum and said that she used to help Miss Pearce prepare the meals. After Mrs Armstrong took to her bed, Nurse Allen took up her food. Miss Rosser said she did not know what arsenic was and had never heard Major Armstrong use the word.

The evidence of the two gardeners at Mayfield was read over to them and Superintendent Weaver also heard the Clerk of the Court read out his testimony. All the witnesses were bound over in the sum of £50 to give evidence to the Assizes if called upon to do so. Finally, the court adjourned until the Friday of the next week.

* * * * *

Friday, 17th February 1922. At 11 a.m. all the participants assembled in Hay's police court for what proved to be the final session of the hearing. As usual the prisoner arrived by car with his regular travelling companions, Superintendent Weaver and P.C. Shakesheff. The Chief Constable of Herefordshire arrived with Chief Inspector Crutchett and to the now familiar faces in court were added those of Sir William Henry Willcox, Doctor Bernard Spilsbury and Mr John Webster.

Major Armstrong, dressed in a brown lounge suit, khaki shirt and red-striped tie, bowed to the court and took his place in the dock. It did not take him long to realize that he was about to come face-to-face with the full might of the Home Office's forensic force. He seemed quite calm but inwardly he was probably thankful that his lengthy ordeal was drawing to a close, at least at Hay. Possibly he permitted himself to wonder whether he would ever again see the familiar scene in the court where he had so often sat as Clerk. During the long days of the hearing he probably also compared the hard, narrow seat of the dock with the comfortable Clerk's chair he had once occupied.

The hearing was to be a short one, and Mr Micklethwait told the Bench that he did not intend to examine the witnesses at any great length. He said that the Director of Public Prosecutions had adopted the somewhat unusual course of submitting the various reports to the defence, an arrangement which would enable the evidence to be shortened considerably.

The first witness was the famous Home Office pathologist Bernard Henry Spilsbury. He was then aged forty-five and already rising to the peak of his unique career so that his appearance anywhere created a considerable stir. The pathologist's greatest years were still to come but the news that 'Spilsbury had been called in' was a virtual guarantee that a case would become a *cause célèbre*. He was dressed in his professional black morning coat and his tall figure with greying hair and fresh complexion looked commanding in the witness box.

Spilsbury gave the customary description of his professional qualifications and told how he was present at the exhumation of Mrs Armstrong's body. He had taken various organs and parts of the body during his post-mortem and remarked on the unusually good state of the corpse, allowing for the time since death. He found no natural disease which would have accounted for the severe vomiting or diarrhoea, and in his opinion the cause of death was acute arsenical poisoning.

The Chairman of the Bench was anxious to clear up a point with Dr Spilsbury. 'We have heard,' he said 'from the Medical Superintendent of the Institution where Mrs Armstrong had been, that she was given a tonic for a period of one month. I think it was from October 5th to November 4th.

The two solicitors' offices in Broad Street, Hay

The magistrates at Hay

Superintendent Weaver leads Major Armstrong
into the Hay Police Court

Exhumed coffin carried into Church Cottage, Cusop

Reburial

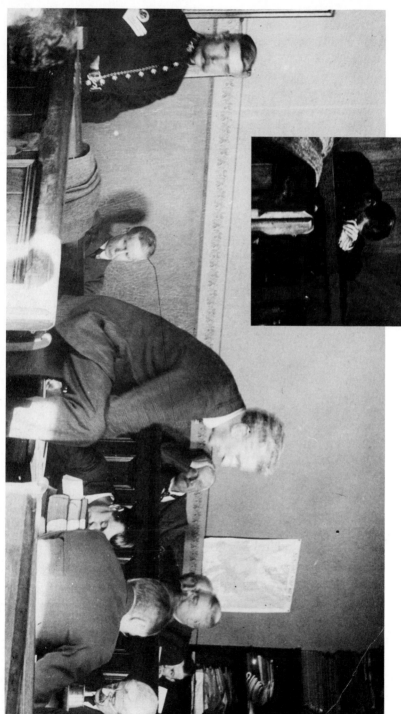

In the dock of his own court

That tonic contained five minims of hydrochloric arsenious acid. She died four months afterwards. Would you expect to find any traces of that arsenic in her body.'

'No sir,' replied Spilsbury, 'with the possible exception of traces in the hair and nails.'

The Senior Official Analyst to the Home Office, Mr John Webster, followed Dr Spilsbury into the witness box. He confirmed that he had received a box of chocolates and a specimen of urine and said that there was one thirty-third of a grain of arsenic in the urine. Out of the thirty-two chocolates in the box, two had the appearance of having been tampered with. Each of these had slightly more than two grains of arsenic in it. Mr Webster then produced the chocolates in question which had been mounted on a block of plasticene. This exhibit was examined with considerable interest, especially by Mr Matthews.

Mr Webster outlined his analysis of the various specimens taken from Mrs Armstrong's body and gave details of the amounts of arsenic found. He said he had received a hamper containing articles taken from the prisoner and from his home. Heading the list was the packet of arsenic found on Major Armstrong at the time of his arrest; this contained three and three-quarter grains of white arsenic.

The final witness was Sir William Henry Willcox, Medical Adviser to the Home Office and Physician to St Mary's Hospital, Paddington. Willcox, only recently knighted in the King's Birthday Honours List, was six years older than Spilsbury and at the height of a brilliant career. His double qualification as both chemist and doctor uniquely fitted him for the role of forensic expert. He had been associated with both Webster and Spilsbury in several famous criminal cases and he made medical history with his identification of hyoscine in the Crippen case and by the quantitative evaluation of arsenic in the Seddon case. He was appointed Medical Adviser to the Home Office in 1919 and quickly became an influential figure, his counsel being highly regarded by the Director of Public Prosecutions.

Willcox told the court that he was familiar with the symptoms of arsenical poisoning and had a wide experience of such cases. In his opinion, the cause of Mrs Armstrong's death was acute arsenical poisoning. Certainly the deceased woman must have had considerable amounts of arsenic in the last few days of her life—during the period she was suffering from vomiting and other symptoms. Two grains was possibly a fatal dose and an amount considerably in excess of this must have been taken during those last days.

Sir William said it was very difficult to make a diagnosis without an analysis, and the death certificate issued by Hincks was correct as regards the symptoms of disease from which Mrs Armstrong was suffering, but in this case the symptoms were not due to natural causes but to arsenical poisoning. He said he had considered the evidence of Mrs Dorothy Martin and agreed that her symptoms, too, were entirely consistent with acute arsenical poisoning. He also considered that Mr Martin's symptoms pointed to the same cause.

Mr Matthews did not cross-examine any of the expert witnesses and, when Sir William Willcox left the witness box, Mr Micklethwait addressed the Bench: 'That concludes the case for the Crown', he said, 'and it is now my duty to ask for a committal to the Hereford Assizes on the charge of murder and also on the charge of attempted murder.'

The Magistrates retired and returned within five minutes. The Clerk turned towards the dock, cautioned the accused and asked if he wished to call any evidence in his own defence. Standing smartly to attention and addressing the court for the first time Armstrong replied in a clear voice, 'I am not guilty of either charge, sir. I reserve my defence.'

The Chairman of the Bench then said he thought the evidence was sufficient for a committal to the Assizes, or other special place where the trial would take place. As the court was rising, Mr Micklethwait thanked the Bench for the courtesy extended by them during the six-week hearing of the case.

Major Armstrong stood rigidly to attention when the court rose. He then turned smartly to the right and left the dock without a backward glance, and for the last time made his exit from the little courtroom and from the town of Hay where he had lived and practised law.

5 Motive and Malady

I may mention that none of the rumours I had heard about Mr Armstrong were to his credit.

Laura Jesse Davies

THE PERIOD between Major Armstrong's committal at Hay and his trial at Hereford Assizes provides a convenient interlude in which to examine his possible motives.

The revelation in the Hay courtroom that Armstrong was being treated for syphilis no doubt caused some coarse merriment in the town's public houses. For some observers it also provided a possible reason for murdering his wife.

The fact that the little man had 'caught a dose' was obvious proof that his wife's domination had turned him to the warm embraces of other women and probably also to prostitutes. Fifty years ago venereal disease was most prevalent in those women who provided comforts to soldiers and seamen, although a few ladies of higher standing but of promiscuous habits might have been unfortunate enough to pick up the disease. At any rate, it seems that Major Armstrong was not too particular about the ladies he consorted with.

Among the theories seeking to provide a motive for Armstrong's behaviour is the contention that he was suffering from general paralysis of the insane (GPI), a late stage of syphilis. GPI is the stage at which syphilis destroys the brain tissue and produces progressive insanity and sometimes leads to violent acts and murder. The disease is characterized by headaches, insomnia, irritability, inability to concentrate, extremes of melancholia and feelings of grandeur. In its most pronounced form it cuts off the sufferer from the real world and reality is replaced by fantasy and illusion.

Some of Armstrong's personality traits might fit into this pattern but he was no Ivan the Terrible. Moreover, the Major himself provided the information which refutes the GPI theory in his case. Where other men would have kept quiet about having syphilis, Armstrong actually made notes about his symptoms. A list of these was found among the papers in his pockets at the time of his arrest. This was in keeping with his egotistical nature, although it is possible that he was asked to make the notes by his doctor.

At any rate he noted the first appearance of a sore on 23rd November 1920 and this makes it possible to date fairly accurately the time at which he became infected with the disease. Syphilis has an incubation period of nine to ninety days, which means that in all likelihood Armstrong became infected during the period that his wife was at Barnwood. As GPI is a late stage of syphilis, not appearing until three years or more after the time of infection it follows that Armstrong could not have been suffering its effects in 1921.

Armstrong's notes on the progress of his complaint covered a period of ten months and he was receiving treatment during the last weeks of his wife's fatal illness.

23rd November 1920	1st sign of sore
9th December	Consulted M.O. Sore aggravated by woollen pants. Treated with oint.
17th December	1st injection at Hford. Sore alright.
23rd January	2nd injection by Dr. H. Muscles very sore afterwards at least 3 weeks before normal movement of legs.
Feb Mar Apr May (middle)	Continuous rash over arms, hands, buttocks and thighs. Very irritable at night. Ointments no use. Gradually worked out leaving slight marks.
May (middle) to June (middle)	Course of Mercury tabloids with Iodide of potash & CwO_3 gargle.
Mid June	Gums began to be sore—salivation—Mercury discontinued.
June (end)	Irritation in palms of both hands. Subsequently skin peeled off and continued till end Sept. At times hands very irritable at night.
Aug (1st week)	Ulcerated throat. Still continues. Spray began and gargle given—no result. Disinclination to smoke.

Dr Arthur Douglas Heath, a Birmingham specialist, to whom Armstrong was sent by Hincks in October 1921, had doubts as to whether the symptoms added up to syphilis at all. Before examining Armstrong, Dr Heath read the case notes and questioned the patient; he learned that two blood tests had been made and that the results were positive. 'I then examined him', said Heath. His throat was sore, but the doctor attributed that to the mercurial treatment he had been given. He wrote to Hincks suggesting discontinuing the mercury and giving intravenous arsenical injections.

Dr Heath admitted that there had been ample time for any symptoms of syphilis to have disappeared since Armstrong first reported sick in November 1920. He also drew attention to the question of the irritant rash and remarked, '. . .this differed from the general run of syphilitic cases. . .'. Dr Heath's conclusion was that as he had not seen Armstrong during the early stages of the disease he was not prepared to say that it was syphilis.

Consideration of whether Armstrong actually had syphilis is academic, for the time factor ruled out GPI and consequently there is no validity in the suggestion that he was insanely motivated to murder. The point is that Armstrong thought he had syphilis, a diagnosis that was corroborated by Hincks, and that was as good as admitting his liaison with women of a type likely to be infected with the disease.

Another theory about Armstrong's mental health was that he suffered from migraine. Violent headaches which are occasionally accompanied by visual disturbances and sickness are the unfortunate lot of the migraine sufferer. Treatment in the 1920s emphasised regular hygiene and clean living and it has been suggested that Mrs Armstrong's rules about no wine or smoking and regular meals and bath nights might be interpreted in this context.

There is no evidence to show that Armstrong was particularly subject to migraine or indeed that he suffered from headaches. If he did quietly suffer, then the regime imposed by his wife, supposedly for his benefit, soon exceeded all sensible limits.

* * * * *

Together with his list of syphilis symptoms, the Major carried three love letters in his pocket. These were taken from him by the detectives and were produced in court. The sender, 'Your loving Marion', was the mysterious Madame X who appeared briefly at the Magistrates' Court. Her name, which was kept from the public throughout the entire case, was Marion Glassford Gale.

Armstrong's relationship with Marion was on a different plane to most of his amorous affairs. She was a fifty-year old widow who lived with her mother and niece at Bournemouth. She first met Armstrong in 1915 when he was serving as adjutant with the Royal Engineers at a camp near Christchurch and was billeted at the home of one of her friends. Marion became friendly with him and he visited her and her mother at their home, Ford Cottage. They knew that he was married, for he often spoke of his family. Like many decent folk at that time, Marion and her mother welcomed into their home a soldier whom circumstances had separated from his family.

This friendship grew and, when Armstrong was posted away from the South Coast, Marion occasionally corresponded with him. In July 1920, after he was demobilized and while Mrs Armstrong was still alive, they met in London and dined together. They did not see each other again until after Mrs Armstrong's death in the following year when the Major went down to Bournemouth on his return from holiday abroad. That was the 29th April 1921. On that visit they just chatted, probably about his trip, but when they met again the next month, Armstrong vaguely raised the question of marriage. A more definite proposal of marriage was made in August but Marion's reply was that she had too great a responsibility looking after her mother and her niece who was her ward. Armstrong was not discouraged, and suggested leaving consideration of the matter for at least a year. There was a tacit understanding that the marriage proposal be reconsidered the following summer.

In October, Marion met Armstrong at Hereford and they drove to Mayfield where she stayed overnight. They also met once or twice in London and at a friend's house in Bournemouth, but the couple were never officially engaged.

In her statement to the police, Marion said that she had not heard from Major Armstrong since 29th December and knew of his arrest only by reading about it in the papers. She said, 'Major Armstrong was to me everything a gentleman ought to be. This news has come to me as an overwhelming shock.'

Chief Inspector William Brown of Scotland Yard witnessed Marion's statement and obviously expected to find a strong whiff of intimacy between Major Armstrong and the widow. His disappointment was such that he sent a sergeant of the Bournemouth Police to take a further statement on the following day. The tenor of the questions was evident from the replies given by Marion. She was at pains to make it clear that when she saw Armstrong in London she stayed the night with married friends whose name and address she gave. She was absolutely certain that after her appointment with Armstrong she returned to her friends, adding, 'I never slept away from them on this visit.'

The contents of Marion's letters were not made known at either the police-court hearing or the trial. As Madame X, she was simply asked to acknowledge that she had sent them. This she did. The letters are here reproduced in full for the first time.

15.12.21.   Ford Cottage

Why this heavy silence? I looked for the usual on Monday or Tuesday but drew a blank. I do hope you are not ill, please do write and tell me, as I get so worried and you know how much I want to hear. I hope the chill is a thing of the past now. The weather is very changeable and here there is a lot of illness about: I do hope I shall keep fit. I am snowed under with work—domestic, and get very little time for anything else. The Pennefathers are pleasant and more reasonable now to Shates, but it's a grind when all's said and done and the getting up early 7 a.m. in the dark—trying!

There is the usual Christmas rush going on here and the tramways are still under repair going to and fro very difficult—I with you, will soon have the holidays upon us, and I am not looking forward to it except that I want Eleanor to have a good rest, she is looking pale and tired when I saw her the other day. So sorry Pearson has fallen a victim to C.P. what a bore but what luck my dear, not getting it at home and the others falling victims also! so thats the right side what. I don't think I have any other news Ina has not been well and stayed in bed sick two days, but is up and out again now. Please do write or else I shall begin to think you are fed up with me—your last letter was rather 'casual'—but I wont say more, as perhaps you weren't up to the mark and didn't mean it! But if you let me down then I shall give up bucking and the rest but you won't, will you? I told you of Willy's engagement didn't I? Everyone muchly surprised and I hear he has it rather badly! At his age too! I shall stop now post this and hope for a nice long one from you. Mother evidently has been on the out look and remarked yesterday you don't hear often from John and I said no I don't! which was true. You will have a long office holiday at Xmas but no doubt arrears will turn up do the family keep you going. I don't think that I quite agree with Miss Pearce, but that is another story—Your ever loving Marion.

The shortest day of 1921
(21.12.21.)

> I wish I could have seen you in town yesterday—don't you want to see me???

I have just time my dearest to send you a few lines, to reach you at I hope on or near the 25th to wish you a Happy Christmas. Of course you will have the children making hay (no joke intended) that always keeps one going. I do hope you are feeling better and worries in the office straightening out. The few days off, so I suppose you will close the office for nearly a week, solicitors generally do I notice, and it ought to give you quite a free time if you can have a free mind. I daresay it is 'the weather and all' that has made you so seedy—moi aussi. I feel so weary daily, but life is really a grind, but I can't like you, get any time off and the Xmas makes it even worse it's meals, meals, meals and washing up and rinsing things and I have to get up ever so early—how would you like that my young friend, to get done at all. However enough of my grumbles —I have got to do it, so what's the use of saying any more.

Eleanor came yesterday, very tired, with a heavy cold, so she has gone to bed for a day or two to get fit to enjoy herself later. She has brought a good report, 2nd in English, which is excellent in the Oxford form and one of her sketches in sepia, is claimed by the school to have the honour to hang 'for ever' in the Staff room so she is *very* bucked and I am awfully pleased. It means so much out of several hundred girl's work for hers to be chosen dont you think so? I hope your Eleanor has also done well and young

Pearson, but the C.P. would put him back of course. It is
strange to feel that Xmas has come round again, and this
year has brought great changes hasn't it, for both of us—I
wonder how next year will find us—Tell me what you
think. I am posting a little book to Margaret, I think it
rather dainty—She probably won't have seen it. My
dearest accept the enclosed tie with my love and wear and
think of me—It is one of the new sort and I rather like the
brown colour and think it ought to go with your things
but if you *hate,* don't say so, only send it back. I wish it
was a bigger 'expression of my regard for you etc etc' as the
saying goes—Much love and again good wishes for the
season, and write soon and often.
Your loving Marion

29 Dec. 21. Ford Cottage

My dearest J, thanks for yours just come today I was so
glad to hear, as I felt jolly depressed all over Xmas time—
(no it was not liver) and everything seemed a bother and I
have an idea in my mind that you aren't thinking of me and
I don't seem to know what your ideas are as regards the
future and altogether I am 'hipped' to use an old fashioned
word. The 25th brought plenty to do in the cooking line
and in the evening I went to a meal (dinner and quite good)
at the McCalls the only real touch of Christmas as we
treated it as an ordinary Sunday more or less. I am so glad
the shops are open again and things once more resuming
their normal course. These holidays are very trying, Eleanor
is not very well, very bored and has to do holiday French
etc, the people in the house are full of their troubles—too
long a yarn to write and the young nephew David aged 16,
is quite near to talk and bike with Eleanor, but his Ma and
aunt pull in the opposite direction, I am really between
the devil and the deep sea and my mother is just at her most
aggravating and worries the young people and I am just
sick of the whole show—I can't exactly describe what I
mean, but perhaps you can understand dearest what I mean.
I didn't know before that you were going in for inoculation,
you never told me, you wretch, what for? is of course what
I want to know so please tell me. Cleaning the silver sounds
jolly useful—don't you feel inclined to come along and clean
at 'Ford Cottage', silver and brass? under the present stress
it has to go very often looking for a willing polisher—I am
glad the children had a pleasant Christmas and that Margaret

got the book safely. Of course we all talk Murder—it is so absolutely baffling and apparently without motive. Of course you realise that the spot is just near the Tanner's house—they heard nothing—it was a wet windy night but they have endless enquiries and people in and out crowds go down to the spot daily, for what reason, no one knows—I had a long letter from Fee at Christmas, they seem very gay and full of doings, and in her letter she says 'What development from Hay, have you told your mother anything yet I am all agog to know' so she evidently is keen for the family to know, but we agreed, didn't we, not to say anything until the holidays were over. What is your real idea, darling? Do write soon. I hope things at the office are better and that you will have all sorts of luck for 1921. At least I hope I shall share some of it, what do you think? Your loving Marion.

Marriage was certainly discussed and Armstrong even mentioned it to his housekeeper in the context of when it would be best to tell the children. One of Mrs Armstrong's friends, Mrs S.J.S. Iredell, wrote to the Major about the death of his wife referring to his loss as 'The Home Call for your dear one'. She also made a clear reference to the possibility of re-marriage: 'I am very glad to know there is a prospect of your going into double harness again. No one will rejoice more than I—and I *believe Katie too*—provided of course that there is real love on both sides. . .'

Armstrong would have been quite a catch for Marion and she was undoubtedly pulled in two directions—by her duty to her mother and niece and by her attraction to the Major and the thought of being a solicitor's wife. Marriage to a prominent citizen of Hay and life as mistress at Mayfield with its household staff to do her bidding would have been infinitely preferable to a continuation of the drudgery expressed in her letters.

The Major no doubt found Marion's company pleasurable in 1915 and she provided a warmth of personality and feeling that was lacking in his wife. But despite the talk of marriage there were signs that Armstrong's interest was cooling off. 'Why this heavy silence?' asked Marion, and again, '. . .don't you want to see me?' There was also a mild rebuke, '. . .your last letter was rather casual.' It was obvious that she was

looking for the postman hoping for letters from 'John' her
special name for Armstrong but few were forthcoming.

Marion's letters were full of mundane domestic details
and grumbles about her life. This may have led Armstrong to
conclude that the prospect of marriage was too distant for
this woman who was unlikely to free herself from the prison
of her responsibilities. An odd topic for discussion in their
correspondence was Armstrong's inoculations. Perhaps he had
planted this information as an oblique reference to an illness
which would be his excuse for breaking off the attachment?

Marion's last letter contained at least two omens. She
wrote, '. . .of course we all talk Murder. . .': this was a
reference to the murder of Irene Wilkins at Bournemouth on
the 22nd December and for which Thomas Henry Allaway
was executed on the 19th August 1922. Regrettably for
Marion, talk of murder was soon to come much closer home.
This same letter also contained New Year Greetings: '. . .all
sorts of luck for 1921', but she was in error with the year—it
should have been 1922. This was indeed an omen, for
unbeknown to her, the police were already on Armstrong's
track and, within a day or two of receiving this letter from his
'loving Marion', he was arrested.

In court both parties played down the intimation that they
were actively contemplating marriage. But these letters suggest
that the idea of marrying Armstrong was firmly founded, at
least in Marion's mind. The same conclusion might also be
read into Armstrong's diary entry for 29th April 1921: 'Stay
Ford Cottage. Ask M.G.'

* * * * *

An incident that was known to have greatly concerned
Armstrong was the Harold Greenwood affair. On 10th
November 1920, the Major travelled by train to Cheltenham.
In the same compartment was another Hay resident, Miss
May Lilwall, whom he engaged in conversation. Armstrong it
seems could talk of little else but the acquittal the previous
day at Carmarthen Assizes of Harold Greenwood. The news
that Greenwood, also a solicitor, had been found not guilty
of the charge of murdering his wife elated Armstrong and the
little man was obviously in high spirits.

Of course, Armstrong might just have been naturally pleased that a fellow solicitor had been cleared of a capital charge. It is also possible that Greenwood's acquittal gave strength to his own ambitions. Certainly the Greenwood case was to have considerable influence on the fate of Major Armstrong. There were many parallels between the two cases and it is worth considering the Greenwood affair in a little detail. To begin with, both men were solicitors, both were charged with using arsenic to murder their wives and in both trials the evidence of the family doctor was critical.

Harold Greenwood, aged forty-five, had a mediocre legal practice in the Welsh town of Llanelly and lived in fairly prosperous surroundings in nearby Kidwelly. His wife, Mabel, was reasonably wealthy in her own right with an annual income of about nine hundred pounds. She was deeply religious and was well liked. Harold, on the other hand, was said not to have a single friend although he had a reputation as a ladies' man.

Greenwood was not such a prominent man in local affairs as Armstrong but he lived comfortably with his wife and four children in Rumsey House together with three family servants. Unlike Armstrong, he was not nagged by his wife and was free to wine and dine as he pleased; his purchases of wines and spirits indicated that he did so quite liberally.

Mabel Greenwood had been in a poor state of health for some time; she complained of pains around the heart and was subject to fainting attacks. She had been very unwell since the beginning of the year 1919 and friends noticed that she was steadily losing weight and complained of sickness and diarrhoea.

Drama came to Rumsey House on Sunday, 15th June. It was a normal Sunday for the Greenwoods and they had a roast lunch with a bottle of Burgundy followed by gooseberry tart. During the afternoon, Mrs Greenwood complained to her husband of diarrhoea which he attributed to the gooseberries she had eaten at lunch. His wife's discomfiture did not seem to get any worse, however, and at 4.30 p.m. she had some tea and bread and butter. At about 6 p.m. she walked in the garden with Irene, her eldest daughter. Shortly after that she felt sick and complained of pains around the heart. Her husband and daughter helped her back into the house and she was taken upstairs to her room in a half-fainting condition.

Just before 7 p.m. Greenwood called in Dr T.R. Griffiths who lived immediately across the street. Dr Griffiths, who was on the point of retiring from the medical practice, came at once. He prescribed a mixture to settle the stomach and by 7.30 he thought the patient was improving. Not long after the doctor had left, Miss Phillips, an old friend of Mrs Greenwood, called at the house and was alarmed to find her friend ill. Later, Miss Phillips, after consulting Harold Greenwood, called on the district nurse and asked her to come and look after Mrs Greenwood.

The nurse, who was well acquainted with Mrs Greenwood's history of heart trouble, came at 8 p.m. and found the patient in a serious state of collapse. At 9 p.m. she thought there was definite deterioration and called for the doctor. Mrs Greenwood was suffering from vomiting and persistent diarrhoea; altogether Griffiths made some four or five visits during the night. At about 3 a.m. Irene, who was sitting up with her mother, sent one of the maids to fetch Miss Phillips who had returned home earlier. By the time Miss Phillips arrived, Mrs Greenwood was dead. Dr Griffiths, who had known and treated Mrs Greenwood for many years, certified the cause of death as valvular disease of the heart.

Shortly after Mrs Greenwood's death, rumours started to spread that all was not as it should have been. There were hints of irregularities concerning the death certificate and gossip about foul play. These rumours were greatly stimulated in October when, only four months after his wife's death, Harold Greenwood remarried. The second Mrs Greenwood was Gladys Jones, the thirty-year-old daughter of a Llanelly newspaper proprietor, whom Greenwood had known for many years.

The names of various women were linked with Greenwood's and eventually serious allegations reached the ears of the authorities. The police advised Greenwood that they would probably wish to exhume his wife's body; Greenwood consented saying, 'Just the very thing, I am quite agreeable'.

Several months elapsed before the police took any action and Greenwood probably thought that the matter had been put aside. However, in April 1920 Mrs Greenwood's body was exhumed and her remains were taken to Kidwelly Town Hall for post-mortem examination. No evidence was found of valvular heart disease but subsequent examination of some of the body's organs revealed the presence of arsenic: the body contained between a quarter and half a grain of arsenic.

Greenwood was represented at the Coroner's Inquest by his solicitor: he did not attend in person. The Coroner's jury returned a unanimous verdict that Mabel Greenwood's death was caused by acute arsenical poisoning and that the poison was administered by Harold Greenwood. Such was the feeling against Greenwood that the verdict brought loud applause from the public seats. In anticipation of this outcome, plain-clothes policemen had already apprehended Greenwood, ostensibly for his own protection. When he was later committed for trial, a large crowd booed and hissed him; this was in marked contrast to the public feeling about Armstrong who received loud cheers when leaving the police court at Hay.

Greenwood was known to have bought some Cooper's Weedicide and the prosecution case against him was that he had put some of this arsenical preparation in the bottle of Burgundy from which his wife filled her glass at lunch. He was brilliantly defended by Sir Edward Marshall Hall whose cross-examination of the prosecution witnesses was devastating. The evidence given by Dr Griffiths, for instance, was shown to be inconsistent and the doctor was obviously confused and forgetful.

The defence attributed Mrs Greenwood's sickness and diarrhoea to the gooseberries* which she had eaten at lunch. Experts were called who agreed that Mrs Greenwood's fatal illness might have been due to the effect of the gooseberry skins. Much was made of this during the trial and some commentators on the case were later of the opinion that the gooseberries secured Greenwood's acquittal.

Marshall Hall worked at every possible advantage for his client but really won the case when he put Irene Greenwood in the witness box. When questioned about lunch before her mother was taken ill, Irene was asked what she had to drink.

* Preserved gooseberries formed part of Mrs Armstrong's last full meal.

She said, 'Mother and I had Burgundy.' She added that she also drank Burgundy at supper and it came from the same bottle that was used at the lunch table.

Thus the prosecution's case disintegrated and after retiring for two and a half hours the jury returned a verdict of 'Not Guilty'. Harold Greenwood was a free man and it was this which so excited Armstrong. But, the 'Not Guilty' verdict did not give complete absolution, for the jury handed the judge a rider: 'We are satisfied on the evidence in this case that a dangerous dose of arsenic was administered to Mabel Greenwood on Sunday 15th June 1919 but we are not satisfied that this was the immediate cause of death. The evidence before us is unsufficient and does not conclusively satisfy us as to how, and by whom, the arsenic was administered.'

Counsel for the Crown applied for this rider to be made public but the judge refused.

Greenwood's acquittal was won by brilliant advocacy which probed the faults in a carelessly prepared prosecution; for example, the police failed to take a statement from Irene Greenwood. Although Armstrong was to be ably defended in his turn, the difference was that the police made very thorough preparations in his case. Sir Archibald Bodkin had been in office as Director of Public Prosecutions for only a few months when Armstrong's papers came before him. This was his most important case to date and his knowledge of the Greenwood verdict and especially of the rider to it set him on a course of meticulous preparation. He believed that if Greenwood's case had been thoroughly prepared, a conviction would have been obtained. Accordingly, he saw to it that the allegations against Armstrong were thoroughly investigated and thus ensured that the prosecution was the strongest possible.

It has been suggested that Greenwood's acquittal was Armstrong's motivation, the Major supposedly reasoning that one solicitor found not guilty of a murder charge involving arsenic would afford immunity to another member of the same profession using the same method.

This proposition does not hold true for the simple reason that Major Armstrong had already begun administering arsenic to his wife when Harold Greenwood was tried. There is no doubt that the Major was inordinately pleased at the news which came from the Assize Court at Carmarthen but there was no connection apart from coincidence.

* * * * *

Katharine Armstrong made her Last Will and Testament on 17th January 1917. She appointed four executors, her husband, Arthur Chevalier, Bessie Friend and Daisy Way. The document, witnessed by Gertrude Hutchins and Elizabeth Parley, contained thirteen clauses. Chief among these were bequests by Mrs Armstrong of £50 to her sister and of £10 each to Arthur Chevalier and Daisy Way. Emily Pearce was to receive an annuity of £12 and the main provisions were for the children each of whom was to receive an equal share of the estate.

Mrs Armstrong bequeathed her husband an annual income of £50 which was to increase to £100 after 1933. This will was made while Major Armstrong was serving in the army and at a time when Katharine was staying at Teignmouth with her sister. The will was properly witnessed, the witnesses signing in each other's presence in front of Mrs Armstrong, and the document was given into the care of Bessie Friend.

When Mrs Armstrong was ill in the autumn of 1920 and was about to be certified as insane, her executors learned that another will existed which superseded that made in 1917. This second will was dated 8th July 1920 and in it the sole executor and beneficiary was named as Herbert Rowse Armstrong; he stood to inherit over £2000 by his wife's death. The provisions of this will were brief:

I KATHARINE MARY ARMSTRONG, wife of Herbert Rowse Armstrong of Mayfield, Cusop in the County of Hereford, Solicitor, hereby revoke all former Wills and testamentary dispositions made by me and by this my last Will devise and bequeath all my real and personal estate whatsoever and wheresoever to my husband, the said Herbert Rowse Armstrong, absolutely and appoint him sole executor of this my Will.

IN WITNESS whereof I have hereunto set my hand this eighth day of July 1920.

I Katharine Mary armstrong wife of Herbert Rowse Armstrong of Mayfield Cusop in the County of Hereford Solicitor hereby revoke all former Wills and testamentary dispositions made by me and by this my last will devise and bequeath all my real and personal estate whatsoever and wheresoever to my husband the said Herbert Rowse Armstrong absolutely and appoint him sole executor of this my will In witness whereof I have hereunto set my hand this Eighth day of July one thousand nine hundred and twenty.

Signed by the above
named Katharine Mary
Armstrong as her last
will in the joint presence
of herself and also of and at
her request and in such
joint presence have
hereunto subscribed our
names as Witnesses

Emily E. Pearce
Lily Candy

K. M. Armstrong —

On the 30th day of March 1921 Probate of this Will was granted at Hereford to Herbert Rowse Armstrong the sole Executor —

Mrs Armstrong's alleged second will dated 8th July 1920, naming her husband as sole executor and beneficiary.

This document was witnessed by Emily Pearce and Lily Candy, both servants at Mayfield. Probate was granted in March 1921 when Major Armstrong inherited the sum of £2278 3s.

After Armstrong was arrested, the newspapers made a point of mentioning his inheritance, with headlines such as, 'Dead woman's will—Everything left to her husband absolutely'. Nor did the significance of the second will escape the Director of Public Prosecutions. He asked Chief Inspector Crutchett to get in touch with Mrs Armstrong's relatives with the object of finding out everything possible about her property, the point of the inquiry being, 'that had she died intestate the whole of her personal property would have gone to her husband. . .so that there would seem to have been some special reason for the making of the will of July 1920, which we do not at present know'. Crutchett was also asked to obtain a specimen of Mrs Armstrong's handwriting to compare with the signature on the will.

Mrs Armstrong wrote to her sister from Barnwood Mental Hospital asking the whereabouts of her 'original will', adding, 'I think all executors ought to know'. It is significant that she used the term 'all executors' for it is obvious that she was thinking of the four executors of her 1917 will and not the sole executor (her husband) of the second. She wrote to her sister again shortly after this and again mentioned her will. 'That is my last, and I should like A.E.C. (Arthur Chevalier) to know where it is and see it. Do write to him.'

Chevalier said that Bessie Friend had shown him a draft of Mrs Armstrong's will and subsequently posted the original of the 1917 will to him after Mrs Armstrong's death. It would seem then that, in January 1921, Mrs Armstrong, admittedly while in a mental hospital, nevertheless considered her 'Last Will' to be the one written in 1917.

When the police took statements from the two witnesses of the second will, Emily Pearce and Lily Candy (she had married and become Mrs Evans), it became evident that the normal witnessing procedure had not been adhered to. This was rightly questioned at the time of the police-court proceedings; after all, when legal documents are signed in the presence of a solicitor it is reasonable to expect that the procedure is flawless.

Emily Pearce said that she remembered signing a document but could not recall whether Lily Candy was there although she knew that she was also going to sign. She could not remember when she signed it but was definite that both Mrs and Major Armstrong were present.

If Emily Pearce was rather vague about the matter Lily Candy was quite definite. She told the police: 'I never signed any paper to my recollection at the request of Mrs Armstrong, and certainly never witnessed her sign any paper, either blank or with manuscript thereon. I know nothing of Mrs Armstrong's will, and no-one has ever asked me to sign a paper as a witness to Mrs Armstrong's signature to any will. I have never signed any document at Mayfield, Cusop, in the presence of Miss Pearce, and I have never seen her sign any document there or anywhere else.

'I have some recollection of Major Armstrong asking me to sign some paper in his study or library. I do not know what that paper was, but I thought at the time it was probably something to do with my National Insurance. Mrs Armstrong was not there at the time, Major Armstrong was alone, and nobody signed that paper in my presence.'

The witnessing clause beneath which these two ladies had signed their names stated:

> Signed by the above named Katharine Mary Armstrong as her last Will in the joint presence of herself and us who at her request and in such joint presence have hereunto subscribed our names as witnesses.

According to the statements of these two women, the witnessing was most improperly carried out. Neither really knew what the paper was which they signed, and Lily Candy could not have witnessed Mrs Armstrong's signature as she said only the Major was present at the time.

Armstrong's version of what happened was that, 'After some general conversation with reference to the previous will, my wife told me of the rather complicated condition she had made. She wished to have a much shorter and simpler one and, at her request, with her knowledge, I drew up a very short document. . .My wife signed that document. Miss Pearce and the servant, Lily Candy. . .were present when she signed it. As far as I remember it took place in the evening.'

Chief Inspector Crutchett, reporting to his superiors, said that both Bessie Friend and Gertrude Hitchins who were familiar with the handwriting of Mrs Armstrong, gave it as their opinion that the signature, 'K.M. Armstrong' on the 1920 will was not in the handwriting of the deceased lady. 'It would seem, therefore,' he added, 'that, if these ladies are accurate, the will of 1920 was forged by Armstrong for the purpose of getting possession of his wife's property. . .'

* * * * *

Armstrong did not like parting with his money as instanced by his attempt to get interest on the fees which he paid for his wife's stay at Barnwood. Penny pinching is not a criminal offence and may even be considered a virtue, but there are signs that Armstrong had to indulge in a little juggling in order to maintain his financial position.

Apart from his business income, which derived chiefly from conveyancing, Armstrong's appointments and clerkships brought in about £250 a year to which could be added his wife's income of about £100 a year. His outgoings, however, were quite steep. There was an office to maintain, stationery to buy and staff to pay on the business side, and he also had to maintain Mayfield with its housekeeper, two maids and a gardener.

Mrs Armstrong was worried about their financial position in 1918 during the time that her husband was in the army and wrote to Arthur Chevalier as a family friend seeking advice. She said, '. . .after all, if I can prevent Herbert's losing all his small fortune I do him a service, even if it necessitates a breach of the ordinary codes of loyalty to him. . .' Her alarm stemmed from a notification that their joint account was overdrawn by £144. Having done a few sums and felt that there was insufficient to cover their commitments, 'Where', she asked,' 'does the balance go?' Mrs Armstrong had a good business sense and her own housekeeping records were immaculately kept; she was mystified, therefore, that her husband's affairs seemed to be in a muddle. She found that Armstrong had lent money on mortgages which had not paid interest for four years, he had overdrawn his private account and she had seen a letter indicating that her husband had transferred £725 of their best investment shares to the bank.

Mrs Armstrong was plainly anxious about their finances and it was only with the greatest diffidence that she approached Chevalier at all. 'If this letter is wrong, please scold me and I will never interfere again.'

Armstrong later brushed aside his wife's worries saying that they had no foundation in fact. He admitted his account was overdrawn but said simply that, 'The trouble referred to in that letter was afterwards put right.'

The fact was that many of Armstrong's business deals left behind a legacy of muddle. Apart from the Velinnewydd sale which was obviously unsatisfactory, there was the question of Armstrong's partnership with Edmund Cheese. When the old man died Armstrong should have paid his share of the partnership into Cheese's estate. The London firm of solicitors dealing with the estate were unable to wind it up because of difficulties with the firm's books which had not been properly closed off. Armstrong reckoned he owed the estate £647 of which he paid £500 on account. The solicitor thought the figure was closer to £1000, but in any event Armstrong did not even pay the balance on the figure he had worked out himself. A characteristic feature of this matter, as in several others, was Armstrong's failure to honour promises of satisfactory completion.

One of Armstrong's clients, a retired Lieutenant Colonel, had such difficulties in getting money due to him from Armstrong that he had eventually to put the matter in the hands of another solicitor. He had tried repeatedly to obtain a statement from Armstrong: 'I have written and had personal interviews with him, always with the same result that he promised to send it along.'

A farmer who had applied to Armstrong for a mortgage of £3000 in the belief that the solicitor himself was putting up the money was surprised to learn, 'that he was lending me somebody else's money'. Armstrong discouraged the man from reading the agreement thoroughly before signing it, assuring him that everything was in order.

When Harriet Price, one of the servants at Mayfield, was awarded £300 compensation for an industrial accident which killed her husband, Major Armstrong looked after her interests. At the court proceedings the judge decided that Mrs Price should have three-quarters of the sum awarded and her mother-in-law the remainder. Subsequently Armstrong said that the girl's mother-in-law was not entitled to any of the compensation claim. Knowing nothing about such matters, Harriet Price left everything to Armstrong. The result was that she actually received only £17, which she used to pay her husband's funeral expenses. Armstrong said he would invest the rest to her best advantage, after deducting his own fees. Harriet Price said she was given no papers to show that the money belonged to her, as Armstrong had promised. She was not told how the money had been invested and no account was ever rendered to her. Armstrong, therefore, had the use of some £200.

Armstrong's bank manager said that a sum of £225 was paid into the Armstrong's joint account on 20th July 1921. 'Armstrong paid Mrs Price on the following day a sum of £12 on account of this money, and no further payment is entered.' He added, 'Some enquiry would appear to be desirable in regard to this matter.'

At the end of 1921 Armstrong used seven bank accounts shared between the Hay branches of Barclays Bank and the National Provincial Bank. The main business account of the firm through which large sums of money passed in and out was the No. 2 account at Barclays. This was in credit at the end of 1921 but showed a declining balance as did the firm's deposit account.

The Armstrongs had a joint account at the National Provincial Bank. This account which was frequently overdrawn was essentially private although some business transactions were put through it. There was also a separate account known as the Vaughan Account to cover Armstrong's transactions with John Williams Vaughan which included the sale of the Velinnewydd Estate. He had been one of Armstrong's clients since 1910 when he had borrowed £1900. At the end of 1920 this account was overdrawn by more than £1000 and by some £600 at the end of 1921. Among securities held by the bank against this overdraft was a policy on Armstrong's life.

There is every reason to believe that Armstrong was in

financial difficulty. In fact the position was put more boldly by the police investigation officers: '. . .we are gradually accumulating evidence which shows that Armstrong's financial affairs are in great disorder, that he is insolvent and has been improperly using his client's money.' Consequently, his wife's money if it were not tied up in the provisions of her 1917 will would provide him with security.

After Armstrong had been arrested, considerable suspicion was thrown on the second will. Inquiries were made but it was not seriously challenged in court, although reference was made to the irregular witnessing of the document. As part of the research for this book, the signature on the second will was analysed with revealing results by the late Mr Henry T.F. Rhodes, a document examiner.

A comparison was made of three handwritings: (a) Major Armstrong's standard signature, (b) Katharine Armstrong's questioned signature on the 1920 will, and (c) Katharine Armstrong's standard signature on the 1917 will.

Mr Rhodes noted the following points about this comparison:

There is a marked general resemblance between the writing of the 1917 will and that of the will of 1920. Formal resemblances of this kind have, however, very little identification value in themselves. The general resemblance of the signature writings does not, therefore, assist in identifying the questioned signature.

The holograph* part and the signature of the 1917 will show a fairly satisfactory line quality and the writing is reasonably fluent. These characteristics are also found in the holograph part of the 1920 will. The line quality of certain parts of the questioned signature of 1920 is, however, poor, particularly in the *K*, and *M* and the terminal *g*. These indications are consistent with the writing's being a forgery, but are not sufficient to prove the fact.

There are other differences which are significant. The small pen movements associated with the base of the *t* and with the *o* are not consistent with the same movements in the writings of Mrs Armstrong. They are, particularly in

---

* A holograph is a document the whole of which has been hand written by the signatory.

respect of the *o*, more consistent with the H.R. Armstrong writing than with that of Mrs Armstrong.

But the most important part of the analysis was in the measurement of the heights of the small letters, or minuscules, in the signatures. Metrical analysis is a standard authentication procedure used by document examiners and consists of measurements expressed in terms of the proportional heights of each character.

When this was applied to the three signatures, Mr Rhodes found:

A metrical analysis of the minuscules proved to be significant in this case, the minuscules of the signature being r, m^1, m^2, m^3, s, r, n^1 and n^2 (the numbers against the n and m refer to the two and three members of these characters each of which can be measured as if it were a separate character.)

The results of this analysis are shown below in graphical form.

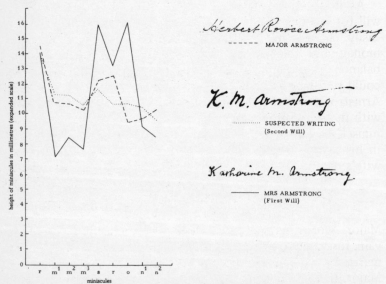

Mr Henry Rhodes's analysis of the suspect signature on the second will. The graph indicates the comparative heights of the characters in the three signatures he analysed. See text for further explanation.

It was concluded from this that, '. . .the metrical values of Mrs Armstrong are quite inconsistent with those of the questioned writing. Those of H.R. Armstrong, on the other hand, are substantially consistent with the values of the questioned signature.'

Mr Rhodes's findings were, '. ..(1) that the probability that the questioned signature was not written by the same hand as the writings attributed to Mrs Armstrong is so high as to amount to a certainty; (2) that the probability that the questioned signature was made by the same hand as the writing attributed to Mr H.R. Armstrong is very high.'

This was the first time that a detailed analysis had been made of the signature on the 1920 will and the results show that the suspicions which the police had at the time were well-founded. There can be little question that Major Armstrong forged his wife's signature on that will and had it falsely witnessed by two servants who were ignorant of the correct procedure.

As it stood there was very little in Mrs Armstrong's 1917 will for her husband. By forging a new will Armstrong could easily change this position in his favour, gaining his wife's money and thereby bolstering up his own sagging bank balance. This was no great feat of imagination for a man who could seriously ask a doctor for interest on nursing fees, and Armstrong probably felt that as a solicitor he could get away with it where others might be detected. But he was exposing himself to considerable risk. The very existence of a new will in his favour might cause a closer look to be made into his wife's death.

* * * * *

Major Armstrong was not a demented syphilitic but he was vain, fussy and to a degree professionally incompetent. Had he married a woman who better understood his personality the Major, likely as not, would have led a dull life which matched his ideals of self-grandeur. But it was his misfortune to court a woman who was every bit as eccentric as he was. Katharine Armstrong's aim in life was to make everyone, and especially her husband and children, conform to her principles. Her methods were blunt, direct and humiliating.

'No wine for the Major' was Katharine's guiding principle added to which there was no smoking and probably no wifely embraces either. Having seen another view of life while in the army, the Major sought affection outside his marriage. The result of this understandable deceit was that his business, which he should have been nurturing carefully in face of competition, was neglected and his financial affairs got into a mess.

As the months passed, Katharine became increasingly hypochondriac and domineering. The Major wanted to continue his double life, but felt it necessary to maintain the myth that he and his wife were an affectionate, devoted couple. With his business on the rocks and confronted also with the problem of juggling his finances to keep solvent, the strain was becoming unbearable.

Herein lay Armstrong's motive. To escape from the tangle enmeshing him he could do away with his wife, thus ridding himself of her intolerable influence, and start a new life. With her out of the way and, as an afterthought, gaining the provisions of her will for himself, he could concentrate on his legal practice and end his financial worries. Moreover, he could bring to Mayfield another woman who would understand him and in whose admiration would be reflected his own image of a man of substance.

6   Rex v Armstrong—The Prosecution

. . .the evidence points conclusively to the fact that she was poisoned by her husband.

Sir Ernest Pollock

WHILE Armstrong was in Gloucester prison awaiting trial, his children were looked after by a neighbour, Mary Tunnard Moore. The eldest child, Eleanor, told Mary, 'When Mummy was so ill she told me to be very careful with the bottles (of medicine) because if she took the wrong one and anything happened Daddy would be blamed.' Possibly recalling that it was his daughter's evidence which largely accounted for Harold Greenwood's acquittal, Mary took Eleanor to the vicar of Hay and made her repeat the story. The vicar related what had happened to Armstrong's defence team but they were against the idea of putting the girl in the witness box. Ronald Bosanquet, one of Armstrong's lawyers, broached the subject to the Major. 'I went to see him in the cramped cell under the Shire Hall and told him what we had decided, to which he replied in a cool, matter-of-fact tone, "Yes, Bosanquet, I quite agree. A little too like the Greenwood case." '

Armstrong's trial* began on Monday, 3rd April 1922 at the Shire Hall, Hereford. The case was to be heard by Mr Justice Darling at the Herefordshire Winter Assizes. The day dawned with weather which was far from seasonal; it was cold and snowing and life was very difficult for the post office engineers who were checking the dozens of extra telephone lines installed for the newsmen. An old Hereford resident told a *Western Mail* reporter, 'It is a curious fact that when a judge comes to Hereford to take assizes we get very bad weather,' By 9 a.m. a crowd, mostly composed of women, had gathered at the entrance to the Shire Hall. A number of pressmen and other spectators had gone to the railway station to meet the first train in from Gloucester in the hope of seeing the accused man. They were to be disappointed, though, for

---

* A full account of the trial of Herbert Rowse Armstrong is to be found in the Notable British Trial series. (Filson Young; *The Trial of H.R. Armstrong*, William Hodge, 1927—now out of print, but may be obtained from second hand booksellers.)

Armstrong was travelling by road.

The crowd of spectators at the Shire Hall grew quickly and many sought shelter from the driving snow and cold east wind in the lee of St Peter's Church, opposite. All approaches to the Shire Hall were guarded by men of the Herefordshire County Police, reinforced by constables from other districts. Occasionally, small parties of ticket holders, mostly pressmen and court officials, were admitted to the Hall.

Mr Justice Darling arrived unobtrusively and entered the court by a side door. He was accompanied by his cousin, Mrs Clive, who was described as his hostess. This lady was a local JP and figured prominently in Herefordshire affairs.

Charles Darling, a weak child who had to be tutored at home, won all his accomplishments in a hurry and lived to be eighty-seven. He was a barrister at the age of twenty-four, a Member of Parliament at thirty-one and a judge at forty-seven. He was called to the Bar in 1874 without passing an examination and soon became known for his verses, which appeared in *Westminster Gazette* and other journals. He was knighted on being elevated to the Bench in 1897, an appointment that was fiercely criticized.

Darling had a wide reputation as a wit and on being appointed to the Bench is said to have remarked, 'Well, I can read and write; what more do you want?' Ronald Bosanquet who knew Darling on the Oxford Circuit, said of him, '. . .he decided from the first to assume the role of the humorous judge and that was his undoing. He never could refrain from joking even in the most serious case.' Joking apart, Darling had presided at some famous trials and appeal proceedings, including those of Sir Roger Casement, Frederick Seddon, 'Chicago May', Steinie Morrison, George Joseph Smith and Hawley Harvey Crippen.

At the time of Armstrong's trial, Sir Charles Darling, P.C., was seventy-three, although he was spritely for his years. He was to preside hawk-like over what proved to be his last murder trial and to stamp his indelible mark on the outcome.

At about 10.30 a.m. the prisoner arrived at the rear of the court building: he also escaped the attention of the waiting crowd. Wearing his inevitable British warm, Armstrong stepped from a covered-in, hired taxi and was briskly escorted into the building by the Chief Constable of Hereford, the Governor of

Gloucester Prison and the prison doctor. The shivering onlookers, denied the privilege of seeing either the judge or accused, had to make do with the arrival of the Crown witnesses. Several of the already well-known names in the case, Bessie Friend, Emily Pearce, Nurse Kinsey and others were shepherded into the large Assembly Hall by Detective Sergeant Sharp.

The lawyers also arrived unnoticed. Sir Ernest Pollock, K.C., the Attorney General, led the prosecution and he was assisted by Mr Charles Francis Vachell, K.C., and Mr St John Micklethwait who had represented the Director of Public Prosecutions at the police-court proceedings in Hay. Sir Ernest Pollock, though voluble in his courtroom manner, was criticized for relying too heavily on intuition in his cases and of being bested by opposing counsel as a result. He was not without humour, however, and there was a story that when he was appointed Attorney General he considered the fee for acquiring the armorial bearings which went with the office too expensive. After lengthy correspondence on the matter, Pollock instructed a College of Arms messenger, 'Tell Garter King-at-Arms with my compliments that he may go to the devil sable in flames gule with a pitchfork ardent stuck in his backside proper.'

Defending Armstrong was Sir Henry Curtis Bennett, K.C., a well known lawyer easily distinguished in court by his size. He was renowned for 'doing a Curtis', which was the name given by colleagues to his characteristic use of legal guile in difficult situations. This big, emotional man, conscious of the strain which his twenty stone imposed on his heart, was prepared to give his all for Armstrong, and his assistants spoke of the great amount of work which he did on the case before the trial.

Curtis Bennett arrived at Hereford in his open Rolls Royce the day before the trial and was met by T.A. Matthews. Together they went to see Armstrong and the prisoner greeted his counsel with the question, 'Were you at Oxford or Cambridge, Sir Henry?' 'Cambridge,' was the reply. 'They won the boat race and we will win this case,' retorted Armstrong, referring to the annual boat race on the River Thames which had just taken place.

Assisting Sir Henry were Samuel Ronald Bosanquet, K.C.

and Mr Edwin Alfred Godson. All three, together with T.A. Matthews, discussed the case with Armstrong in his cell on the morning of the trial and if there was any anxiety it was Armstrong himself who made light of it. Speaking to Bosanquet, with whom he had been on friendly terms since student days at Cambridge, he said, 'Bosanquet, I can tell you something that will interest you very much. A Cat's man (St Catherine's College) is president of the Union for the first time this term'. Events were thick with omens for those who looked for them, and possibly Armstrong drew encouragement from what to took to be good signs.

Inside the courtroom there was an unusual lighting effect caused by reflection from the snow which lay outside; it was an effect which added to the atmosphere of excitement. Seats which were not occupied by the large contingent of newsmen were filled by members of the public who counted themselves fortunate to have been admitted by the police. Counsel were in their seats talking and arranging papers when, just before 11 a.m., the buzz of conversation was silenced by the arrival of the High Sheriff dressed in scarlet uniform and wearing military decorations. He took his place on the left of the judge's seat and was joined by the Chief Constable of the County. Members of the Grand Jury filed into their seats and at ten minutes past eleven the assembly rose as the judge entered the court. Mr Justice Darling was a slight, almost shrunken figure, but he represented the full dignity of the law in his scarlet and ermine robes and full bottomed wig.

The function of the Grand Jury was to decide whether there was sufficient cause to believe that a person had committed a crime. It usually consisted of twenty-three persons summoned for the whole period of an assize to fulfil an advisory role. It was often said of the Grand Jury that it merely endorsed the aims of the prosecutors and the system was abolished in England in 1933 although it still flourishes in the USA.

The first words at the trial were spoken by the Clerk of the Assize, 'Members of the Grand Jury,' he said, 'please to answer your names.' Among those called were two baronets, four colonels, two majors and two captains. Armstrong was not in court at this moment but no doubt he would have felt that his fate was at least in the hands of his peers. The Grand

Jury was duly sworn in and Sir Richard Harrington was elected foreman.

Mr Justice Darling then outlined to the jury the three indictments against the prisoner. Major Armstrong was charged first and foremost with the murder of his wife. But, in addition, there were the two accusations of attempted murder of Oswald Martin : the alleged administration of arsenic during the tea party at Mayfield and the sending of poisoned chocolates to Martin's home. The judge advised that the last of these charges be dropped as it had not been satisfactorily shown that Armstrong had posted the chocolates to Martin. The Judge asked the Grand Jury 'to say whether you find a "True Bill" or "No Bill",' and at 11.45 they retired to make their decision. Whether or not the trial proceeded depended on the decision of the Grand Jury but there seemed little doubt of the outcome as the clerks continued their preparations, toing and froing with books and piles of documents which were placed on the table in the well of the court.

At 12.15 the return of the Grand Jury was announced and silence settled on the court as the judge returned to hear their decision. 'Gentlemen of the Grand Jury,' said the Clerk of the Assize, 'do you find a True Bill against Herbert Rowse Armstrong for murder?' Almost in an undertone, the foreman answered, 'We do.' They had taken thirty minutes to find a True Bill against Major Armstrong for the murder of his wife and the attempted murder of Oswald Martin; as expected, the third charge was rejected. Having done their duty, the members of the Grand Jury were thanked for their services and were discharged by the judge, their Assize duties completed.

The trial jury were waiting to be called outside the courtroom but first the prisoner was summoned to face his moment of destiny. The accused man, flanked by two warders, was led to the dock. Here was no common felon or brute killer but a dapper little man in a brown tweed suit, spats and brown boots who bowed courteously to the judge. Armstrong's heavy moustache was waxed at both ends and his intense blue eyes shone alertly through gold-rimmed spectacles. The Clerk of the Assize addressed him: 'Herbert Rowse Armstrong, you are charged in this indictment with the wilful murder of your wife, Katharine Mary Armstrong, at

Cusop, on February 22nd, 1921. How say you? Are you guilty or not guilty?' Armstrong standing to attention, replied in a firm voice, 'Not guilty.'

The prisoner was informed that the members of the trial jury would now be called and that if he objected to any one of them he should say so as they took the oath. Armstrong gave a polite bow indicating that he understood and he relaxed to the 'stand easy' position as the first of the jurors came into the court. There were two women among them and the judge told them that they could step down if they wished as the case was likely to be a painful one. They both asked to be excused and their places were filled by male jurors. No objections were raised as to the eligibility of any of the jurors and Armstrong was faced by his real judges, mostly farmers, who elected Tom Hopkins, a broad-shouldered, John Bull-like figure, as their foreman. The jury were reminded of their duty which was 'To inquire whether he (the prisoner) be guilty or not guilty, and to hearken to the evidence.'

With the preliminaries over, the tall figure of Sir Ernest Pollock rose and he began to present the opening statement for the Crown. Armstrong leaned forward attentively in the dock as the Attorney General's voice resounded throughout the courtroom. Sir Ernest described the symptoms of Mrs Armstrong's illness and said that she had been submitted during the last weeks of her life to a course of poisoning, with a final dose within twenty-four hours of her death when she was lying in bed unable to move her limbs or her hands to feed herself. 'Who poisoned her? . . . I am going to submit to you that the evidence points conclusively to the fact that she was poisoned by her husband.'

The first challenge came when the Attorney General wanted to bring as evidence the allegation of Armstrong's attempt on Martin's life. Sir Henry Curtis Bennett immediately objected to the admissibility of this evidence and contended that any symptoms of arsenical poisoning suffered by Mr Martin could not possibly throw any light on whether or not Mrs Armstrong was poisoned by her husband. The jury withdrew while this legal argument was battled out. This was clearly an important decision for the judge. If he ruled against admitting the evidence then a large part of what was relevant

Mr Justice Darling is driven to the Assizes at Hereford

The jury arrive too

For the Defence: Bosanquet, Toogood and Matthews

Defence and Prosecution, Curtis Bennett
and the Attorney General

The crowds assemble for the trial at Hereford's Shire Hall

Defending himself in court

Leaving Shire Hall after sentence of death

The crowd assembles outside Gloucester
Prison for the execution

about Armstrong's character and conduct would have been lost. On the other hand he could be criticized on the grounds that such evidence might work unfairly against the prisoner on the main charge.

After listening to both sides of the argument. Mr Justice Darling ruled that the evidence was admissible. He did not think it necessary to give detailed grounds for his decision, he said only that if he was wrong there was the Court of Appeal which could set him right. There was clearly an omen here for Armstrong's defenders and it did not bode good.

Sir Ernest Pollock resumed his statement, dealing with Armstrong's relationship with Oswald Martin, and he made special reference to the arsenic found on the prisoner at the time of his arrest. The Attorney General then laid down the guidelines of the fight that would decide Armstrong's guilt or innocence. He contended that the prisoner had the *means*: arsenic bought from a chemist; *opportunity*: frequent occasions to be alone with his wife; and *motive*: namely the benefits to be derived from her will, all of which added up to Armstrong as his wife's murderer. The Crown was to call witnesses, including medical experts, to support this contention and the defence would strive to show that there were other explanations of Mrs Armstrong's death, such as accidental poisoning or suicide.

When Sir Ernest had completed his opening statement the court was adjourned. The first day of the drama was over and the participants withdrew to their various quarters: Mr Justice Darling to a friend's house near Hereford, counsel to their hotels in the town, the jury to accommodation at the Hereford Training College and the accused to his cell at Gloucester Prison. This was a ritual which was repeated at the end of each day of the trial.

Sir William Willcox, accompanied by Bernard Spilsbury and John Webster, had travelled down to Hereford by train earlier on this first day of the trial. They stayed at the same hotel as the Attorney General and the representative of the Director of Public Prosecutions, Gerald Paling. All the principals involved in the prosecution took part in an after dinner council of war that same evening; Willcox took a leading part in discussing the likely tactics of the defence.

* * * * *

The following day, the first Crown witnesses were called: Mrs Armstrong's sister, her nurses and the servants from Mayfield. They related their now familiar stories under examination and then cross-examination. Mr Justice Darling frequently interrupted to put questions and to clarify various issues. Miss Pearce was virtually treated as a hostile witness by the prosecution because under Sir Henry Curtis Bennett's cross-examination she said that she signed the July 1920 will in the presence of Mrs Armstrong. This conflicted with what she had said in previous statements but she explained it by saying, '. that has only just occurred to me.' She told the court that Mrs Armstrong put her hand on the paper and said, 'You put your name there'. The old lady's memory was plainly not of the best and later on she told counsel, '. . .I am sorry, but my memory is getting dreadful; I am getting old and it is getting worse'—or perhaps she suddenly realized the awful predicament her employer was in.

The defence drew out several issues which suggested they were building up the idea of suicide as an explanation of Mrs Armstrong's death. Emily Pearce, for instance, was questioned about Mrs Armstrong's remark concerning the likelihood of anyone breaking their back by jumping out of the bedroom window. And Nurse Eva Allen, who was in the witness box for over three hours, was asked by Mr Vachell if the sick woman had indicated whether or not she wished to live. Eva Allen said Mrs Armstrong's exact words were 'Nurse, I am not going to die, am I? Because I have everything to live for my children and my husband.'

Pursuing the vital question of how much the sick woman could do for herself a few days before her death, the judge put several questions to Nurse Allen.

'During the last four days did she get out of bed at all?'

'No, not to my knowledge, she did not.'

'Do you believe she could have done it?'

'I do not think she could have.'

'. . .As I understand it it is suggested that she could after the 13th have got out of bed and have got a bottle out of the cupboard above the fireplace. What do you say to that. . .?'

'I do not think it was possible.'

'You have said you did not think it possible that she could have done it after the 13th, that is the Sunday; but what do you say to any time during the last four days?'

'I do not think it was possible then because she was so much weaker.'

If Nurse Allen's evidence was the most important during the early days of the trial, the testimony given by Madame X was the most dramatic. This witness, who had appeared at the Hay Police court proceedings veiled and anonymous, was equally mysterious at the trial. As before, her name was not used in court but it was written on a piece of paper which was handed to the jury.

Madame X, Marion Glassford Gale, told how she had met Major Armstrong and she answered questions about her relationship with him. 'Were you then on the footing of his fiancee?', asked prosecuting counsel. 'No, certainly not', replied the witness. Similar questions were asked by the judge and by Sir Henry Curtis Bennett. The reply was the same—there was no promise of marriage, merely a discussion of the possibility.

The prosecution then raised the question of correspondence between the witness and Major Armstrong: 'You did correspond with him?' asked Mr Vachell. 'Yes', was the short reply. 'I do not want to be embarrassing,' counsel continued, 'but there were certain letters of yours found on Mr Armstrong when he was arrested, you know that do not you?' 'I did not know that,' replied the witness.

There followed a minor row between counsel concerning the admissibility of such letters as evidence. After all, as Sir Henry Curtis Bennett pointed out, the prisoner was not responsible for letters written to him. Mr Justice Darling ruled that the letters could not be considered as evidence at this time but he asked the witness to initial them if she acknowledged that she had written them. Marion Glassford Gale was handed each letter and envelope which she initialled without question.

There was a stir of expectancy in the court when Oswald Martin was called to testify. He looked ill-at-ease and answered questions in such a low voice that he was asked to speak up. He recounted the sequence of events leading up to the invitation to tea at Mayfield and gave details of what took place there. In his cross-examination, Sir Henry Curtis Bennett tried to show that Martin was not well-disposed to Armstrong, 'Am I right in saying that from time to time you had received acts of kindness from Major Armstrong? He proposed you, did he not, for the Herefordshire Law Society?'

'That is quite true, yes, but that would have been a matter of form in any case.'

'That is the way you look at it, do you?'

'That is the way I look at it.'

'. . .Am I right in saying that up to October that was the position between you two—perfectly friendly?'

'One would wish to be courteous.'

'Is that the only reason?'

'Well, there is no need to be rude.'

'Let us have it out—did you dislike Major Armstrong before October 1921?'

'No, I did not dislike him.'

'What do you mean then by disinclination to be rude?'

'My feelings were neutral as far as he was concerned. I never liked nor disliked him.'

The way in which the witness fenced with these questions did not create a good impression and defence counsel was later able to convey the impression that Martin was vindictive.

* * * * *

On the fourth day, when Dr Hincks was called to the witness box, the trial entered a new phase. Up to this point, the background of the case, which was already known in great detail, was covered routinely. With Hincks and his eminent colleagues giving evidence, the court was to embark on the medical aspects of the case which would dominate the rest of the trial.

Dr Hincks gave a careful account of Mrs Armstrong's illness referring from time to time to his record books. He said that during the last few days of her life his patient could not move her legs at all and she had a loss of co-ordination in the muscles and could not use her arms. There was a general condition of paresis; she could not lift herself up and the most she could do was to be propped up in bed. The doctor explained that when he made out the death certificate he had no suspicion that the toxaemia was caused by an outside agency. He had subsequently changed his opinion and he now believed that Mrs Armstrong's illness when she went into hospital was due to arsenical poisoning.

Anticipating the line the defence would pursue, the Attorney General tried to make Sir Henry Curtis Bennett's task more difficult. Sir Ernest asked Dr Hincks, 'Supposing this lady had within her reach or in a cupboard in her room a number of bottles containing anything, do you think in her condition it would be possible for her to have administered them to herself during the last three or four days of her life?' With considerable emphasis, Hincks replied, 'Absolutely impossible.' Thus Hincks underlined the view stated earlier by Nurse Allen.

Not for the last time in the trial, Mr Justice Darling, put questions to a witness which seemed to identify the judge as prosecutor. The record shows judge and Attorney General working together very effectively in examining Hincks.

Attorney General:	'Let me put this period to you. You visited her on the 16th, 17th, 18th, every day from the 16th onwards up to the 22nd. What was her physical condition during the last few days of her life; was she able to get out of bed?'
Dr Hincks:	'Oh no.'
A.G.:	'That is what I want you to tell me about.'
Dr Hincks:	'No, she could not possibly get out of bed.'
Mr Justice Darling:	'From when did you say?'
Dr Hincks:	'I doubt if she ever left her bed after the 16th when I first saw her; certainly after the 18th she never left her bed.'
A.G.:	'Do you mean for any purpose at all?'
Dr Hincks:	'For any purpose.'
A.G.:	'We have heard from the nurse.'
Dr Hincks:	'She can give better evidence on that point than I can, but from my knowledge of her and her condition I should say it was impossible for her to leave her bed certainly from the 18th onwards.'
Mr Justice Darling:	'For any purpose whatever?'
Dr Hincks:	'For any purpose whatever.'

Dr Hincks had given his evidence in a calm, authoratitive way and Sir Henry Curtis Bennett knew that he would have to probe deeply to seek out the slightest weakness. He asked the doctor if there was anything he could see in Mrs Armstrong's condition, including her death, which was inconsistent with natural causes. Hincks said there was nothing. The certificate which he had issued certified death as due to heart disease which he considered to have been caused by long-standing rheumatism.

Sir Henry then went on to ask questions about toxaemia and the doctor agreed that toxaemia could result from some poison either taken or administered. It could also arise from auto-intoxication such as blood-poisoning due, for example, to a badly decayed tooth. Defence counsel contended that Mrs Armstrong's early illness could have been due to toxaemia following years of ill health and rheumatism. This condition in turn could have led to the multiple neuritis which Mrs Armstrong suffered when she went to Barnwood. Dr Hincks was bound to agree in general terms that such a course of events was possible if somewhat unlikely. Sir Henry was trying to show that Mrs Armstrong's illness to within a short time of her death could have been due to natural causes such as auto-intoxication. If he could establish this point, the way would be clear to suggest that Mrs Armstrong killed herself later with self-administered arsenic.

Counsel now turned to the Oswald Martin affair and tried to shake Dr Hincks's belief that arsenical poisoning was the cause of Martin's illness. He asked, 'There are many ways, are there not, in which a very small trace of arsenic can be found in a person's body without that arsenic having been wilfully administered as arsenic?' Hincks replied, 'It can.' Sir Henry continued by asking Hincks if arsenic was one of the impurities of bismuth. The doctor replied a little tetchily, 'I am not a chemist: I do not know.' Defence counsel was suggesting that the bismuth mixture given by Hincks to settle Martin's 'biliousness' contained arsenic as an impurity which explained why arsenic was subsequently found in the patient's urine. This was a not very convincing thesis and the Attorney General rightly brought out the point that bismuth mixtures were very commonly used without complaint or ill effect.

Dr Hincks's cross-examination was lengthy, tense and

probably tedious, but he was faced by a lawyer trying to carve a defence out of very little material. Sir Henry framed his points well and Hincks was bound to agree with many of them in principle although he continually forced counsel to modify his questions and thereby reduced their effect. Some of those in court thought that Sir Henry Curtis Bennett had got the country doctor on the run, but Hincks was not a witness to be rattled and the defence gained very little from him in the four hours that he was in the witness box.

Hincks was followed by Dr Arthur Townsend, the Medical Superintendent at Barnwood. He was questioned about Mrs Armstrong's admission to the asylum and the Attorney General asked him about the tonic medicine containing arsenic which was prescribed for the patient.

'What was the purpose of that?'

'For anaemia and as a general tonic.'

'...Is that a preparation or a tonic which you use commonly at the hospital?'

'Very commonly.'

'...While she was in the asylum did her condition improve?'

'Yes.'

Dr Townsend was next questioned about the conditions which applied to a patient given leave of absence from the asylum. He explained that should a patient released on leave of absence suffer a breakdown, he or she could be returned to the hospital without recertification. During the period of absence, reports would be required by the hospital as to the patient's mental state and if at the end of three months the patient was well he or she would be discharged. If the patient became seriously ill during leave of absence the doctor said, 'I should probably go down and see the patient myself or send one of my medical officers.'

'Were you surprised to hear of Mrs Armstrong's death?' asked Sir Ernest Pollock.

'Yes, I was surprised.'

'From her physical condition when she left the hospital on January 22nd had you any cause to anticipate her early death?'

'I had no cause to anticipate her early death.'

In the interval between Dr Townsend's evidence and that of the Crown's expert witnesses, there was a period of rather dull, formal questioning. The Hay chemist and his assistant

told how they had sold arsenic to Major Armstrong, and the
police investigating officers gave evidence of arrest. In his
cross-examination, Sir Henry Curtis Bennett asked Chief
Inspector Crutchett to relate the details of searches made at
Mayfield after the arrest. The study was searched in detail
and Crutchett told how Major Armstrong had directed him
to the drawer in the study's bureau where the keys to the
safe were to be found: 'We pulled out the drawer and made a
thorough search,' said Crutchett. Sir Henry interrupted
dramatically with the question, 'Would it surprise you to
know that Mr Matthews, with Doctor Ainslie, found that
arsenic which I have produced here this afternoon, at the
back of that little drawer?' 'It would surprise me,' replied
Crutchett.

Defence counsel later told the court that after Armstrong
was arrested he remembered that he had not told the police
about some arsenic which was in the drawer of that bureau.
He told his solicitor, Mr Matthews, who at once went to
Mayfield to look for it but could not find it. He assumed that
the police had taken charge of the poison, but three weeks
later, when the police provided a list of the articles they had
taken, this item was not shown. Matthews decided to have
another search and this time he took out the drawer completely and put his hand at the back of the cavity where he found
the packet of arsenic.

This arsenic which was alleged to have been missed by the
police during their searches was the subject of considerable
debate, in which Mr Justice Darling inevitably took a part.
Superintendent Weaver, who had accompanied Crutchett at
the time of the search, was recalled. He was quizzed at some
length by the judge who ascertained that no police guard was
left at Mayfield after the search. 'Then for all you know
anybody might have gone there?' he asked Weaver.

'Quite so, my Lord.'

'Do you believe it possible that that little packet of two
ounces of arsenic could have been in that drawer, or in the
cavity behind it, at the time you searched?'

'I say it was absolutely impossible. . .I don't think we left
an inch of the bureau untouched.'

'And Inspector Crutchett was with you when you searched?'

'Yes, my Lord.'

'A Scotland Yard man?'
'Yes.'
And there the matter rested for the time being.

* * * * *

As the first week of the trial drew to a close the prosecution
called the first of its expert witnesses. This was Dr Bernard
Henry Spilsbury whose wealth of experience coupled with the
precise way in which he gave evidence made him a formid-
able witness. Examined by Sir Ernest Pollock he told of his
findings when he carried out the post-mortem on Mrs
Armstrong. He said that several organs of the body were in a
remarkable state of preservation; this was subsequently fully
explained by the amount of arsenic found in them. There
was no evidence of natural disease and the condition of the
liver and kidneys was consistent with arsenical poisoning.

Spilsbury was asked for his opinion regarding the effect of
the arsenical tonic mixture given to Mrs Armstrong while she
was a patient at Barnwood. He replied that the amount
prescribed totalled between four and five grains over a period
of thirty-one days. The Attorney General asked him directly
if this could have had any bearing at all on the arsenic which
was found in the exhumed body. 'No, it is quite impossible,'
replied Spilsbury. Asked at what time a dose of arsenic must
have been given in order to account for that later found in
the body, Spilsbury said, '. . .it is clear that a large dose of
arsenic must have been taken, I mean a poisonous dose,
possibly a fatal dose, must have been taken certainly within
twenty-four hours of death, and from the amount of arsenic
which was found in the liver. . .the poison must have been
given in a number of doses extending over a period, certainly
of some days, possibly not less than a week.'

When Spilsbury was questioned about the condition of
Mrs Armstrong's body it was clear that the court were in some
difficulty as to the names and positions of many of the
organs referred to. To assist the jury the Attorney General
produced a drawing of the human alimentary system with the
stomach inked in, the small intestine coloured blue and the
large intestine coloured red. With this drawing held up for
the jury to see, Dr Spilsbury marked in the ileum, jejunum

and caecum, those parts of the intestines from which he had
taken fluid for analysis.

Sir Henry Curtis Bennett then cross-examined Dr Spilsbury.
He put it to the pathologist that there were cases on record
where large doses of arsenic had been taken four, five, six or
even seven days before death and where large quantities of
the poison were later found in the corpse. Spilsbury agreed
that such cases were not entirely unknown. There followed a
considerable debate about the course of such a case particularly
with regard to the symptoms of vomiting and diarrhoea and
their abatement. Sir Henry well knew that a single fatal dose
of arsenic caused vomiting and purging for two or three days.
These symptoms then eased off and death ensued. Now, in
Mrs Armstrong's case there was vomiting right up to the time
of death; a feature which suggested continuous doses of
poison to within about twenty-four hours of death. As
witnesses had already testified that Mrs Armstrong was too
weak to have taken the arsenic herself at this late stage of
her illness, defence counsel's task was to account for the
symptoms of continuous poisoning in some other way.

Sir Henry pressed Spilsbury again. 'Am I right in saying
that in very extreme cases and only in very extreme cases, a
person may live up till fourteen days after a fatal dose of
arsenic?'

'It is conceivable and I dare say cases have been recorded.'

'That is all I put, fourteen days. Would you agree that it is
quite likely cases are reported to that effect?'

'I dare say; that is to say under special conditions.'

Trying to build on this slender foundation, defence counsel
suggested it was possible that a large dose of arsenic could
produce immediate symptoms of poisoning, then abate for
two or three days and restart without further arsenic being
taken into the body. Death would result and a post-mortem
examination would be expected to reveal fatty degeneration
of the liver and kidneys and dilation of the heart. Spilsbury
would not concede that such an outcome was likely without
the existence of some disease. He was equally insistent that
Mrs Armstrong's body had shown no condition not accounted
for by arsenical poisoning.

The need to demonstrate that Mrs Armstrong's symptoms
could have resulted from a single, fatal self-administered dose

of arsenic was vital, and Sir Henry pursued it vigorously. He had to find an alternative explanation for the continuous vomiting in Mrs Armstrong's case. A possible explanation for a remission of the symptoms in such a case was, he suggested, that the arsenic did not fully dissolve but became encapsulated with mucus in the stomach and ceased to be absorbed. The result was that the violent symptoms of poisoning ceased temporarily and then restarted when the arsenic became free. Spilsbury agreed that instances of encysted arsenic had been reported, but the most he would commit himself to was that he would '. . .not like to exclude it entirely'. As always, he backed up his opinion with facts and in this instance he said that the two grains of arsenic found in the liver showed that a great deal of poison had been thoroughly absorbed. This weighed against the theory of encysted arsenic as did the findings of the post-mortem which revealed no signs of this phenomenon.

Having made little progress in this matter, Sir Henry Curtis Bennett switched his attention to the treatment Mrs Armstrong received while at Barnwood. He asked Dr Spilsbury if one seventh of a grain of arsenic prescribed daily might not have aggravated the condition of someone already suffering from arsenical poisoning. The pathologist thought it would tend to retard recovery. Defence counsel was not easily put off and he persisted with his line of questioning:

'The case here is that Mrs Armstrong in August 1920, when she entered that home [Barnwood], was suffering from the effects of arsenical poisoning?'

'Yes'.

'Assuming that is correct—I am disputing it, but assuming that it is correct—would you not expect the giving of one seventh of a grain every day for thirty-one days to such a person would aggravate the symptoms?'

'No, I should not. I think the course of the patient in the asylum shows that this was not so in this case. . .'

'Exactly, because I suggest to you that she was not suffering from arsenical poisoning; that is why one seventh of a grain for thirty-one days had no effect upon her.'

'I am afraid I do not agree with that,' was Spilsbury's reply. The important clue to this matter was the albuminuria which Mrs Armstrong had when she was admitted to Barnwood. Albumen in the urine was caused by the damaging action of the arsenic on the woman's kidneys. After a few days in hospital, however, the albuminuria cleared up, indicating that Mrs Armstrong's body was no longer being poisoned.

Finally, Sir Henry questioned Spilsbury about the arsenical impurities of bismuth. He took the same line that he adopted with Dr Hincks and received much the same answer—although arsenic might occasionally be found in bismuth, the compounds supplied by chemists were free of such impurities. Sir Henry also tried to cast doubt on the suitability of the bottle chosen to collect Martin's urine sample in. It had previously contained hydrogen peroxide which Spilsbury admitted had been known to contain contaminating traces of arsenic. It was a pity that John Davies, the Hay chemist, did not think of saving for analysis a washing from the bottle before it was filled with urine. That would have put the matter beyond doubt: as it was, this minor deficiency provided the defence with its only victory in an otherwise unrewarding examination.

Defence counsel had been unable to shake the prosecution argument that Mrs Armstrong, too weak to help herself in any way, had received a large dose of arsenic twenty-four hours before death.

The next expert witness was John Webster, the Senior Home Office Analyst, who, like Spilsbury, had wide experience in forensic investigations. He had been involved in such work for twenty-two years and was regarded by Sir William Willcox as a man of meticulous accuracy and brilliant technique. Webster and Willcox had worked together on the Seddon and Greenwood cases and their testimony frequently proved unassailable.

In reply to the Attorney General's questions about the amount of arsenic found by analysing the organs taken from Mrs Armstrong's exhumed body, Webster said simply. . .'this is the largest amount of arsenic I have found in any case of arsenical poisoning.' A total of 208 milligrammes of arsenic was found in the organs but the amount actually taken in must have been very much larger.

Sir Henry Curtis Bennett questioned him about the way in which the analyses were carried out. Webster explained in some detail how the amounts of arsenic were calculated. He said the tests used were ones which he always carried out, adding, 'The test is a reliable one.' With regard to the arsenic found in Martin's urine he considered that was certainly not a minute trace. In his opinion one thirty-third of a grain could not be introduced by a mere impurity of hydrogen peroxide in the bottle.

The last of the trio of expert witnesses for the prosecution was Sir William Henry Willcox, Medical Adviser to the Home Office, and another man of enormous experience. Sir William and Bernard Spilsbury had been friends for twenty years and with John Webster had worked together on numerous occasions. Willcox had been involved in the case from the very beginning. His advice had been sought by the Director of Public Prosecutions before Armstrong was arrested in December 1921. Having studied the early reports on the case, Willcox had told Sir Archibald Bodkin that, 'Since, in Mrs Armstrong's case, acute symptoms occurred during the last six days of the illness it appears probable that arsenic was administered during this period and if this be the case arsenic will certainly be found on analysis of the dead body.'

Willcox had considered all aspects of the case and the evidence he gave at the trial was clear and precise. He cleared up much of the confusion about medical matters which must have troubled the jury and he crystallized the important issues. Answering questions put by Sir Ernest Pollock, he defined auto-intoxication as an accumulation of poisons in the body due to the kidneys or liver failing to work properly; a common form of auto-intoxication was diabetes. He agreed with Spilsbury that, in Mrs Armstrong's case, it followed from the clearing up of the albumen in her urine while she was in Barnwood that the cause of the trouble had ceased. '. . .If the cause of this illness had been auto-intoxication,' said Sir William, 'it would still have been operating.'

Asked to explain why the albuminuria should stop and the peripheral neuritis develop he said, 'In arsenical poisoning the action of the arsenic on the kidney is a quick one; it occurs in twenty-four hours. The action on the nerves is a slow one, and takes ten days to a fortnight, or perhaps longer, to commence.'

Willcox also corroborated Spilsbury's view that a fatal dose of arsenic was taken within twenty-four hours of death and added, '. . .there must have been a good deal of arsenic absorbed during the last few days of life. Two grains was an unusually large quantity to find at the post-mortem in the liver. Regarding the suggestion that Mrs Armstrong had committed suicide, Sir William's view was that in a suicide attempt one would expect a large dose to have been taken. In this case there was continuous dosing, causing painful symptoms, which he thought was not in the least indicative of suicide. Mr Justice Darling had intervened frequently during the medical evidence and he did so again at this point to put a direct question to Willcox. The judge asked if, in view of all the medical evidence given, Mrs Armstrong could possibly have taken that final dose herself. Without hesitation, Willcox replied, 'No, certainly not.'

Sir Henry Curtis Bennett was faced with the unenviable task of trying to gain some advantage from a prosecution case that was growing in stature with each successive witness. Again, he tried to explore the suicide angle and covered the same questions he had put to Spilsbury. Would Sir William Willcox agree that a person may take one large fatal dose of arsenic, suffer from vomiting for two or three days, and then die after five or six days?

'Yes, that is an abstract proposition,' answered the witness.

'Is it possible?'

'Yes.'

Willcox had already said that the several doses of arsenic which Mrs Armstrong had received ruled out suicide on the basis of common sense, but Sir Henry suggested that a person who was not sane might take several doses. Willcox agreed, but it was plain that the defence was grasping at straws. Questioned about the delaying effect of encysted arsenic, another important plank in the suicide theory, Sir William said, 'I cannot deny the possibility, but it is extremely unlikely.'

The last question put to Sir William Willcox was by Mr Justice Darling. Referring to the defence's theory of Mrs Armstrong's death, he asked '. . .is that hypothesis, in your opinion, a possible one . . .?.

Willcox replied simply, 'Quite impossible.'

* * * * *

The evidence given by the Crown's three expert witnesses and backed by their combined authority and experience, had been factual and uncompromising. As the court adjourned for the weekend, Sir Henry Curtis Bennett must have felt that the legal tug-of-war was pulling away from him. When he returned to his hotel it was not to relax but to prepare his opening speech for Monday morning and to muster all the arguments at his command for the defence of Major Armstrong's life.

The jury were able to spend the Saturday and Sunday in a more light-hearted fashion despite being accommodated at the Hereford Training College. Some of them played football on the college lawn or played cards, and on the Sunday they were all taken for a long drive in the country. In the evenings the more conscientious of them made use of the college library to look up some of the terms used in court: they had not heard the last of words such as 'encysted' and 'encapsulated'.

Hay residents who had been lucky enough to get into the Shire Hall, chattered about the pros and cons of the trial as they were driven home in Humphrey Webb's brake. The Hay undertaker also ran a garage, and the motor chassis which he used as a hearse could easily be converted to a passenger-carrying body. The enterprising Mr Webb was only too willing to satisfy the demand for trips into Hereford and his brake was driven in each day of the trial. It was ironic that the vehicle which in all probability carried Mrs Armstrong to her funeral also took sightseers to her husband's trial for murder.

7 Rex v Armstrong—The Defence

*Do not be too hard on Major Armstrong because he did
not do what a wise man would have done.*

Sir Henry Curtis Bennett

WEEKS before the trial began the police gathered opinions
as to how Major Armstrong and the charge he faced were
regarded in and around Hay. Sergeant Worthing of the
Herefordshire Constabulary reported hearing a conversation
about the case between two travellers at Hereford Railway
Station. At the time, the Sergeant was escorting Armstrong
to Worcester Gaol after one of the remands at the magistrates'
hearing at Hay. The view expressed by both travellers, who
failed to recognize the presence of the man they were
discussing, was that the Major was guilty but would not be
convicted because there was insufficient evidence.

The general opinion was that Armstrong was a much
injured person and he was regarded by many local inhabitants
as something of a martyr. Superintendent David Evans of
the Breconshire Constabulary noted that '. . .many of his
[Armstrong's] friends are betting upon the verdict of the
trial, and are giving odds upon his being acquitted.'

A similar view was reported by Superintendent Weaver who
knew Armstrong personally. He said the majority of people
had already made up their minds that the prosecution would
fail to make a strong enough case to get a guilty verdict.
There was a common feeling, too, that it was a flimsy case
made up out of spite by Oswald Martin and his father-in-law.

Local feelings then were such that when Sir Henry Curtis
Bennett rose to make his opening speech for the defence on
Monday 10th April, he carried with him the support and
hopes of many local people. He began by expressing something of the strain he himself was experiencing: '. . .I have
never wondered more than during the last three days whether
anybody realizes the terrible anxiety and responsibility which
rests upon the shoulders of a member of the bar when he is
defending a man for his life.' With this reference to his own
burdens Sir Henry quickly went into the attack.

The prosecution he contended had failed to show how or

when Major Armstrong had administered the arsenic and no real motive had been put forward. He said he would attempt to show that Major Armstrong did not murder his wife and he made it clear that he did not consider it part of his task to prove who did.

He believed that the Attorney General had worked backwards from the post-mortem. 'Everyone', he said, 'has become extraordinarily wise.' His view was that the history of Mrs Armstrong's illness showed her poor health was due to natural causes and in no way reflected suspicion on her husband. The facts showed a highly hysterical woman who had for years suffered from rheumatism and ill health and had finally reached a stage where a family friend thought she might commit suicide. Mrs Armstrong then went to Barnwood where, according to the prosecution, she developed multiple neuritis. It was Sir Henry's contention that she had multiple neuritis in 1918, months before the alleged poisoning began. Moreover, as a patient in hospital, Mrs Armstrong was given an arsenical tonic which the defence experts believed would have revived any symptoms of poisoning.

When Mrs Armstrong came home from Barnwood she had every hope of getting better but when this did not happen and her health deteriorated, she lapsed into a suicidal frame of mind. Defence counsel reminded the jury that Nurse Kinsey was so concerned that she left the Armstrong home saying that the patient needed a full-time mental nurse.

Sir Henry was scathing about the motives put forward by the prosecution; they were ludicrous, he said. He faulted the suggestion that Major Armstrong killed his wife in order to benefit from her will, on the grounds that Mrs Armstrong had told her sister she was thinking of altering the terms of the will in her husband's favour. In any event, when the will was proved and Major Armstrong inherited his wife's money he did not, 'spend a farthing of it'. The alternative suggestion, that Armstrong murdered his wife in order to leave him free to marry 'that respectable lady' (Madame X), he described as 'fantastic'.

Defence counsel was inclined to dismiss the Martin incident; his opinion was that if Major Armstrong tried to poison Oswald Martin he must have been insane. It would have been more likely that Martin should have wanted to poison Major

Armstrong; after all, Martin was the newcomer and Armstrong was the man with an established position. With regard to the tea party at Mayfield, Sir Henry said there was simply no evidence to show that Major Armstrong put any arsenic in the food. Moreover, the fact that Martin went home and was not sick for four hours suggested that the cause of his illness was something he had taken at dinner.

The one thirty-third of a grain of arsenic found in Martin's urine was quite possibly accounted for as an impurity in the hydrogen peroxide which the sample bottle had previously contained. 'That sample', said Sir Henry, 'was in my submission. . .in the highest degree unsatisfactory.'

Finally, defence counsel said he would call medical witnesses whose opinion was that Mrs Armstrong died as the result of one large fatal dose of arsenic taken on 16th February. There was no evidence connecting anyone in the case with the administration of arsenic and there was certainly no evidence that Major Armstrong gave his wife poison.

Sir Henry's opening speech, in which he had made his strategy quite clear, lasted three hours. After a brief adjournment the prisoner was called and there was an eager, excited atmosphere as Major Armstrong stepped into the witness box. It is always an intense moment when the accused gives evidence, for it is then that he becomes to some extent master of his own fate. It is his chance to speak for himself instead of through others and an opportunity to tell his own story in his own way. There are also the pitfalls of cross-examination and the interpretation of his demeanour by judge and jury. Every reaction and reflex is observed and measured; arrogance, indignation, humility, innocence or self-pity are recorded in the minds of jurors and influence the final reckoning.

* * * * *

Throughout the trial, Armstrong had been attentive and unemotional as if he were detached from the proceedings rather than its central figure. When he was examined by Mr Bosanquet, he answered in a clear, firm voice that was audible right around the court. He gave an account of his business and domestic life and mentioned that his wife suffered from rheumatism when they were first engaged to be married. After that she had constantly recurring attacks of rheumatism and was also a 'martyr to indigestion'.

He first became aware that his wife was unwell in August 1920 when she indulged in self-recrimination about not looking after her children and of defrauding tradesmen. Referring to Mrs Armstrong's admission to the asylum, Bosanquet asked the witness, 'Is there any truth in the suggestion that you administered arsenic to your wife prior to her removal to Barnwood?'

'Not the slightest', came the firm reply.

Counsel then led Armstrong on to the subject of Madame X: '. . .will you tell the jury your relations with her—what they have been?'

'Perfectly friendly relations. I used to visit at her house where her mother lived, and they were extremely hospitable and kind to me during the time while I was on service and quartered in their neighbourhood.'

'Did you discuss the fact of your having a wife and children with her?'

'Yes, and I showed her a photograph both of my wife and my home and children.'

These answers were well composed and no doubt Armstrong had thought them out in advance. Certainly his reply concerning his relationship with Madame X reflected his legal training.

Bosanquet then dealt with the tea party at Mayfield:

'You have heard Mr Martin's evidence with regard to your taking up a scone in your fingers and handing it to him, saying to Mr Martin 'Excuse fingers' or something of that kind. What do you say with regard to that?'

'Oh, that is incorrect.'

'Do you remember using any expression of the kind?'

'I remember simply leaning across to help myself, and saying 'excuse me' but nothing further.'

'To help yourself to what?', asked Mr Justice Darling.

'To a scone, my Lord. It was necessary for me to stretch in front of him to do so.'

Armstrong was asked to give an account of his gardening activities and of his use of arsenic. He explained how he had put a packet containing white arsenic in a drawer of the bureau in the study at Mayfield. This now notorious piece of furniture was to feature in a little courtroom drama at the end of the trial's seventh day. The bureau which had been brought from Mayfield and locked up in the Hereford Under-Sheriff's Office was moved to an ante-room in the Shire Hall. Mr Justice Darling instructed that during the tea interval Armstrong should be escorted to the bureau and place in it the packet of arsenic in the manner which he had described in court. This was duly carried out in the presence of the jury, all the counsel engaged in the trial and the judge—all witnesses were excluded. After he had played his part, Armstrong was taken back to the witness box and Mr Matthews went out to show where he had found the packet of arsenic.

The story was that despite not having told the police specifically about the arsenic in the bureau, Armstrong was sure they would find it during their searches. When it did not feature in the police inventory, Armstrong told Matthews who went to Mayfield to make a search himself. He pulled open the central drawer of the bureau to its fullest extent of about four inches and ascertained that it was empty.

When it became clear that this arsenic was still not accounted for, Matthews went back to Mayfield, this time accompanied by his managing clerk. Again he pulled out the drawer to its fullest extent and this time decided to take it right out—but it was stuck. Feeling at the back of the drawer with his hand he found a piece of paper jammed there; on freeing it he revealed a folded paper packet and its removal allowed the drawer to be pulled right out. Matthews knew then that he had found the arsenic spoken of by Armstrong.

The packet was of white paper folded with a blue paper inside it; it was labelled, 'Arsenic, poison: J.F. Davies'. Matthews put the packet back as he had found it, closed the bureau and locked the room. A few days later he demonstrated his discovery in the presence of Dr Ainslie. The packet was then taken away and an analysis of its contents confirmed that the powder was indeed arsenic. This discovery was announced for the first time in court by Sir Henry Curtis Bennett.

Reporting on this courtroom incident to his chief, Crutchett wrote, '. . .I understand from one who was [present] that as soon as the drawer was opened the packet immediately caught one's eye.' He went on, 'The judge and jury then removed the drawer completely from its slide as they were anxious to know about the cavity at the back where Sir Henry Curtis Bennett had said the packet was found, but on investigation it was found that there was no cavity at the back at all, as the drawer just fitted the space, leaving no room for anything to have got behind or to lodge at the top or on either side.'

* * * * *

After some more questions, Bosanquet sat down and Armstrong was then cross-examined. Sir Ernest Pollock went on the offensive immediately with questions about Mrs Armstrong's suicidal tendencies, recalling that Mr Chevalier had mentioned the possibility to the witness.

'Then it was that you put away your razors and your service revolver?'

'Yes.'

'Did you think that was necessary?'

'It came as a shock to me to hear that from Mr Chevalier as I had never contemplated such a possibility.'

'Mr Chevalier not being a doctor and being a solicitor might urge precautions that might be greater than necessary. I want to know what your view was.'

'From the arguments that he put forward as to her then state of health it seemed to me that he was justified.'

'You took a serious view of it?'

'I took a serious view of it then.'

'You were afraid that there was a suicidal tendency?'

'At that moment.'

Then came the moment that the Attorney General's questioning had been leading up to. Referring to the questionnaire on his wife's health which Armstrong completed and signed on 23rd August 1920 as part of the procedure to admit her to the asylum, Sir Ernest read out a single question and answer.

'Question: Has she threatened or attempted self-destruction; if so, when, and by what means? Answer: No. Did you think it fair to the asylum not to make any disclosure of your anxiety as to this suicidal tendency?'

'I answered that question correctly; she had never made any attempt,' replied Armstrong.

It must not be forgotten that Armstrong was a solicitor and consequently knew better than most men how to anticipate a question and have a ready answer. His reply on this occasion was clever but not very convincing; the prosecution had pointed a finger at a weakness in the prisoner's own testimony.

Explaining why he had been anxious for his wife to be completely released from Barnwood rather than to come home on leave, the Major said he thought that if she were given leave someone would have to come to examine her. He had since heard that would not have been necessary. He said that he had no further anxiety regarding her possible suicidal tendencies after she came out of the asylum.

Armstrong was questioned at great length about a supply of white arsenic, part of which he had used for weed killing. This was the four ounces of arsenic bought from Mr Davies, the Hay chemist, on 11th January 1921, which had not been coloured with charcoal in the normal fashion. The significance of this white arsenic was exploited by both sides. The prosecution contended that because it was the last arsenic to be bought and turned out not to have been coloured, there was every reason why Armstrong should have remembered all about it. The same reasons were used by the defence to reach a different conclusion: they argued that, as the prisoner could account for every scrap of arsenic in his possession, Mrs Armstrong must have taken a fatal dose from some other source, possibly weed killer, to which she had access.

Sitting in the study of Mayfield one June afternoon in 1921, Armstrong had divided up this four ounces of arsenic. He said he first roughly divided the bulk into two lots and then, taking one of these he sub-divided it with his penknife into twenty parts, each of which was wrapped in a piece of paper to make a little packet. These little packets were used that same evening to kill dandelions. His method was to make a hole next to the dandelion with a piece of metal and then to tip the contents of one little packet into it. Each weed was dosed separately but only nineteen packets of arsenic were used; the twentieth being found in the pocket of his jacket when he was arrested.

'Can you tell us how you came to use nineteen of the score and not the twenty?', asked the Attorney General.

'I do not know. I did not count the number that I was using.'

That accounted for half of the original four ounces of arsenic but what of the second two ounces? In his statement to the police Armstrong said he had used some of that arsenic to make liquid weed killer by boiling it up with caustic soda. Now he said that was wrong—he had confused the 1921 arsenic with that bought in 1919.

It was only after he had been arrested and the twentieth little packet of arsenic was found among the things taken from his pockets, that he remembered where the other two ounces were—they were in the drawer of the bureau at Mayfield. 'It all came back to my memory when I saw this little packet. . .', he said in reply to a question by Mr Justice Darling. The packet in question was entered as Exhibit 32 and lay on a table in the courtroom. It was a folded paper packet measuring about one and a half inches by three-quarters of an inch; the paper itself was similar to that used by chemists for putting up powders.

The Attorney General now proceeded to give the witness a gruelling time on this subject and he was assisted, if not actually outdone, by the judge. Sir Ernest read out part of the statement made by Armstrong to the police, 'This arsenic I speak of is the only poison in my possession anywhere, excepting, of course, any contained in medicine.' The Attorney General continued,

'Within an hour of signing that statement, by finding the little packet of white arsenic you knew that statement was all wrong?'

'Yes.'

'And although you knew it was wrong, you took no steps with the police to correct it?'

'In the meantime I was arrested.'

When the judge intervened, pressing home the same question, Armstrong explained '. . .it was a very great shock, the arrest, naturally; and then I decided to say nothing further until I had seen my solicitor.'

The prosecution had the bit between its teeth now and relentlessly pursued the same questions seeking to gain damaging admissions from the prisoner.

'. . .to allow the police, to whom you had promised to render every assistance, to go away with a misleading statement in their possession. This statement is quite misleading is it not?'

'When that statement was made, I did not know I was going to be arrested.'

'We have passed that. You were allowing the police to go away with what you knew was a misleading statement in their possession?'

'I am afraid I did not think very much about it, about what the police were going to do. I was too much overcome by the position I had been placed in.'

'. . .you know these last three lines in your statement were untrue: "This arsenic I speak of is the only poison in my possession anywhere excepting of course any contained in medicine". You knew that to be untrue?'

'I do not think I had those particular words in my mind at the time.'

Finally, the admission was clearly wrung from Armstrong:

'Then may I take it from you, first that the statement that you made to the police was before they left to your knowledge untrue?'

'The original statement that was made before arrest was incorrect.'

But the most searching questions were put by the judge: 'Why did you want to consult your solicitor before you should say anything further?'

'I was met with having found this little packet, and I was not at all sure how it would affect my defence.'

The prisoner's long ordeal was nearly at an end. He was preparing to stand down from the witness box when Mr Justice Darling motioned him to remain. Doubtless to Armstrong's utter dismay, the judge decided once again to go into the question of how he had used the arsenic.

He found it difficult to understand that Armstrong who had been so careful about other details in his police statement should have forgotten about the arsenic in the bureau.

'Do you tell the jury that you absolutely forgot about that white arsenic?'

'I do.'

The judge thought this was remarkable and said, damagingly, 'You are a solicitor. Does not it occur to you it would have been a very, very bad case for you if you had to tell the police that you had got not only weed-killing arsenic, but white arsenic in your possession?'

'But I did not remember it.'

'That is not what I asked you', snapped Darling, and he repeated the question.

'It would have to be explained', admitted Armstrong.

His Lordship seemed to be enjoying the role of questioner, or perhaps he thought the prisoner was weakening. At any rate, the questions continued: '. . .did you realize that it was just a fatal dose of arsenic, not for dandelions only but for human beings?'

'No. I did not realize it at all.'

Mr Justice Darling told the prisoner that it was suggested the moment he remembered there was arsenic in the little packet taken from his pocket when he was arrested that 'you tried to get it back.' Armstrong denied this. 'You know now what you saw there [in the little packet] was a fatal dose of arsenic?'

'I know since the evidence in this case.'

'And you realize what you had given the dandelions was a fatal dose of arsenic for a human being?'

'I have realized it since. I did not know it at the time.'

'Why go to the trouble of making twenty little packets, one for each dandelion, instead of taking out the ounce you had got and making a hole and giving the dandelions something from the one ounce?'

'I do not really know.'

'Why make up twenty little packets, each a fatal dose for a human being, and put it in your pocket?'

'At the time it seemed to me the most convenient way of doing it. I cannot give any other explanation.'

Finally, as he had done throughout Armstrong's examination, the judge switched his questions. Referring to the arsenic found in the bureau, he asked, 'You are a man accustomed to criminal procedure?'

'Yes.'

'Would not it have been better to make a clean breast of it

and say "It is in the drawer of the bureau"?'

'It did not occur to me, my Lord.'

Shattering as the judge's final onslaught of questions must have been, Armstrong nevertheless missed an opportunity to give a more convincing account of why he had divided up the arsenic into little packets. He could have said with irrefutable logic that the method he used ensured that every particle of arsenic powder was dosed directly onto the dandelions' roots and prevented the danger of the powder blowing away in the wind.

As it was, these last questions, put at the end of the prisoner's six-hour ordeal in the witness box, were probably the most destructive of the whole trial. The impression left with the jury was probably one of Armstrong struggling at the last fence to give a plausible reason for using arsenic innocently for weed killing in a manner which would also account for the packet found in his possession.

When Armstrong stepped down, the trial was as good as over in many people's eyes. He had not broken down; in fact he had conducted himself with considerable calm, but his replies had not convinced the sceptics. There was perhaps even a sneaking admiration for the little man whom the trial had cast as underdog; he had answered over two thousand questions and most of the judge's interventions, which had been frequent, had been against him.

* * * * *

While the conclusion of the prisoner's evidence seemed to make what followed an anticlimax, there was important testimony still to be heard. An early witness to follow Armstrong was his solicitor, Mr Matthews. He gave his account of the white arsenic found in the bureau at Mayfield. He expressed his surprise at finding it: '. . .it was the last thing in the world I expected to discover.'

The prosecution was uneasy about this whole matter if only for the reason that the discovery had been made after the police searched the house. Consequently, Matthews was asked several questions about other persons who had been to the house. It seemed that two of Matthews's clerks and one of Armstrong's had been to Mayfield for various reasons after the police had completed their searches.

There was no direct imputation that the arsenic might have been planted, but Sir Henry Curtis Bennett intervened, as he put it, 'to see that no attack was made'. The Attorney General made it clear that no such suggestion was made and all agreed that Mr Matthews was a man of the highest reputation. So, the strange affair of the arsenic missed by the police, but discovered by the defence on the accused man's instructions, was accepted.

Then came the defence's medical witnesses. The first was Dr Frederick Sherman Toogood, a practitioner with varied experience in mental illness and pathology who had given evidence for the defence in the Greenwood trial. In answer to Mr Bosanquet's questions he gave it as his opinion that between 1915 and 1920 Mrs Armstrong was suffering from auto-intoxication caused by chronic indigestion. This was associated with the presence of gallstones which he thought indicated faulty digestion. She also suffered from neuritis which in his view was an effect of auto-intoxication.

Dr Toogood thought that Mrs Armstrong's condition when she went to the asylum was due to acute melancholia accompanied by the physical symptoms of vomiting and albuminuria. He did not think that she was suffering from any arsenical poisoning at that time. '. . .I say there was no evidence consistent only with arsenical poisoning up till the 16th February. . .in all probability the cause of her death was arsenical poisoning caused by arsenic taken about the 16th February, but none before. It must have been a large dose.' Questioned about the size of the dose by Mr Justice Darling, the witness said he thought it must have been more than six grains because of the amount found after death. It was his opinion that a large portion of the arsenic became encysted in the stomach. Continuing his examination, defence counsel, asked, 'Supposing that this large dose was given on the 16th February, would that, in your opinion account for what was found at the post-mortem?'

'Quite'.

The 16th of February was a date which repeatedly came up in the defence version of Mrs Armstrong's last illness. It was on that day that Dr Hincks was called to Mayfield to see Mrs Armstrong who was very ill and had been vomiting badly.

Only the symptoms seen from that day until her death were recognized by the Defence as indicating arsenical poisoning.

Dr Toogood was doubtful that the circumstances of Oswald Martin's illness added up to arsenical poisoning. He said, 'Assuming a fatal dose of arsenic was taken at about five-thirty in the afternoon, I think it would be exceedingly unlikely that the person would be likely to be able to eat dinner at seven-thirty.' He also thought that Martin's return to work was very quick for someone who had received a near fatal dose of arsenic. He described the sample of Martin's urine as not having been 'taken in a scientific way' and he maintained that arsenic was a constant impurity of hydrogen peroxide. 'By implication, therefore, the arsenic may not have been in the urine at all but in the sample bottle itself. He made the point that a sample of the washing water should also have been sent for analysis; no doubt that was also the private view of the prosecution.

The witness was cross-examined by the Attorney General and was taken through Mrs Armstrong's symptoms in detail. 'With all these symptoms,' asked Sir Ernest, 'the heart, the albumen which cleared away, the subsequent peripheral neuritis, why do you prefer auto-intoxication to arsenical poisoning?'

'I prefer auto-intoxication, and the condition of acute melancholia. I never heard of arsenical poisoning emphasising melancholia.'

A number of specialized medical matters were raised by the defence in an attempt to support their contention that Mrs Armstrong died of one fatal dose of arsenic taken six days before death. The analysis of the body organs pointed very strongly to poison being taken right up to the time of death. The jejunum (upper part of the small intestine) contained 1.6 milligrammes of arsenic; the ileum (lower part of the small intestine), 9.1 milligrammes, and the caecum and ascending colon (beginning of the large intestine), 37.6 milligrammes.

A possible explanation for this, although rated only a bare possibility by Spilsbury, was the encysted arsenic theory. The gradual release of arsenic from the stomach into the intestines days after the initial dose could explain the arsenic found in the alimentary canal after death. Another possibility was the migration of arsenic from one part of the body to another. Sir Henry Curtis Bennett had posed this idea to Spilsbury earlier on in the trial, suggesting migration of arsenic from the liver into the caecum after death; he supported the theory by quoting from Witthaus's work on toxicology. Spilsbury disagreed with the theory except where the organs had collapsed through putrefaction; then arsenic might pass in a fluid condition from one organ to another. He pointed out that in Mrs Armstrong's case the bowel was intact.

Dr Toogood, on the other hand, thought that encysted arsenic with subsequent migration of the poison was quite feasible. He was asked about this by Sir Henry Curtis Bennett; 'If you found arsenic being encysted in the stomach, and gradually coming away, would you then find that arsenic going on down through the jejunum and the ileum into the caecum? Which is what was found in this case? Having heard the whole of the evidence . . . , having considered carefully the evidence which has been given by the other doctors, in your opinion was the arsenic from which Mrs Armstrong died given in one big dose on the 16th?'

Witness replied, 'I believe it was given in one big dose.'

Dr William Ainslie, who practised in Hereford and had represented Major Armstrong's interests at the post-mortem, gave evidence next. He concurred with Dr Toogood on all the major issues and was mildly critical of Spilsbury for not making a post-mortem examination for rheumatoid arthritis and for not opening any of the joints. He was closely questioned by the Attorney General about encysted arsenic.

'. . .did you or did you not find any encysted arsenic in the stomach at the post-mortem examination?'

'I did not expect to.'

'Perhaps you will answer the question. . .you did not?'

'No, I did not.'

Several historical cases of arsenical poisoning were referred to including one in Blythe's *Poisons and their Detection,* where a suicide took a large dose of arsenic and lived for six days with symptoms of arsenical poisoning the whole time.

Counsel were by now used to Mr Justice Darling intervening with the last word before witnesses stepped down and he did so in this case. 'How did you fix on six days before her death for the dose that killed her?', he asked. Ainslie replied,

'Because, as I answered before, I did not think the symptoms occurring before the 16th were due to arsenical poisoning.'

The last defence witness was John Steed, a doctor with a practice at Staunton-on-Wye. He added his opinion to those of his two predecessors: there was no evidence of arsenical poisoning before the morning of 16th February, when a large dose was taken.

* * * * *

The trial, now in its ninth day, was approaching its final phase: closing speeches by Counsel, the judge's summing up and the jury's verdict. Sir Henry Curtis Bennett took an hour and a half to make his final speech to the jury. He made his address a short one as he was aware that the proceedings had already been drawn out; he probably also realized that the jury were bored with expert witnesses. His contention was simply that Mrs Armstrong's illness up to the 16th February was due to natural causes. She was known to have suicide in mind and took a fatal dose of poison on that day. Addressing the jury, he asked, 'Are you going to say in the face of that evidence that she did not take poison herself?' He said that the Prosecution had failed to establish a motive on Major Armstrong's part for murdering his wife.

The Martin incident was virtually brushed aside by the defence. It was not shown that Armstrong had the opportunity to put arsenic in the scones served to Martin, and in any event there was nothing to prove that Martin had suffered from arsenical poisoning. The symptoms of his illness were compatible with a natural complaint and the arsenic in the urine could have got there from other sources.

Sir Henry made a play on the fact that Armstrong went into the witness box even though he was not obliged to. 'Did you not think,' he asked the jury, 'that Major Armstrong gave his evidence in the box like an honest man? Do you not think, and I put this before you as strongly as I can, that he emerged from four hours, I think it was, of cross-examination by the Attorney General, absolutely unscathed? . . .in my submission to you Major Armstrong was an excellent witness.'

Knowing that the weak replies given by Armstrong to the judge's questions were likely to have made a firm impression on the jury, Sir Henry set about repairing the damage. He said that with hindsight it was easy to say that the prisoner should have told the police about the white arsenic in the bureau immediately he remembered it. But it was an understandable human reaction in someone who had been in the position of administering justice and is suddenly arrested and taken to the police station. '. . .I cannot see what the criticism of it is,' said Sir Henry. 'If Major Armstrong had been trying to deny that he had got arsenic upon his premises at all, then I could understand it. He knew they were inquiring about arsenic, and told them where they could find one packet. . .do not be too hard on Major Armstrong because he did not do what a wise man would have done.'

Finally, there was the criticism of Armstrong's method of killing dandelions using his prepared packets of arsenic. Curtis Bennett suggested the method was quite sensible. 'That is what he said he did; is there any reason to disbelieve him? There is no sort of evidence that he did not.' Counsel thought the explanation of the packet of arsenic found in Armstrong's jacket was quite reasonable. 'As I say, nobody is safe in possession of arsenic, because if you happen to be arrested, and you have some in your pocket, it is going to be said you are carrying it about for the purpose of poisoning somebody. . .'

Sir Henry said the jury's verdict would be read by many who were merely interested in sensations, 'But for the friends of Major Armstrong it means, I hope, his freedom, for his children the restoration of their father to his home; and for Major Armstrong it means life,' Sir Henry Curtis Bennett had done all he could for Armstrong and when he sat down the responsibility which he had carried—to argue for the prisoner's life—passed to the jury.

* * * * *

Thursday, 13th April was the last day of the trial. As on the previous nine days, Armstrong was brought to the Shire Hall from Gloucester Gaol. Mr R.L. Ball, a Hereford resident, remembered seeing Armstrong's arrival: 'I thought how intensely blue his eyes were and I saw no sign of foreboding in his face.'

In his closing speech for the Crown, Sir Ernest Pollock said the prosecution's case had been strengthened during the trial. It was agreed by everyone that Mrs Armstrong died as the result of arsenical poisoning; what had to be decided was who administered that poison. The defence's thesis that there was no arsenical poisoning prior to 16th February and that her illness before then was due to natural causes, was not borne out in the document which described her condition on admission to Barnwood. This was the questionnaire completed and signed by Major Armstrong. Despite the contention that she was suffering from rheumatoid arthritis and auto-intoxication, Mrs Armstrong's health was described as 'fairly good'. And the question 'Has she ever suffered from any serious disease, or is she subject to any particular constitutional or bodily ailment?'was answered with a 'No'.

The Attorney General criticized the defence for overlooking a good deal of evidence in maintaining that Mrs Armstrong took a fatal dose of arsenic on 16th February. Nurse Kinsey said she was told the patient had vomited on 27th January; and on 10th February, Mrs Armstrong herself complained of vomiting badly. Sir Ernest said this suggested that the prisoner had commenced once more to give his wife small doses of arsenic. As regards the suicide theory, both Dr Hincks and Nurse Allen had said that Mrs Armstrong was anxious to get better, and in his testimony Major Armstrong said he had ceased to be anxious that his wife might commit suicide.

Sir Ernest had no doubt about the prisoner's motive in wanting to be rid of his wife: '. . .it was abundantly clear on this evidence that the prisoner was minded to get for his advantage under the new will immediate possession of his wife's goods.' The new will had one remarkable feature—everything went to the prisoner—whereas the previous will was drawn with particular regard to the children and provided an annuity for the faithful Miss Pearce.

There was a remarkable concurrence of testimony concerning the details of the tea party at Mayfield. Both Miss Pearce and Mrs Price said the scones provided from Mayfield's kitchen were uncut and unbuttered; Martin, however, said the scones were buttered and this was corroborated by Armstrong himself in his first statement; 'The food consisted of buttered scones. . .' The implication was clearly that the scones were buttered at some stage after leaving the kitchen—that was the opportunity chosen by Armstrong to poison one of them.

Finally, there was the prosecution's interpretation of Armstrong's statement and the offending packet of arsenic. The Attorney General said there was 'a meticulous particularity' about that statement and Armstrong knew that it was misleading as soon as the packet of arsenic was found on his person. The whole story of this busy solicitor making up a score of little packets of arsenic to dose individual weeds was merely to explain away that sinister discovery in his jacket pocket. 'Gentlemen', said Sir Ernest Pollock, 'If I am confident of one thing in this case, I am confident that no one will believe that story. . .I shall ask you to find a verdict that the prisoner is guilty.'

Opposing Counsel had made their final assessments of the evidence, and who was to say which way the verdict would go? Was one set of experts more convincing than the other? Were there reasonable doubts about connecting Major Armstrong with the arsenic from which his wife died? These and other questions were not to be settled quickly. Above all else, the law takes its course and it now fell to the judge to make his charge to the jury.

* * * * *

Mr Justice Darling began his direction to the jury by saying, '. . .I doubt whether any of us engaged here today have in recollection so remarkable a case in its incidents.' He dealt first with the Martin case, explaining that he believed it had a bearing on Mrs Armstrong's death: '. . .it is of value as showing that the defendant had arsenic in his possession, and that he would use it to poison a human being.' When asking the jury to consider how Martin might have taken in the poison, the judge let it be known that they need not confine themselves to thinking only about scones, '. . .there were other victuals', he said. The defence doctors who believed that Martin's urine sample was not properly taken might be correct but, equally, Mr Davies, the chemist, was a man of experience who did not let his corks roll about in arsenic powder and he knew how to wash out bottles. 'Therefore,' Mr Justice Darling told the jury, 'you try and come to a conclusion as to whether Martin really did suffer from arsenical poisoning. If he did, of course that does not prove that the defendant gave it to him.' He added, however, that, according to his own evidence, Armstrong had arsenic in his possession at the time.

The judge permitted himself one indulgence in the kind of humour for which he was so well known. 'Many, many people', he said, 'have been poisoned and poisoned with arsenic. . . but, of course, these people did not see what was being done. No-one who had been asked to dine with Cesare Borgia would have eaten anything if they had seen him putting white powder on the victuals.' This was an ace for the prosecution which, though suspecting the buttered scone, had been unable to prove exactly how Armstrong was supposed to have administered the poison to Martin.

In his summing up of Mrs Armstrong's death, the judge made a strong argument of the evidence which went against the idea of suicide. Referring to the dying woman's stated wish to live, he said, '. . .if you believe she said that (and it is not questioned that she said it)—do you believe that woman had already, with intent to kill herself, taken a fatal dose of arsenic?' Mr Justice Darling placed great emphasis on the testimony of Dr Hincks, 'a perfectly competent doctor', who never heard a word spoken about a tendency on the part of his patient to commit suicide. Moreover, on the 16th and 17th of February, when the defence said Mrs Armstrong took a fatal dose, Dr Hincks had testified 'she could not hold up a cup to her lips, and she could not use her arms, she could not grip anything perfectly.'

He referred to 'the contest' between Dr Spilsbury and Sir William Willcox on the one hand, and Dr Toogood and Dr Ainslie and Dr Steed on the other. Speaking of Spilsbury's view that a large dose of arsenic must have been taken twenty-four hours before death, the judge appealed to the jury to consider Spilsbury's manner as much as the evidence which he gave. 'Do you remember Dr Spilsbury, do you remember how he stood and the way in which he gave evidence? . . .Did you ever see a witness who more thoroughly satisfied you that he was absolutely impartial, absolutely fair, absolutely indifferent as to whether his evidence told for the one side or the other. . .?'

Such statements of confidence in the ability of the doctors were not extended to the defence experts and Sir Henry Curtis Bennett could have been forgiven for thinking that the summing-up was becoming one-sided. The views of Dr Toogood and his colleagues were given little more than a passing reference although the judge missed an opportunity to point out their lack of experience in cases of arsenical poisoning which had come out during cross-examination. Instead he chose to remark rather acidly that Dr Ainslie's criticism of Hincks's vagueness about dates was, 'a very confident opinion, by one who never saw the deceased during her life, as against Dr Hincks, who had seen her during life.' He dwelled at some length on the implications of the packet of arsenic in Armstrong's pocket: 'He realized, the moment he saw the little packet . . . it was a very awkward thing.'

Finally, the judge crystallized the case for the jury: 'He is charged with murder by administering arsenic to his wife. She had an administration of arsenic, and if you are satisfied beyond doubt that he gave it to her intending to kill her, he is guilty. He had the opportunity to give it to her, you can see on the evidence. The question is whether he did give it. . . Take the whole case into your consideration and say how you find it.'

Mr Justice Darling's summing-up had lasted nearly four hours and at eight minutes past five the jury filed into the assembly room to consider their verdict. The judge retired to his private room and the prisoner was taken down to the cells to await the decision which would settle his destiny.

The courtroom, previously so silent when the judge had been speaking, now erupted with sound as everyone began talking at once. The corridors of the Shire Hall filled with court officials and pressmen avidly discussing the case and weighing up the prisoner's prospects for an acquittal. Sir Henry Curtis Bennett told a newspaper reporter: 'I have been in forty-eight murder trials, for and against, and I have never known the verdict so open.' People in the crowd gathered outside the court and in the streets of Hereford were quoting odds of five to one in favour of an acquittal.

* * * * *

In his book on the Armstrong trial in the Notable British Trials series, Filson Young wrote, 'Sir Henry Curtis Bennett himself was so confident that he went for a walk, expecting to come back either to hear the verdict for acquittal or to meet Armstrong himself and find that he had already been released.' Indeed, Curtis Bennett's optimism led him to sign the following note to enable a photographer to take pictures of Major Armstrong when he was released:

Shire Hall,

Hereford,

April 13th 1922

H. R. Armstrong Esq.

Would you kindly assist bearer if possible, to take photographs of yourself and children

Curtis Bennett's note for a photographer during Armstrong's trial.

After they had been out forty-eight minutes, the jury signalled that they had reached a decision. Armstrong was escorted back to the dock and was seated as the jurors walked to their places. The members of the jury seemed to show more signs of strain in their faces than the prisoner who eyed them keenly as if trying to elicit their secret in advance. Leaning over to one of his warders, the Major asked, 'Shall I stand up while the jury give their verdict?.

The formalities were rigidly adhered to and for the last time the jury answered their names. Then, in a quavering voice the Deputy Clerk of Assize asked them, 'Gentlemen of the jury, have you all agreed upon your verdict?'

The foreman replied, 'Yes.'

'Do you find the prisoner at the bar, Herbert Rowse Armstrong, guilty or not guilty of the wilful murder of Katharine Mary Armstrong?'

Whitefaced but with a controlled voice, the foreman answered, 'Guilty'.

'You say he is guilty and that is the verdict of you all?' 'Yes'.

The only sounds were a few stifled gasps around the court. The Deputy Clerk of Assize now addressed the prisoner: 'Herbert Rowse Armstrong, you stand convicted of the wilful murder of Katharine Mary Armstrong. What have you to say why the Court should not now give you judgment to die according to law?'

Armstrong, standing to attention, answered quietly, 'Nothing.'

The court was absolutely silent and all eyes focussed on the judge as slowly, deliberately the black cap was placed on his head. He then passed sentence. Before uttering the final words that would decide the prisoner's fate, Mr Justice Darling announced that he concurred with the jury's verdict and considered as absurd and unsupported by any evidence the suggestion that Mrs Armstrong had committed suicide. He continued, 'You have had a fair trial; and been brilliantly defended; and a jury of your countrymen have carefully considered their verdict. It is my duty now merely to pronounce the sentence of the Court. It is that you be taken hence to the place from whence you came; that you be taken thence to a place of lawful execution; and that you be there hanged by the neck until you be dead; that your body be buried within the precincts of the prison in which you shall last be confined; and may the Lord have mercy on your soul.'

Throughout this final ordeal, Armstrong remained at attention, heels together and arms straight at his sides. He looked directly at the judge and the only hint of inner torment was the white knuckles of his tightly clenched hands. When sentence was passed, he turned about smartly at a nudge from one of his warders, and disappeared from public view down the steps to the cells.

The last act was complete. After the formality of excusing the jury members from further service for twelve years, the judge allowed the Martin indictment to stand over to the next assize in the event of a successful appeal against the verdict. The court then rose and Armstrong's trial was officially over.

* * * * *

Sir Henry Curtis Bennett's walk had taken him out along a country road and he stopped at a small village post office. The counter assistant told him that her husband who had been in Hereford had just telephoned to say the jury had found Armstrong 'Guilty'. Sir Henry was shattered. He later told his family, 'I shall never do a case like that again. I know that I have never done a better case and never will do. It was unjust—a poor show.'

A special edition of the *Hereford Times* was quickly on the streets proclaiming the verdict. The reaction among the several hundred people gathered outside the court was one of stunned silence. When Mr Justice Darling was driven from the court building many people respectfully raised their hats; then there was a great surge of spectators to the gaol gate of the Shire Hall to witness Armstrong's departure.

It was rumoured that Armstrong collapsed in his cell after sentence was passed, but within half an hour he was ready to be driven back to Gloucester Prison. He looked drawn as he walked the few steps across the inner yard to the waiting car. The double doors to the street opened and the car reversed out; press photographers were perched at every vantage point; they hung from pillars and windows and even from hastily procured ladders. The camera shutters clicked at the face in the back of the car as the vehicle sped away from the court. Like the other moments of drama that day, the departure of the man under sentence of death was witnessed in complete silence.

8 Appeal and Execution

The Armstrong who was hanged at Gloucester was not the Armstrong that we knew.

Dr Lisle Carr—Bishop of Hereford

THE NATIONAL newspapers had a field day when the news of Armstrong's conviction was announced. The facts of the case were garnished with opinions about the rightness of the verdict, the relentless logic of the judge and the moral degeneration of the nation.

Those who had thought the prosecution's case against a respected local figure was too weak, had reckoned without the telling interventions of Mr Justice Darling. During the ten days of the trial he interrupted counsel countless times to put questions which invariably told against the prisoner and he asked Armstrong himself over a hundred questions. The only ploy available to Sir Henry Curtis Bennett was the suicide theory which he argued brilliantly, although, in the end, ineffectually. His use of the discovery of white arsenic in the bureau at Mayfield might have gained the defence some advantage but again the judge destroyed it in his summing up. Sergeant Sharp who attended the court throughout the trial thought that the defence's use of this arsenic recoiled rather badly: '. . .when it arrived his Lordship could see that the piece of furniture was so well made that nothing could have jumped over the back of the drawer, and that even if it had then the drawer could not be closed properly. . . Even the stolid Herefordshire farmers on the jury could not stomach this obvious attempt to deceive them and I believe it went a long way towards Armstrong's downfall.'

The impact on the jury of Mr Justice Darling's conduct of the case could not be measured, but when he charged them it is likely that they had already made up their minds about Armstrong's guilt. The public are not permitted to observe the workings of juries but the newspaper revelations of the foreman of Armstrong's jury revealed the background to how the decision was made. Two days after the verdict was given at the trial, Tom Hopkins gave an interview to an *Evening News* reporter, an action for which he was subsequently reproved by the Lord Chief Justice.

When the twelve good men and true retired, 'We first of all had tea,' said Hopkins, 'then we went to another table, where twelve chairs had been placed for us and I tore a sheet of paper into twelve pieces for a ballot. Each man was asked to write either "guilty" or "not guilty" on his paper, fold it and hand it to the foreman.' When Hopkins announced the result there were eleven votes for 'guilty' and one for 'not proven'; the odd man out identified himself and said, 'Well Tom, you can guess whose the "not proven" is. I really believe the man is guilty.' Apparently this man bore a grudge against Mr Justice Darling and was trying to be obstructive. As he was obviously of the same mind as his colleagues, there was never any real doubt about the verdict. Hopkins said, 'We have heard enough of the case and need not discuss it any more. Let's have a quiet smoke before we go back to court.'

Looking back on the trial, Hopkins's impression was that it was very monotonous. He thought Armstrong's worst day was when the Home Office experts gave evidence. 'I don't think there was ever any chance of a verdict of 'not guilty' after that.' Armstrong created a generally favourable impression as a witness but the jury thought many of his answers were too 'pat'; the most damning piece of evidence was the arsenic found in the prisoner's possession. The jury thought the speeches of leading counsel were brilliant and Hopkins concluded that the judge 'had a great faculty for putting things very clearly in a few words. . .'

Criticism was directed at Mr Justice Darling from various quarters and his impartiality was certainly questioned. *The Times Literary Supplement* reported that his summing up was most able but wondered whether it had come from the right part of the court. Understandably, the defence lawyers were upset; Bosanquet wrote later, 'The judge assumed from the very beginning that Armstrong was guilty and it was disturbing to see the way in which he pounced on every point which told against the prisoner and underlined it. His summing up contained many phrases to which strong exception was taken by the defence, and to many it read as a speech for the prosecution.'

Apart from making humorous remarks during the trial, it was said that Darling used the occasion of the trial to entertain his friends, and hired a room in the Shire Hall for that purpose. There were allegations, probably spiteful, that sounds of laughter at times reached the courtroom during the progress of the trial. Sir Henry Curtis Bennett did not criticize the judge but was reported as saying that Darling's questioning of Armstrong was '. . .like the words of destiny.'

Major Armstrong and his defenders, who at the outset of the trial had shared such bold optimism about an acquittal, were left now with the wreckage of their plans. There was one remaining hope of salvation and the indefatigable Sir Henry Curtis Bennett immediately set about preparing an appeal; official notice of appeal against the death sentence was lodged on behalf of the condemned man on 20th April 1922.

A week later, the much adjourned inquiry into the cause of Mrs Armstrong's death was concluded before Mr Southall and a Coroner's Jury. Only one witness was called. Dr Hincks said it was his opinion that Mrs Armstrong had died of arsenical poisoning. The jury returned a verdict of death in accordance with the medical evidence.

A curious feature of the Armstrong case was the way in which it touched that of Harold Greenwood, the solicitor acquitted at Carmarthen on a murder charge. If anyone understood the feelings of the man in the dock it was Greenwood, although he never had to face the ultimate penalty. In an article which appeared in *John Bull* on 22nd April 1922, Greenwood let the public know what it felt like to stand accused of murder. The article was called, 'Armstrong's fight for life.' '. . .I know what the prisoner felt. Helpless, trapped, overborne. He steals a glance at the jury and sees that every word is telling. That is almost the worst moment in the trial . . .I remember that when a telling point was made by the Crown against me I simply dared not look at the jury.' Remembering that both Greenwood and Armstrong were solicitors it can be seen that the judge's summing-up would have, for them, added poignancy. Greenwood wrote that this '. . .is more painful than can be described. For a trained legal mind can appreciate exactly the effect upon the jury. As minute by minute the cultured, measured voice flows on, hope seems to evaporate. . .'

But Armstrong's hope did not evaporate completely. The

hearing of his appea against sentence of death commenced on
11th May before the Lord Chief Justice, Lord Hewart, and
Mr Justice Avory and Mr Justice Shearman. Armstrong did
not attend the Criminal Appeal Court but, if he was looking
for omens, the inclusion of Shearman on the Bench might
have comforted him—Mr Justice Shearman had presided at
Greenwood's trial.

The lawyers representing prosecution and defence were
the same as at the trial. There were five grounds of appeal.
The main complaints were that Mr Justice Darling wrongly
permitted the Martin evidence to be admitted and that he
misdirected the jury on several important issues. Sir Henry
Curtis Bennett pleaded his case forcibly and his speech of
twelve hours was the longest of his career. A great deal of
the three-day sitting was taken up with discussion of legal
precedents.

Judgment was given on the 16th May by Lord Hewart. He
gave it as the opinion of the court that the evidence was
amply sufficient to justify the trial jury's verdict, even if
nothing relating to Martin had been considered. Among other
things, the court found that the evidence in the case proved
that a fatal dose of arsenic was administered to Mrs Armstrong within twenty-four hours of death; that she suffered
from arsenical poisoning both before and after going to
Barnwood; that Major Armstrong purchased arsenic shortly
before each of those occasions; that he was the only person
on both occasions with the opportunity of giving arsenic to
his wife. And, finally, that his possession of arsenic, made up
in small packets of fatal doses, including the packet found on
him when arrested, was inconsistent with any legitimate
purpose. 'In these circumstances,' said the Lord Chief Justice,
'this appeal is dismissed.'

* * * * *

After the trial was concluded at Hereford's Shire Hall, Armstrong had been escorted back to Gloucester Prison by two
warders. One of the escorts was William Paradise who later
spoke about the events which as he recalled, made up Armstrong's last days. When the appeal was dismissed Paradise
brought the news to Mr Mobberley, the chief officer at the

prison. Mobberley said, 'Go up to The Gresham, Bill, and
get Mr Smiley to let you have a bottle of Guinness and a nice
plate of steak and chips.' Armstrong, after this treat. was
allowed only ordinary prison food. 'He was extra dejected
when his appeal failed,' said Paradise.

The condemned cell was really two ordinary cells knocked
into one; at Gloucester Prison it was always called 'Number
Twelve'. The cell, which had one window, contained a bed,
table and chair for the prisoner and a table and two chairs
for the warders. There was a WC and hand basin in one corner.
The wall opposite the entrance to the cell had a concealed
door in it which led to the execution shed.

Armstrong was now under constant surveillance: two
warders accompanied him both day and night. Paradise and
his fellow warder, Nash, worked 'nights', going on duty at
8.50 p.m. and being relieved by the day staff at 6.50 a.m.
The warders were not allowed to speak to condemned prison-
ers on matters concerning the trial but they tried to interest
Armstrong in ordinary conversational topics. Paradise found
Armstrong very quiet and curt in everything he said; he
appeared to be lost in thought much of the time. After the
appeal had been dismissed Armstrong asked Sir Henry Curtis
Bennett to apply to the Attorney General for his case to go
to the House of Lords. This was refused and Armstrong
mentally had to prepare for the end; the execution was fixed
for Wednesday, 31st May 1922—Derby Day.

For a man facing the scaffold Armstrong ate and slept
well, indeed his weight never varied from the moment he was
admitted to prison. Before settling down to sleep he always
smoked two small cigars, and Paradise observed that he
never talked in his sleep. Every night the Governor of the
prison, Mr Harry Whyte, together with his chief officer,
visited the condemned cell on their rounds. Armstrong used
to watch them but never spoke.

W.G. Val Davis, author of *Gentlemen of the Broad Arrows*,
claimed to have been an inmate of Gloucester Prison while
Armstrong was under sentence of death. Davis worked in the
prison library and he alleged that the Governor allocated him
to special duties which included cleaning the condemned cell.
'I remember some of the books I issued to him,' wrote Davis,
'. . .and the last book given him had awful significance in the

circumstances—*The Sleeper Awakes* by H.G. Wells.'

The day before his execution, Armstrong gave final instructions to T.A. Matthews regarding his property and care of the children. A condemned man has no power under the law to make a will because his body is forfeit to the Crown but he can give power of attorney to his legal adviser; this Armstrong did and he made provision for his property to pass to his children. He also asked that Miss Pearce should stay with the children as long as she could.

The Major added a Codicil to his Last Will and Testament. Dated 30th May 1922, it read, 'I appoint my two executors A.E. Chevalier and R.H. Lee* to be the Guardians of my infant children.' He also wrote a letter on prison paper to T.A. Matthews, his friend and solicitor.

Matthews had indeed been a faithful friend. From the time of Armstrong's arrest to his trial, Matthews's firm worked on little else, and the case proved to be a costly one. This letter was one of the last opportunities Armstrong had to confide in a close friend, but it contained neither confession nor protestation of innocence.

The vicar of Hay, the Reverend John Jefferys de Winton, visited the prison at Armstrong's special request. The vicar who had been a friend of the family for many years said he would not believe Major Armstrong was guilty unless he confessed to the crime. He described the condemned man as, '. . .very brave and quite cheerful.'

The protocol for execution required that an official notice be fixed to the main gate of the prison announcing to the world that which it already knew:

Capital Punishment Amendment Act, 1868
The sentence of the law passed upon Herbert Rowse Armstrong, found guilty of murder, will be carried into execution at 8 a.m. tomorrow.

> Ed. Marten Dunne,
>   Sheriff, Herefordshire
> H. Whyte
>   Governor

May 30th, 1922
Gloucester Prison

---

* R.H. Lee was Surveyor of Taxes, of Derby and a close friend.

In replying to this letter, please write on the envelope:

Number   Name

Gloucester   Prison
30 May   1922

My dear Matthews.

My heart was too full today to say all I wished. Thank you, my friend, for all you have done for me. No one could have done more. Please convey also to all your staff my gratitude for the unsparing work they put in. No team could have shown more loyalty, or will always remember it.

Ever your grateful friend

Armstrong's letter to his friend and solicitor T.A. Matthews, written from Gloucester Prison on the eve of his execution.

On the eve of execution, the Governor, together with his chaplain and chief officer went to the condemned cell to tell Armstrong that he must prepare to die as his appeal for clemency had been rejected. They were amazed at his calm.

In these last hours Armstrong did not forget those who had fought so hard to defend him. From the prison came a note of gratitude to Sir Henry Curtis Bennett and with it a diamond tie pin: Edwin Godson, the defence junior, received a silver cream jug. Ronald Bosanquet, Armstrong's old university friend, was the last outsider to see the condemned man. After his visit the relentless preparation for hanging began. The executioner, Ellis, and his assistant, Taylor, arrived at the prison within whose walls they were obliged by law to spend the night. Later that evening, Ellis went to the condemned cell and spoke to Paradise through the grill in the door. 'Is everything all right?' Paradise said that it was. Armstrong, though awake, was unaware of the identity of the man behind the door.

There was a story that Armstrong spent most of his last night tossing about on his bed and often getting up and pacing about his cell. 'It's hard to wait to die,' he is supposed to have said when being told by his warders what the time was. In any event he was awake at 6 a.m. and his own clothes; the reddish-brown tweed suit he wore at the trial, had been laid out for him in preference to prison uniform. It was one of the peculiar customs of the law that a murderer must be hanged in his own clothes. He asked Paradise, 'Where's my collar?', adding quickly, 'Oh! I quite understand.' After he had dressed he was given a cup of tea and some dry toast. He told Paradise and Nash that he had nothing to give them but after a moment's thought handed them his spectacles and pipe.

The two warders were then instructed to take the prisoner into the exercise yard where, after a short while, they were relieved by the day staff. After forty-five minutes' exercise Armstrong was returned to his cell where he formally thanked the prison officials for the kindness they had shown him.

* * * * *

The 31st May was a cloudless day with a brilliant blue sky;

at about 7 a.m. a small crowd started to gather outside the prison. It consisted mostly of men, including some workmen whose maintenance work on the prison walls had been suspended until after the execution. The crowd swelled quite quickly and pressed up to the prison gates, a number of women were present, some carrying babies in their arms.

At 7.30 a.m., the Under Sheriff of Herefordshire arrived at the prison in the company of a Church Army chaplain. They were immediately besieged by pressmen who were told by the Under Sheriff that they would be permitted to enter the prison to attend the inquest at 11 a.m. A strong force of Gloucestershire police constables was on duty to see that the officials went unhindered, and the next arrivals, the prison chaplain, vicar of nearby St Mary de Lode, and Dr James Bell, the prison doctor, were quickly admitted to the prison.

The large crowd, now numbering some two thousand, pressed even closer to the prison gates as if mere proximity would enable them to see through the walls and witness the final act itself. Some sightseers even climbed on to housetops overlooking the prison and there were also a number of people waiting on the towpath of the River Severn which runs along the south wall of the prison. If any of those gathered in anticipation of the hanging had a feeling for history they might have reflected on an event which took place outside Gloucester a hundred and forty-five years previously. Then, a man named Joseph Armstrong was hanged for murdering his employer's wife: he was the footman and carried out his crime by poisoning the woman's drink with arsenic.

Just before 8 a.m. the prison chaplain and the executioner entered the condemned cell. The concealed door in the far wall of the cell was opened and Armstrong was escorted the short distance to the place of execution. Standing by the scaffold were the officials: the Under Sheriff of the County, the prison governor, the prison doctor and various warders. Asked by the Governor if he wished to make a statement Armstrong was reported in the *News of the World* as saying, 'I am innocent of the crime for which I have been condemned to die.' Armstrong's steps were unfaltering; as he stood at the drop his legs were strapped together and a white cap which completely covered his features was placed over his head. The chaplain began to intone the prayers for the dead.

The eerie tolling of St Mary de Lode's church bell stopped on the stroke of eight as Ellis placed the rope around Armstrong's neck. The bolt was drawn and Armstrong disappeared through the drop into the pit beneath; the rope quivered with his dead-weight at its end.

Only a minute had passed from the time he had been taken from his cell to the moment he hung limp and lifeless. What that minute meant to the condemned man can only be surmised, but for the officials gathered at the scaffold it probably seemed an eternity. The Governor had special cause for reflection, for according to Bosanquet, he had said on one occasion, 'I don't like this hanging business, Armstrong,' and Armstrong with that strange detachment which ran so strongly in his personality, replied calmly. 'Yes, I am sure it must be most unpleasant for you.'

Armstrong left no confession, although some have construed his letter to Matthews as such. However, there was a story that as Ellis pulled the lever Armstrong shouted out, 'I am coming, Katie.' This has never been authenticated and sounds very much like a traveller's tale; it would certainly have been very much out of character for so passionless a man—even at the scaffold.

Being a very light man, Armstrong was given the unusually long drop of eight feet eight inches. When the body was taken out of the pit it was put into a simple, whitewashed coffin to await the inquest.

At 8.30 the following notices were fixed to the doors of the prison:

Certificate of Surgeon

I, James A. Bell, surgeon of his Majesty's Prison of Gloucester, give and certify that I this day examined the body of Herbert Rowse Armstrong on whom judgement of death was this day executed in the said prison, and that on examination I found that the said Herbert Rowse Armstrong was dead.

Dated this 31st day of May 1922.

J.A. Bell

Declaration of Sheriff and Others

We, the undersigned, hereby declare that judgment of death

was this day executed upon Herbert Rowse Armstrong in His Majesty's prison at Gloucester in our presence.
Dated this 31st day of May 1922.

Francis R. James
Under-Sheriff of Herefordshire
H. Whyte
Governor of the said prison
W.C. Maclin
Chaplain of the said prison

The Prison's Execution Book, a thin, oblong volume, was filled in with the details of the hanging and the behaviour of the executioner and his assistant—there is only one entry after Major Armstrong. By 9.30 a.m., their assignment completed, the executioner and his assistant were on their way to Gloucester Railway Station. The crowd which had gathered at the prison gates, not to protest or even to witness a public hanging but merely to satisfy some unspoken fascination with sudden, calculated death, melted away.

Excerpt from the front-page report of Armstrong's execution in the *Hereford Times* of 31st May 1922.

Fifty miles away in Hay, the centre of Major Armstrong's life and crimes, Oswald Martin, still anxious and rather poorly, was driving down to his office with Trevor Griffiths. On the Cusop Road they met an old woman known locally for her dealings in second-hand clothes. She stood, arms akimbo, in the middle of the road and stopped the car. Speaking to Martin she said, 'They hung him today, have thou seen his ghost?' Poor Martin was so taken back that he had to return home and go to bed.

The blinds in Armstrong's office in Broad Street remained drawn and no business was done on the day of execution. At Mayfield, loyal Miss Pearce looked after the now orphaned children; they were unaware of the drama which had been enacted early that day. Reverend de Winton told reporters that Armstrong on the eve of his execution had said, 'I feel better now than ever I did. I realize that the end has come and I am prepared for it. I have no confession to make. I am an innocent man.'

Later that day, the Derby was run and the winner was Lord Woolavington's *Captain Cuttle*, ridden by Steve Donaghue and trained by F. Darling. Armstrong was supposed to have tipped the winner to his warders—perhaps he got his hunch from the trainer's name, but Darling was no winner for him.

In accordance with the Capital Punishment Amendment Act, an inquest was held in the prison's boardroom at 11 a.m. on the death of the offender. Mr J. Waghorne, Coroner for the Northern Division of Gloucestershire, conducted the proceedings which were officially to seal the end of Major Armstrong's life. The jury viewed the body of the executed man, clad in its brown tweed suit, which was afterwards made ready for burial. Their duty was to ascertain the identity of the body and to say whether judgment of death had been duly carried out. Also present at the inquest were the Governor, the prison doctor and six representatives of the press. Dr Bell was questioned by the coroner:

'You examined the body after death?'

'I did.'

'And the cause of death was?'

'Dislocation of the vertebrae.'

'That is dislocation of the neck?'

CERTIFIED COPY OF AN ENTRY OF DEATH

The statutory fee for this certificate is 3s. 9d.
Where a search is necessary to find the entry,
a search fee is payable in addition.

	REGISTRATION DISTRICT				Glouces

1922. DEATH in the Sub-district of _Glouces_

Columns :— (1)	(2)	(3)	(4)	(5)
No. When and where died	Name and surname	Sex	Age	Occupation
483	31ˢᵗ May 1922 His Majestys Prison Gloucester U.D.	Herbert Rowse Armstrong	Male	53 years	of Cusop Herefordshire R.D. Solicitor

CERTIFIED to be a true copy of an entry in the certified copy of a Register of D

Given at the GENERAL REGISTER OFFICE, SOMERSET HOUSE, LONDON, under the Seal

DA 465450

This certificate is issued in pursuance of the Births and Deaths Registration Act, 1953.
Section 34 provides that any certified copy of an entry purporting to be sealed or stampe
or death to which it relates without any further or other proof of the entry, and no certifi
is sealed or stamped as aforesaid.
CAUTION.—Any person who (1) falsifies any of the particulars on this certificate, or (2) us

Armstrong's Death Certifica

'Yes.'

'Caused by hanging, that is?'

'Yes.'

'Death was practically instantaneous?'

'Quite instantaneous.'

The jury concluded that '. . .the sentence was duly and satisfactorily carried out.'

Armstrong's execution may have provided a happier conclusion than if he had been acquitted. The burden of innocence gained by trial or appeal is often too great and neither Harold Greenwood nor William Herbert Wallace lived long after the courts had pronounced them free men. In

....ern in the   County of Gloucester C.B.

(6) Cause of death	(7) Signature, description, and residence of informant	(8) When registered	(9) Signature of registrar
....ted pursuant ...dgment of	Certificate received from J Waghorne Coroner for Gloucestershire (Upper District) Inquest held 31st May 1922	Second June 1922	H. A. Barrett Registrar

: District above mentioned.

.. Office, the   22nd day of   September 1954.

f the General Register Office shall be received as evidence of the birth
..ng to be given in the said Office shall be of any force or effect unless it

..tificate as true, knowing it to be false, is liable to prosecution.

Greenwood's case, being found 'not guilty', and in Wallace's,
having his sentence quashed on appeal, carried a stigma that
involved them in loss of reputation and livelihood and
premature death. Greenwood died a broken man, aged fifty-
five, nine years after his acquittal, and Wallace died, aged
fifty-four, two years after his conviction was quashed on the
only occasion that an Appeal Court judged the conviction was
against the weight of the evidence.

Had he been acquitted or his verdict reversed, Armstrong,
perhaps more than most, would have suffered the misery of
trying to live down his notoriety and regain even a small
part of his former status. His hanging at least saved him from

that ignominy.

*   *   *   *   *

Did Major Armstrong, beyond any doubt, poison his wife? The answer to this question lies in what we know of the man's personality. To be born small was bad enough but to be both small and married to a woman whose aim seemed to be to make him smaller, was unbearable. Armstrong overcame his inferiority feelings with the classic device of egoism. He liked to talk at great length, mostly about himself, he was fussy about his appearance, was fastidious over all kinds of trivial matters and indulged in flights of fancy.

His craving for attention was partially satisfied while he was in the army, and his personality changed as a result. No doubt the authority and aura of an army officer did wonders for his ego and he emerged a new man in 1919. Where he had once accepted his wife's domination with timid compliance, he now determined to have his own way. The army had taught him the privilege of rank and he decided to be the new master of Mayfield.

The Major had a clear motive for murdering his wife and it was one that was passed over by the prosecution at his trial, although Mr Justice Darling hit on it when he referred to Mrs Armstrong as a 'tiresome invalid'. Equally, the defence might have made use of the knowledge that was common gossip in Hay—Katharine Armstrong was a nagging, neurotic wife. There is no doubt about this and a revealing remark was said to have been made about her character by Mrs Chevalier, a long-standing family friend, 'I could have murdered her myself, she was an overbearing, difficult woman.' This was an honest opinion coming not from someone with a grudge against Mrs Armstrong but from a real friend who, after the execution, took the Armstrong children into her home for a period and raised them with her own family.

Because murder is so final and repugnant, there is a tendency to regard murderers as so far removed from normality as to be insane — insanity being the only possible explanation that a reasonable man can find to account for a Heath or a Christie. Major Armstrong's thought processes may have been twisted but he was certainly not insane—he knew perfectly well what he was doing. He elected to do away with his wife because he could no longer bear the humiliation to which she subjected him—that was sufficient motive.

There were various reasons why he might have chosen poisoning, and arsenic in particular, as his tool of destruction. He had used arsenic for killing weeds in his garden as early as 1912 and it might easily have suggested itself as a suitable method when he decided to kill his wife. Sir William Willcox, however, believed that Armstrong's use of arsenic merely imitated that of Harold Greenwood. At any rate, Armstrong shirked the knife or gun and elected to use the secret ways of the poisoner which were cloaked by the ordinary routines of meal-times and cups of tea. With every poisoned plate of food, given under the guise of affection to a wife wasting to destruction before his eyes, he could have pulled back. But he chose to go on and in so doing earned the opprobrium reserved for the vile poisoner.

The opportunities for administering the poison were legion; every cup of tea, every dish of food was a potential vehicle—provided he could doctor it secretly. What would be more normal in the sick household than that the husband should from time to time take food to his invalid wife? The link between cause and effect is not always easy to establish in poison cases—poisoning is a slow, thoughtful business and the administration of it is the most secret part. The unseen hand disguises the almost tasteless powder in some food which passes into the body leaving no mark save that which can be construed as natural illness.

Any small departure from normal routine in the sick room where every activity is centred on the invalid might escape attention or, if noticed, not seem significant. But many years after the events of February 1921, Inez Rosser, the nineteen-year-old who was cook-housemaid to the Armstrongs, spoke about her employer. Inez was appointed to the staff at Mayfield during the period that Mrs Armstrong was at Barnwood. She was known to everyone in the house as Mary and described the atmosphere at that time as happy and cheerful. She got on well with Miss Pearce who was 'a nice old girl' and she also liked the children. But this pleasant atmosphere changed when Mrs Armstrong came home. Obviously there was anxiety about the sick woman but it appeared that the Major became quiet and furtive.

Mary often cooked Mrs Armstrong's meals and took them up to her bedroom but the Major gradually took over this duty in a way which caused Mary to be suspicious. He would intercept the girl on her way to the sickroom with the food, take it from her, and then, instead of going straight to his wife's room, go into his study. He would be there for two or three minutes, and Mary, who lingered curiously, could hear the sound of stirring. The Major stayed with his wife while she ate the meal and he would bring the plate or bowl down to the pantry, 'rinsing it again and again under the running tap.' Mrs Armstrong was invariably worse the day after the Major carried her food up.

Mary was upset by her suspicions and confided to her mother, '. . .I'm sure Major Armstrong is helping Mrs Armstrong out.' Her mother told her never to repeat her suspicion and made her promise 'not to mention it to a living soul.' None of this was mentioned at the trial and the reluctance of a junior servant to speak out against her master when everyone else was expressing loyalty, is understandable.

Mrs Armstrong had been having poison for so long that she was actually developing a tolerance to it. The continued purging, pain and wasting went on in varying degrees for several months, unequivocally ruling out suicide.

A feature of chronic arsenical poisoning that was not fully understood at the time was the victim's discoloration. Dr Hincks said that Mrs Armstrong had some discoloration, of the face and abdomen when she went to Barnwood, and months later, on 10th February, Nurse Kinsey described Mrs Armstrong as looking like a jaundice case. On 16th February, Dr Hincks said, 'She had a deep discoloration of the skin, a sort of bronze or coppery colour,' and Nurse Allen remarked that the skin was going 'very dark and copper coloured.' At the time this was not thought to have any special significance and was regarded only as part of the general deterioration. Writing in later years, Sir William Willcox, said, 'The effect of arsenic on the liver is sometimes shown by the development of toxic jaundice. This is now recognized as a definite effect of arsenic.' Jaundice had frequently been observed in cases of criminal arsenical poisoning but had not been fully understood. Modern textbooks on forensic medicine list pigmentation of the skin, ' "rain-spot" flecks, yellow to deep brown', as one of the symptoms of chronic arsenical poisoning.

This addition to medical knowledge came too late to aid the Attorney General in dismissing the defence's suicide theory. Obviously Mrs Armstrong's history of discolouration, which went back to August 1920, completely invalidated the suggestion that the only arsenic she had was a fatal dose on 16th February 1921.

Where Mrs Armstrong was concerned, the Major's motive was straightforward enough and derived from his intolerable domestic situation. The forging of her will was a naive after-thought to finance his freedom. Although the anomaly remains that having become legally entitled to his wife's money in March 1921, Armstrong did not touch a penny of it until forced to do so to pay legal costs at the time of his trial. But the Major was to find that the art of being masterful was not without difficulty. He picked up syphilis as a result of his philandering while his wife, already eaten up with arsenic, was away in the asylum. There was also the necessity, which he disregarded, to pull his business out of the doldrums.

He took delight in Harold Greenwood's acquittal. It was the Major's private joke—after all he had committed the perfect murder. With his wife dead and buried, he went on a continental spree and then courted Marion Glassford Gale. Unwittingly he was preparing a trap for himself. His business affairs were deteriorating into a mess and confrontation with his rival, Oswald Martin, was inevitable.

As events unfolded, Armstrong was placed in an inferior position—the kind of situation from which he thought his wife's death had rescued him. The Major's freedom turned into a nightmare. High noon in his affairs came with the challenge which Oswald Martin made over his procrastination in the sale of the Velinnewydd Estate. This was a tangled situation but to Martin there must have seemed at least two honourable courses of action open to Armstrong: he could have explained to him the reason for the delay or he could have used his own money to pay back the deposits in question.

But to Armstrong there was more than professional integrity at stake and he resolved to kill Martin. When his ill-conceived poisoned chocolates failed he tried the more direct method of the scone. When it also failed his methods became stupid in the extreme. Gone were the care and cunning with which he had contrived his wife's death and in their place was the arrogant disregard forsubtletywhich proved to be his undoing. His intentions were so badly concealed that his victim was alerted to the danger. After the poison attempt on 26th October he could not, next morning, even wait to go to his own office first. He had to rush into Martin's office to find out how successful he had been.

He was so confident of his own actions and invulnerability that when he walked into his office on New Year's Eve 1921 he carried a small packet of arsenic in his coat pocket. He was prepared for the moment when he could overcome Martin's countless refusals to tea. It was suggested by Inez Rosser that the packet of arsenic might have been a suicide dose to be swallowed in the event of detection. This hardly seems likely as Armstrong was not the type to fall on his sword. When the three police officers marched unheralded into Armstrong's office and arrested him it was as much a surprise to him as it was to the whole of Hay.

There was never really any doubt that Oswald Martin had been given arsenic although the defence made the most of the one imperfection in the method of taking the urine specimen —the failure to send a sample of the wash water for analysis also. If this had been done, and provided its analysis showed no arsenic, it would have proved beyond any doubt that the arsenic in the urine indeed came from Martin's body and not from some impurity in the sample bottle. Dr Toogood's contention that the one thirty-third of a grain of arsenic found in Martin's urine could have got into his system as an impurity in the bismuth mixture given him by Dr Hincks, had no foundation at all. Mr Justice Darling had raised laughter in the court when questioning Dr Toogood on this point. The doctor referred to a case where medicinal bismuth contained .44 (of a grain) of ordinary white arsenic. 'It must have been very, very bad bismuth', said the judge drily.

Taking the limit of arsenic in bismuth given in the *British Pharmacopoeia* as two parts per million, Sir William Willcox calculated that Martin would need to have taken a pound of bismuth to account for the quantity of arsenic found. Indeed, because the portion excreted would have been only a small part of that ingested, the total amount of bismuth would need to have been higher still. Beyond doubt then Martin received arsenic and there never was any suggestion in his case that he tried to commit suicide.

One of the key features of the whole case was the part played by Dr Hincks. He certainly made mistakes—his diagnosis of Mrs Armstrong's illness was proved wrong by subsequent events and Martin's symptoms were also incorrectly interpreted. Moreover, Mrs Armstrong's certification of lunacy was very casual and the second opinion given by Dr Jayne was certainly open to criticism. He could not remember any details of the conversation he had with Mrs Armstrong and he was not even sure if he gave her a physical examination. The only mitigation here was that both doctors practised in areas where mental disease was prevalent and familiarity made them careless with procedure and dulled their perception.

When Mrs Armstrong was admitted to Barnwood there was a great opportunity for the doctors to detect arsenical poisoning. The fact that they did not was no reflection on their competence but simply a lesson in the elusive nature of arsenical poisoning. No doubt with the Armstrong case fresh in his mind, Sir William Willcox told a medical audience in 1928 that 'in many cases the symptoms of poisoning so closely simulate natural disease that it is almost impossible to make a diagnosis on clinical grounds alone.' He added that toxicological analysis was usually necessary.

Where Hincks brought great credit to his profession was in admitting that his diagnosis of Martin's symptoms was in error. Had he lacked the courage to change his mind there might have been another death in Hay. Armstrong would probably have continued his naive attempts against Martin even though suspicion was mounting. But the fact that Hincks was prepared to listen to John Davies's suspicions and lend his authority to them averted a possible tragedy and was instrumental in bringing Armstrong to justice.

One of the modern inheritors of Dr Hincks's medical practice has provided an ingenious theory to explain Mrs Armstrong's death. Shortly after her husband returned from the war, Katharine Armstrong, a recognised hypochondriac, began taking a wide variety of homeopathic medicines. It is suggested that Armstrong's army experiences had broadened his sexual appetites and that his wife consequently lost her attraction. Katharine, who was a very plain woman, realized this and sought to remedy her unattractiveness by using arsenical preparations to improve her complexion.

When she became mentally ill and was admitted to Barnwood, Katharine was given an arsenical tonic which had the side effect of contributing to her peripheral neuritis. On returning home she found out that her husband was being treated for syphilis and she at once increased her intake of arsenic believing that this would prevent her contracting the disease. There was certainly no shortage of arsenic in the house, as subsequent events revealed.

The theory now takes a sinister twist, for Armstrong learned what his wife was doing and decided to help her by making sure there were always ample supplies of arsenic available to her. Thus, Katharine unknowingly slowly killed herself and Armstrong never administered a grain of arsenic to her himself. This could have accounted for the arsenic which was found in several places around the house; hypochondriacs are known to be secretive. There was also Mrs Armstrong's expression of shame at what she had done—was this a result of her real knowledge rather than some delusion?

Of course this imaginative theory does not explain the Martin episode, but then Armstrong was tried for the murder of his wife and his defence might possibly have made better use of this than of the suicide theory.

The mass of circumstantial evidence by itself might still leave room for doubt as to Armstrong's guilt but, taken together with what we know about the man's personality, all doubts are dispelled.

Many writers and observers have found it difficult to understand the mentality of Herbert Rowse Armstrong, whose character oscillated between that of the affable country solicitor and the odious poisoner. Filson Young, for example, was concerned about Armstrong's complete disregard for the effect his behaviour would have on his children and he concluded that the man lacked imagination, 'otherwise' he wrote, 'how would it be possible for a man engaged with life in all its ordinary relationships not to recoil from contemplation of the effect of his conduct on these little lives?'

No-one can say that Armstrong did not ultimately experience remorse, although he showed no signs of it, but he was certainly not lacking in imagination—imagination that is of a one-sided, egotistical kind. His experiences in the army may have affected his personality; certainly it was after the war that all his actions were diverted to feed his self-glorification. The cravings of this man's vanity made him stand apart from and out of touch with the real world; he lived in a vacuum of egotistical fantasy that made it impossible for him to consider others in the commission of his plans. Who does not tremble at the thought of what he might have become, this little man who tinkered with death-dealing poison, forged his wife's will, read the lesson at the memorial service after murdering her, and terrorized Oswald Martin with his telephone calls?—these were the signs of a small-scale paranoia.

* * * * *

In an article in *John Bull* shortly before Armstrong was hanged, Edgar Wallace strongly criticized what he called, 'this precedent of conviction without proof'. He contended that Armstrong may have been thoroughly guilty but it had not been proved that he alone had the opportunity of committing the crime. What concerned Wallace was the real possibility that an innocent man might one day be convicted, for as he pointed out, 'If some of us were on trial for our lives and our eccentricities were produced against us, I daresay that they would seem even more absurd than Armstrong's.'

It is true that no-one saw Armstrong actually mix arsenic with his wife's food and give it to her, but the circumstantial evidence was overwhelming and no satisfactory answer to it was provided by the defence. And the chances of Mrs Armstrong taking suicidal doses of arsenic were ruled out by the colossal amounts found in her body. These could only have been accounted for by administration without her knowledge; if she were bent on suicide she would surely have used a more expedient method than poisoning which went on for months and produced terrible suffering.

An article in *The Lancet* discussed some of the important public issues which arose out of the medical side of the Armstrong affair. It was pointed out that Dr Hincks gave a perfectly proper certification of death in Mrs Armstrong's case but added that the law offered no guidance to the medical man in cases where there might be a doubt. The medical journal suggested that the procedure for investigating a death prior to cremation might be instituted before ordinary burial. A tragedy had been caused as a result of the ease with which the public could obtain large supplies of deadly poisons. The article concluded, 'The changes suggested might not lead to the detection of many cases of murder by poisoning, for the excellent reason that the certainty of enquiry would have a deterrent effect and would tend to prevent poisoning.'

Lord Russell of Liverpool, discussing the detection of poisoning in his *Though the Heavens Fall*, thought it strange that more poisoners did not arrange for their victims to be cremated. After all there was always the risk of detection by exhumation. With cremation, the sole possible evidence of the fatal use of poison, its presence in the body itself, would be destroyed. Although the Cremation Act of 1902 and subsequent regulations require an 'authority to cremate' in the form of a special certificate signed by the dead person's own doctor and another signed by an independent doctor who must see the body, there is no requirement for a post-mortem. Had Armstrong elected to have his wife cremated he might never have been brought to trial on a charge of murder.

As it was, Herbert Rowse Armstrong, an officer and gentleman and the only British solicitor to be hanged for murder, was buried in the front yard of Gloucester Prison. Paradise said '. . .there is nothing to show except a number on the wall. He was eat up with lime.' Like her husband, Katharine Armstrong has an anonymous resting place. When she was re-interred, the grave was levelled in order to discourage morbid sightseers, but there is a patch of soil in Cusop churchyard forever contaminated with the arsenic which drained from her body.

Well dear, if 'e done it 'e done it and if 'e didn't do it 'e didn't do it and e's a solicitor and 'e ought to know.

Hay resident

After Major Armstrong was executed, Hay had to get back to normal—the busy social and commercial life of the town had to be resumed. The disappearance of the newsmen and curiosity seekers allowed the townspeople to reflect on recent events and to come to terms with the fact that a respected citizen had been plucked from their midst and put on justice's scaffold.

Armstrong's disgrace was like some pestilence which had infected every corner of the community leaving no-one untouched. Even those not directly involved were affected to the extent that they had given their trust and respect to a man who had betrayed them. The lives of a number of people were drawn together in the web that Armstrong had created. Some, like the lawyers, detectives and doctors, were professionals for whom the case was just another piece of experience. But others, local people, friends and acquaintances, were to have their lives unutterably changed.

Major Armstrong's affairs and personality were so woven into the local fabric that the reminders of his position and influence lingered on after his death. There was the search for a successor to his legal practice and for someone to fill the office of Clerk of the Justices; there were empty seats at the Loyal Hay Lodge of Freemasons and at the local Territorial Army Detachment; there was a vacant position for churchwarden at Cusop Church and, sadly, there was a large house peopled only by his children and servants.

Dear old Miss Pearce could not bring herself to think of her former master's guilt. Looking very drawn and sad she remained at Mayfield until arrangements were made to look after the three children. On 8th September 1922, a sale was held at Mayfield for their benefit. The Armstrong estate was bankrupt and the sale of furniture and effects on Mayfield's lawn was well-attended. The Major's bureau, Mrs Armstrong's bed and the three-tier cake stand were among the items for sale. T.A. Matthews attended and bought for Sir Henry Curtis Bennett a medicine chest which had been exhibited in court during the trial. Chief Inspector Crutchett also attended the sale. The detective bought one or two small items as mementoes of the case but the famous bureau went to a bidder from Scotland for £41.

Mayfield itself was bought by Trevor Griffiths, Martin's young partner, and he renamed it Brynglas. Griffiths gave a great deal of help to Filson Young who compiled *The Trial of H.R. Armstrong* in 1927. During a visit to the house, Young remarked that the dandelions were thicker than ever and seemed eventually to have triumphed over the Major. Recalling the visit, Young wrote:

> The sun shone, the doors and windows were wide open, so that the summer breeze stirred through the house, and the voices of children at play sounded in the precincts. A saner and more normal life, and a happier set of children had taken possession of the place. But my thoughts were with those other little children whose voices, more repressed and not quite so happy, had sounded there at the time of this story.

Those other children, made fatherless overnight, were in the care of servants and relatives under the supervision of Arthur Chevalier. Even before the execution, there was difficulty finding money to maintain them although they were later helped by the Loyal Hay Lodge. The Royal Masonic Institution for Girls made grants to both girls and eventually all three were taken into the Chevalier family and lived first at Birkenhead and then Colwyn Bay.

The children changed their name, possibly on the advice of Chevalier who could foresee the difficulties that an inquisitive world would impose on their future. In later years probably all they wished to do was forget, and it was reported that they went to Australia. In June 1955 a BBC broadcast on the Armstrong trial, one in the series, *Prisoner at the Bar*, was withdrawn at the last moment. The BBC said, 'We have received a valid private request that this broadcast should be withdrawn. . .'. The wish of those intimately connected with painful events not to have them raked over can be respected, but guilty and innocent alike live in a real world which has a right not to pry but to know and to understand.

The Armstrong children were the innocent victims of their father's crimes and their plight brought them considerable sympathy. But poor Oswald Martin who had been made to suffer physical and mental torment, gained little of the sympathy normally visited on the victim in such cases and, strangely, seemed to be blamed for spite. The whole affair was a very great shock to sensitive people like the Martins. They had become unknowingly involved in a sinister plot, had notified the authorities quite correctly, suffered agonies of illness and waiting, realized the irony of the murderer buying his poison from a member of his intended victim's family, and behaved throughout with considerable dignity.

Martin sold his share of the legal practice in Broad Street to Trevor Griffiths and he and his wife moved to East Anglia in 1924. They tried to make a fresh start and to put all the unpleasant memories behind them. It was not a success. Oswald was never the same man again; he suffered periods of depression and was afraid of the dark. The couple moved again, this time to Cheltenham, where Oswald worked for a firm of well-known solicitors. He died after an operation for cancer of the rectum on 10th May 1946 at Cheltenham Hospital—he was aged fifty-six, and he left £13,429 gross.

Not all of Armstrong's victims were poisoned. There were others such as his children and Marion Glassford Gale (Madame X), to whom he proposed marriage, whose lives were left in ruins as a result of his actions. Marion was one of those people whom life seems repeatedly to injure. She had been widowed before the First World War and then, unselfishly made a home for her mother and for a nephew and niece who had been orphaned. Denied a life of her own, Marion spent her days looking after her dependents.

The possibility of marriage to Armstrong offered hope of another life, but the shattering of this dream was yet another sorrow she had to bear. The niece, Eleanor, remembered seeing her aunt seated at the kitchen table with her head in her hands and spread on the table before her a newspaper containing the news of Armstrong's arrest. It must have been a bitter blow. Marion died, aged 91, at a home for the elderly in Bournemouth in 1960.

The Armstrong's young servant girl, Inez (Mary) Rosser, is

now in her seventies. She remembers meeting Marion Glassford Gale at the trial and found her a likeable person. Mary felt that there were unvoiced suspicions at Mayfield about the Major's activities; she thought Miss Pearce was suspicious and also Miss Friend who was very curt in her attitude to Armstrong. On the other hand, she was sure that Mrs Armstrong had no idea what was going on, an ignorance which was shared by her nurses.

Dr Tom Hincks who played such a key role in the events which led up to Armstrong's arrest, survived the Major's death by only ten years. He died suddenly while out hunting on 8th November 1932. For much of his professional life in Hay, Hincks had worked single-handed to maintain a strenuous country practice. This involved long rides or walks over the mountains in all weathers, irregular, hastily eaten meals between crowded surgeries, and the jarring note of the night bell for urgent calls. Hincks had the robustness of physique and outlook to match the demands of his work and he was a first-rate country doctor.

In the late 1920s Hincks experienced the first signs of heart trouble and he was told to take things easy or indeed, to give up his demanding practice altogether. Apart from having an assistant he made no concessions and gave up neither his practice nor the hunting of which he was so fond.

The circumstances of his death were curious. As was his custom, Hincks had a half-day off on Tuesday, 8th November to ride with the hounds. He was seen riding alone at the top of Cusop hill behind Mayfield along a track which Mrs Armstrong and her children had often walked. One of the doctor's patients watching from the meadow below saw Hincks rein in his horse and lean forward as if to speak to someone; then he dismounted, staggered and fell to the ground. The onlooker in the meadow went up the hill to help, fully expecting to find the person Hincks appeared to have been talking to getting the doctor back on his horse. Instead, he found only Hincks who was dead; there was no-one else nearby and the horse had cantered off; Hincks was only fifty-seven and his reputation in Hay was secure in the hearts of the people he had served so well for thirty-four years at the sacrifice of his own health.

Armstrong's affairs were eventually put into the hands of

a receiver and applicants were invited to take on his legal practice. In the meantime, Arthur Phillips, Armstrong's chief clerk, carried on the business and fulfilled the office of Acting Clerk to the local justices. The authorities were very dilatory about paying his salary and Phillips had to remind them more than once. In answer to a potential purchaser of Armstrong's practice Phillips wrote optimistically about the prospects. 'There is. . .every opportunity for an energetic and *sociable* man to make a good mark. I have every reason to believe that old clients would remain and a good many more could be secured. . .'. (The emphasis on the word 'sociable' was Phillips's own.)

The remarkable nature of Major Armstrong's crimes ensured that they could not remain the secret property of a small market town; they acquired a classic status, which would have pleased their perpetrator. All the professionals involved in the affair had reason to remember the trial of Major Armstrong, an event which they could view with an air of detachment not possible for the people of Hay.

The person least moved by the case was Mr Justice Darling. Armstrong was the last murderer to be subjected to his wit and coldly dispensed logic, for he retired from the Bench in 1923. He wrote a few lines to commemorate the occasion.

Mantle and stole laid by; and cap of doom;
Bereft, alone, I wear no ermine more.

The following year he was created Baron Darling of Langham and became an active participant in debates in the House of Lords. Darling noted some of his opinions about criminal matters in a little volume called *Musings on Murder*, which was published in 1925. Concerning the deterrent value of punishment, he wrote, 'Whoever kills by poison, whoever kills for gain, whoever kills to gratify long-cherished hatred, whoever, in short, is guilty of prepared, premeditated crime— is untouched by this tolerant philosophy.' His Lordship might even have had Armstrong in mind when he wrote this particular 'musing'. Seemingly untroubled by misgivings about the men he had sent to perdition, Darling enjoyed his versifying and country life until his death in 1936 at the age of eighty-seven.

Sir Archibald Bodkin, the Public Prosecutor, retired to Sidmouth in 1930 to live for twenty-eight years in retirement. There was said to have been 'no politer man in the Temple than Bodkin', and probably few more meticulous. During his ten years as Director at the Department of Public Prosecutions he set high standards of excellence and pressed for better recognition of the work done by his counsel and solicitors. The words, 'Excuse fingers' uttered at meal times by the Bodkin children were said to provoke gales of laughter throughout the house. Sir Archibald died suddenly in 1958 at his home; he was ninety-six. *The Times* spoke of his unsparing industry and accuracy for detail.

Of the two leading counsel at the trial, Sir Henry Curtis Bennett was most affected by the verdict in the Armstrong trial. He took his defeat badly, not just because he didn't like losing but because, as his biographers put it, 'more than in any of his other cases, he felt that he had not deserved to fail.' He had worked tremendously hard on Armstrong's behalf without, it seems, a great deal of help from the prisoner. Curtis Bennett's clerk said that Armstrong was a difficult client; he would not discuss the charge of poisoning his wife and beyond denying it would give no details until the trial had actually begun.

During the first week of the trial, Curtis Bennett's biographer said, that he and Matthews drove up to Cusop church one afternoon to see Mrs Armstrong's grave. It was cold and there was snow still on the ground and Matthews decided to stay in the car. Curtis walked off to the graveyard but returned within a few minutes looking white and shaken. He explained that as he approached he was suddenly confronted by a mongrel dog which stood on the mound of Mrs Armstrong's grave and snarled at him. He was fond of dogs and made befriending moves to the animal which responded by baring its teeth in a savage fashion. Curtis did the wise thing and retreated but he was vexed by the thought that he, the defender of the man accused of murdering the woman who lay in that grave, should be forcibly kept away. He was so struck by this that he made inquiries locally but no-one was able to identify a dog such as the one he described.

Doctors who lose a patient do not give up practising medicine and defence lawyers who have verdicts given against them do not stop their advocacy. Curtis Bennett went on to defend Edith Thompson, Ronald True, Jean Pierre Vaquier and others. He was rather proud of the tennis lawn at his country home and used to show it off to his visitors who more often than not pulled his leg about the conspicuous absence of dandelions.

Like several others closely connected with the Armstrong case, Curtis Bennett died suddenly. In October 1936 he spoke at the dinner of the National Greyhound Racing Society at the Dorchester Hotel. 'I feel this is the last time I shall speak in public,' he said. He joked about his size, and suddenly lurched sideways and fell dead. He was fifty-seven and his heart, weakened over the years by his excess weight, had finally given way. Lord Donegal, the journalist peer, sat next to him at the dinner. Afterwards, he said that Sir Henry told him, 'I shall speak for exactly nine minutes—time me.' It was exactly that to the second and never, remarked Donegal, had so much big news fallen so heavily into one journalist's lap! Curtis Bennett was a likeable man and his early death was a sad loss to his profession.

Sir Ernest Pollock, Curtis's great courtroom rival at Hereford, died twelve days before Sir Henry collapsed at the Dorchester. In a distinguished but perhaps not distinctive career, the Attorney General was made Master of the Rolls in 1923 and raised to the peerage as Baron Hanworth in 1926. He resigned office through ill health in 1935 and died in Hythe, Kent, the following year. Pollock's handling of the prosecution in the Armstrong case was much criticized and it was said that, 'he appeared to prefer intuition to close reasoning in his arguments, a course which did not assist the court.'

The prosecution was also criticized for winning a verdict on purely circumstantial evidence. This was recognised by Sir Ernest but he in no way thought it weakened his arguments at the time, '. . .circumstantial evidence is best in this case,' he said. 'It does not depend upon the veracity of one or two witnesses. It relies on a multiplicity and accumulation of facts which point in one direction and to one conclusion and no other. It fits together like a puzzle and when fitted, each piece falls into its appropriate place and forms one connected and complete whole, cogent and convincing.'

The medical experts, those seekers after hidden truths, played their part according to rules which permitted different interpretation of the same signs. Inevitably the court recognized the collective wisdom of men like Willcox, Webster and Spilsbury. They enjoyed the privilege of high reputation, deservedly won, but which made them oracles in a sense that competent doctors, like the defence witnesses, Toogood, Ainslie and Steed were not. William Ainslie, the Hereford doctor, who had represented Armstrong's interests right from the beginning, showed up the shortcomings of Spilsbury and Hincks when he gave evidence. Although, as a local man, he was known and probably admired by most of the men on the jury, his criticism was too late and too little. Ainslie seldom spoke about the Armstrong case but he was known for his feeling that the prosecution depended more on names than on facts.

Ainslie was an innovator who became better known for his advanced medicine than for his participation in a murder trial. He ran the first X-ray unit at Hereford and devised a portable machine for diagnosing fractures at the scene of road accidents. Like many others he gave of his best for Armstrong, but in truth he was up against a mass of forensic evidence as well as those big names.

Sir William Willcox, the detective physician, often quoted the Armstrong case in his lectures to learned societies but for him the affair was really just one experience in a long career in forensic medicine. The famous poisoned chocolates, which featured in the early part of the affair, were regularly shown by Willcox to students at St Mary's Hospital, London to enliven his lectures there.

Willcox, active to the last, died of a stroke on 8th July 1941. The *Daily Mirror*, using the affectionate nickname given to Willcox by crime reporters over the years, said simply, 'The King's Poisoner is dead.' The much exhibited poisoned chocolates also suffered the ravages of time and a few years after Willcox's death they were so crumbled that they were eventually destroyed.

It might be said of Sir Bernard Spilsbury that his career had all the acclaim but none of the honours. The man and his work reached almost legendary proportions in the popular imagination but he was accorded only a grudging esteem by his own profession and the Royal Colleges ignored him.

As in so many criminal cases, Spilsbury's evidence played a decisive part in Armstrong's trial. Harold Dearden wrote, 'If only Sir Bernard had not exploded that cyst! In so doing he blew the little Major as surely to perdition as could one of those shells which the pasteboard officer had so sedulously avoided in the past.' This was rather extravagant language but there was no denying the weight of Spilsbury's opinion.

Sadly, Spilsbury's career ended on a low note as his technical performance declined following the tragic death of two of his sons in the space of five years. One was killed during the London blitz of 1940 and the other died of tuberculosis. Spilsbury tried to immerse himself in work but a stroke and the onset of arthritis cruelly reminded him that his powers were failing. He took his own life in his Gower Street laboratory on the 17th December 1947. Douglas G. Browne and E.V. Tullett said in their biography of Spilsbury, 'Fame did not alter him, and its rewards interested him not at all. Truth was what he most cared about. . .'

Chief Inspector Crutchett and his assistant, Sergeant Walter Sharp, were rightly praised by the Deputy Assistant Commissioner for Crime for their work in the Armstrong case, 'The officers concerned have done us the greatest possible credit,' he wrote. Crutchett received a commendation for 'skill in a difficult case of murder' and Sharp was awarded two pounds for 'valuable assistance. . .' The Assistant Director of Public Prosecutions, speaking for Sir Archibald Bodkin, was even more generous in his praise. 'It is not too much to say', he wrote to the Commissioner of the Metropolitan Police, 'that the whole attitude of the Police—both Metropolitan and Provincial—in this important and memorable case has been one of conspicuous fairness, tact and discretion.'

Crutchett's last major assignment, like that of Mr Justice Darling, was the Armstrong case. Three months after the trial he resigned from the Metropolitan Police Force after nearly thirty years' service. Questioned about the case Crutchett said there was no truth in the story that he and Sharp had disguised themselves as tramps during the investigation, 'That sort of thing is all right in detection fiction. . .', he said. He did reveal though that, as it was essential not to be seen in Hay, they worked from Hereford travelling by car and interviewing witnesses after nightfall.

With regard to Armstrong's demeanour, Crutchett said the man's self-control was amazing. 'When I arrested him he changed colour and trembled from head to foot. But it was only momentary, in an instant he seemed to make up his mind about his line of defence and became, and was until the end, completely self-possessed.'

Crutchett was a thorough professional whose talents were recognised and depended upon by men such as Sir Archibald Bodkin. He was articulate with doctors and lawyers and his reports on the Armstrong investigation were models of clarity and good sense. In a chapter on 'The Detective at Work' contributed to a book on crime detection, Crutchett extolled the virtue of thoroughness in a police officer. His own service had been a model of this virtue but perhaps mindful with hindsight of the famous 'arsenic in the bureau', he wrote about searching premises: 'Every drawer should be taken right out and the aperture behind explored, any paper lining of a drawer or other article should be removed, and the drawer or other article turned over to see if anything is fastened to the underside.'

Before retiring he suggested that the Police Museum had a number of the Armstrong exhibits; these included the diaries, Armstrong's original statement to the police and the small packet of white arsenic. Crutchett died at his home in Bognor Regis in 1954; he was eighty-two.

Detective Sergeant Walter Sharp retired to Malvern, not so very far away from Hay where as Crutchett's assistant he took down all the witnesses' statements in long-hand. His firm, fluent hand covered hundreds upon hundreds of foolscap sheets which formed the basis of the police investigation of the Armstrong case. Mr Sharp assisted the researchers of this book by recalling some of the highlights of the investigation which are still vivid in his memory. As a police officer he knew how fickle the public could be and he remembered how he and Crutchett were hooted at by the crowds before the trial but acclaimed after it.

While the detective officers were commended for their work, one of their local colleagues, Sergeant Walter Worthing, received a reprimand. Worthing, thoughtfully, did not handcuff Major Armstrong on their journeys to and from the railway station. This misdemeanour was reported and the sergeant's respect for his prisoner cost him dear—he was severely reprimanded and lost six shillings a week from his pay with a corresponding reduction in his pension.

A man who played an important but often overlooked role was the coroner, Henry J. Southall. His daughter, Mrs Evelyn Whiting, said the police called at night, getting her father out of bed and pressing on him the need for secrecy: they were afraid that Armstrong would abscond if he got the slightest hint of what was going on.

Southall told his family of the local reaction to Armstrong's arrest. A solicitor friend told him, 'You won't be able to convict Major Armstrong. The Freemasons will see to that.' The coroner believed otherwise but he came up against the obstinate refusal of some local people even to consider the case. There was a wide belief that Major Armstrong had come under undesirable influences while in the army which undermined his character; as one local shopkeeper put it, 'We all liked Major Armstrong and couldn't believe our eyes [when he was arrested]. We liked him much better than his wife. But the war changed him.'

Eric Southall, the coroner's nephew, formed the impression that his uncle was anxious to spare the Herefordshire farmers any expenses on the inquest that could properly be avoided. With this in view, Southall decided to adjourn the inquest until the result of the trial was known. This was certainly an unusual practice at that time and considerable comment was excited in legal circles. In view of the way in which the police-court proceedings at Hay dragged on, there was obvious sense in Southall's decision and his judgment was later endorsed when Parliament amended the law concerning the conduct of coroner's inquests.

Southall believed that the coroner's obligation was to determine the cause of death and not to allow the inquest to be turned into a commission of inquiry for the prosecution. Questions could be asked at a coroner's inquest which would not be permitted in a court of law and Sir Archibald Bodkin was said to be furious that he had been denied the opportunity to ask such questions. (Perhaps he had it in mind to raise questions about other deaths which had been associated with Armstrong's name.) In the event, Southall won approval for his decision from the law officers, Mr Justice Darling and even from Sir Archibald who sent him an appreciative letter after the trial.

Mrs Whiting knew Constance Martin, Oswald's wife, quite well. She described her as, 'an attractive girl, pleasant and obviously unusually intelligent'. It was Constance whose training as a nurse caused her to make the first warning noises about her husband's illness and perhaps her foresight was really the start of Armstrong's downfall.

Only a very few people could claim to have known Armstrong well and chief among these was T.A. Matthews, his solicitor, Matthews did not stint himself on his client's behalf and there are those who say the Armstrong case broke him. Another view has the opposite: that the case made him, but the truth more likely lies between these extremes. Certainly his legal practice in Hereford became well established and he was widely recognized as a leading West of England lawyer.

The highlight of Matthews's career was undoubtedly the Armstrong case in which he instructed distinguished counsel for the defence. If the admiration won for his skill on this occasion served him in later years, it was no more than he deserved. Matthews thought highly of that last letter of gratitude sent to him by Armstrong and he carefully preserved it along with photographs and other mementoes of the case. Mr Matthews was still working in his seventy-sixth year when he was taken ill in his office and died a few days later in March 1952.

Arthur Chevalier, who had known Armstrong from his youth and was friend and counsellor to Mrs Armstrong, died in 1939. The Reverend John de Winton, who saw the Major on the eve of his execution, died in 1973 at Lymington in Hampshire. He was ninety-eight and had been vicar of Hay for thirty years.

These three men were better placed than most to gain an insight into Armstrong's character. But beyond the distress they must have felt at his decline, the quality of their friendship was such that they left no record of their feelings.

Most of the principals connected with the Armstrong affair are now dead. Those who remain have memories blurred by time and the passage of countless other events; their recollections are often disjointed and the trick of remembering brings out strange highlights. For example, E.A. Godson, the defence junior, vividly recalled Armstrong's heavily waxed moustaches which he disliked intensely, and Walter Sharp, as one of the arresting officers, remembered the labour of taking down Armstrong's statement in long-hand. Mrs Constance Martin, even at this distance in time, still found it too painful to recount details of the case and declined to assist the researchers of this book. Understandably she had not the slightest liking for Armstrong and scathingly recalled his obsequious manner when he was a guest at her home.

There remains but one mystery in the Armstrong case. Why did the Major not complete the Velinnewydd sale? What was the compelling reason which he could share neither with his own client nor his fellow solicitor? None of the accounts of the affair has given a satisfactory explanation of this incident, indeed few have bothered to try. Yet the solution is a vital factor in gaining a full understanding of Major Armstrong's behaviour.

Fading memories of an unimportant legal tangle and incomplete files have combined to make a thorough explanation elusive. But sufficient of the records remain to make possible a new perspective of the events which led up to Armstrong's attempted murder of Oswald Martin.

The only reason ever offered by Armstrong for not completing the sale was at his trial when the question was put to him directly. He replied, 'Several questions had arisen on the title.' Martin's understanding of the matter bore this out: 'I believe there was some complication with the Yorkshire Penny Bank who were mortgagees of this property.' But Armstrong's agitated behaviour at the time leads to the inescapable feeling that there was more to it than this. Martin drew a similar conclusion suggesting that Armstrong was personally involved although he had no idea how.

The Major's actions were both extraordinary and unprofessional. Pleading for time with another solicitor's clients is, to say the least, unusual, and not giving adequate answers to his own client's repeated inquiries is unprofessional. What becomes abundantly clear is that Armstrong was fighting for his business life. He was on a desperate merry-go-round to keep solvent and the person sharing the ride was his landowner client, John Williams Vaughan.

Armstrong's business affairs had long been in a mess. For reasons which may never come to light, or perhaps only from force of circumstance, his professional survival became inextricably mixed with the affairs of Williams Vaughan. The landowner, as it turned out, was not the best client for a solicitor in Armstrong's position. Williams Vaughan's assets were heavily mortgaged and he did not always properly inform his solicitor of changes in his legal and financial arrangements. Moreover, despite the fact that he was himself in financial difficulty, Armstrong continued to lend money to the landowner. Very often the money was not even his to lend and repercussions followed. For instance, Lieutenant Colonel John James, another of Armstrong's clients, was furious when he learned that his solicitor had lent money due to him to Williams Vaughan. 'I was annoyed and have made repeated demands for the return of this money, but without success,' stated the Colonel. 'I have from time to time tried to get a statement from Armstrong. . .but have never succeeded.'

The result of these transactions meant that the Williams Vaughan estate owed Armstrong £4500. The Velinnewydd sale, for which Armstrong held the deposits amounting to £500, would gross £4585 on completion. Together with his costs this would easily enable Armstrong to recoup his losses from Williams Vaughan. In fact, so precarious was Armstrong's position that his sole source of financial salvation lay in the successful completion of this deal.

The only obstacle in the path to success was the problem over the mortgages. Armstrong had waged a dogged stalling operation for a year and ten months and, in the circumstances, the intending purchasers had shown considerable patience. But then the solicitor handling the purchase side of the deal died and Oswald Martin stepped into the scene. The new man, already clearly established in Hay as Armstrong's rival, began with a zest for clearing away the difficulties. Why had the conveyances not been sealed? Why had there been such a long delay? The pressure was on and clear demands to complete were soon forced on Armstrong.

The Major continued to stall but it was an action which he must have realized was to be short-lived. When Martin threatened to rescind the contracts if the sale was not completed within a stated time, Armstrong faced an appalling prospect. If the sale were lost he would have to repay the deposit money and his chance of recouping his loan would slip away, perhaps for good. He could not cover a loss of nearly £5000, for his own resources were practically non-existent; even the money gained from his wife's will was inadequate. He would be utterly ruined.

What could he do? The only possible course was to gain more time in the hope that the legal impediments blocking the sale would be finally resolved. When his distressed plea to Martin's clients failed he could think of only one further manoeuvre. That was to incapacitate Oswald Martin and gain the breathing space he so badly needed from the ensuing confusion.

The thought of going bankrupt must have been a recurring nightmare for Armstrong at this time; it certainly lent desperation to his actions. He didn't like Martin anyway, so the prospect of poisoning him presented no difficulty. Moreover, he possessed knowledge which no other could conceive of—he was already an experienced poisoner. But so great was his frenzy that he did not anticipate the problems involved in secretly administering poison to someone not a member of his household. The trick was to create the right opportunity. But everything about Armstrong's attempts on Martin's life was stupid and ill-considered—his poisoner's cunning was usurped by his desperation.

After his plotting against Martin had failed so miserably and he had unknowingly laid himself open to detection, Armstrong declared that he was ready to complete the Velinn-ewydd sale by 6th December 1921. Even if this was genuine, it was too late because Martin had already broken off negotiations. On 13th December, Armstrong appeared at Martin's office and served him with High Court writs for specific performance. These were issued on behalf of John Williams Vaughan and demanded reason for non-completion of the sale and claimed for damages and costs. This was an unusual course for a solicitor to take in this kind of dispute and is clearly seen as a last-ditch effort by Armstrong to retain a feeble grasp on his legal right to costs from his own client. But again it was too late.

The Velinnewydd sale was still not completed by the time Armstrong was hanged. It was further complicated by a legal tangle over the priorities of Williams Vaughan's mortgagees, whose estate, like Armstrong's, went into bankruptcy.

It can be seen now that the attempt on Martin's life was less of a personal vendetta than an effort by Armstrong to avoid professional disgrace. Ruination stared him in the face as he contemplated the Velinnewydd sale slipping away from him. That sale was a matter of life or death to him. To protect his future he was driven to frantic, foolhardy measures. The extraordinary events surrounding the Martin chapter in the Armstrong story are thus shown in a new light. They are no less amazing but perhaps they afford the Major a small degree of sympathy.

Poor Armstrong was a born loser. He never really enjoyed the freedom which he hoped his wife's demise would earn him. The slow disintegration of his business and professional life through a combination of neglect and incompetence left little chance of escaping with dignity. He no doubt spent many sleepless nights struggling for a miracle to overcome the mess he was in. The little man with his egotistical fantasies was dreadfully alone. Any means that could secure his survival would have been acceptable. The awful dilemma presented by Martin's initiative in the Velinnewydd affair triggered that malignant area of his mind wherein lurked the idea of murder. From that moment, the road to total ruin was swift and sure.

* * * * *

No story as intriguing as Major Armstrong's is complete without its legends. Despite the wealth of records describing the case and its principal characters, there are still some areas of incomplete knowledge. Perhaps the greatest of these concerns Armstrong's extraordinary personality. It is here that there is most room for speculation and here too that half truths, embroidered memories and pure fantasy have combined to weave a legend around the man.

For example, Fred Stokoe, a Hereford journalist who knew Armstrong, was entertained by the Major at Mayfield a few weeks before his arrest. Stokoe related that during conversation over drinks, various local affairs were discussed and Oswald Martin's name was mentioned: 'Between you and me,' said Armstrong, 'the man's not a gentleman.' This was probably a straightforward attempt by a local journalist genuinely caught up with history in the making to explain the crime against Martin.

There is another class of journalist who claim that Providence puts them at the centre of every drama and arranges a chance meeting with every celebrity. William Le Queux was one of these and in his *Things I Know*, claimed among various kings, celebrities and crooks he had known, to have met Armstrong.

One cold March afternoon, Le Queux was sitting in the smoking room of a London Club when a fellow member, a country solicitor, came in. The two men had chatted before and Le Queux knew him to be, 'a man of refinement and taste, a good talker, a golf enthusiast and somewhat humorous.' The author told his fellow member that he was due to attend the annual dinner of Our Society sometimes called the Crimes Club that evening. 'In my profession I am constantly dealing with petty crime,' replied the visitor: '. . .he was none other than the notorious poisoner, Herbert Rowse Armstrong,' declared Le Queux. As a matter of accuracy the Club records show no meeting for the date mentioned!

Another man who always claimed to be in the right place at the right time was, W. Harold Speer, author of *The Secret History of Great Crimes*. 'For the first time in the history of criminal cases in this country I was actually permitted to have an interview with Armstrong after his arrest, in the cell of the police station in the little Welsh market town of Hay,' was Speer's modest claim. When Speer was admitted to the cell, 'Major Armstrong was revealed half reclining upon a comfortable looking bed.' He confided in the stranger, speaking of his innocence, and then with 'a cruel, vicious look' in his eyes, declared, '. . .as soon as I am free I will make someone sit up for this indignity.' 'The impression I carried away,' wrote Speer, 'was of a vain, cruel man. . .'

E. A. Bell, in *These Meddlesome Attorneys*, wrote of meeting Ellis, a powerfully-built man with pendulous hands, who was Armstrong's executioner. Ellis it was who alleged that when he was on the scaffold Armstrong cried out, 'Kitty, I'm coomin' to ye', or at least that was the version quoted in this account. Ellis added that after making this utterance, Armstrong began to crumple and, had he not been quick with the lever, 'would have nose-dived and hurt himself' (*sic*).

One of the facets of Armstrong's personality which caught everyone's imagination was the little man's cool, unflustered behaviour even when everything was against him. This has been interpreted as everything from courage to indifference and at least one crime reporter from one of the national daily newspapers was so struck by this that he decided to follow it up. He observed Armstrong's composure during the police-court proceedings at Hay and wondered if the little man had some idea at the back of his mind of 'getting out of it all'.

After each remand of the hearing at Hay, the prisoner was taken back to Worcester Gaol by train. Wondering if Armstrong might see a 'fall under a passing train as a way out', the reporter followed him and his escort party to the railway station; but Armstrong did not make any dramatic gestures. Before the train arrived, he asked his escort if he might buy a newspaper; he was allowed to do so and took it on the train with him. The reporter watched through the carriage window as Armstrong glanced at the front page of the paper and then leafed through its pages in a rather bored sort of way. The paper which Armstrong seemingly found so uninteresting carried on its front page a full-length photograph of himself and his wife on their wedding day.

Of course the prestige which Armstrong still commanded locally was reflected at the police-court proceedings in the deference paid him by the officials. Perhaps at this stage he really thought he would get off for his attention to the running of the court seemed to override consideration of his own position. Apart from reminding the Clerk about the times of trains. Armstrong actually offered to take down the evidence as there was difficulty in finding someone to do it. He was also able to assist the court officials when they ran out of foolscap notepaper by smilingly telling them where the stock was kept. W. Harold Speer related the story of how T.A. Matthews and a colleague were startled at the end of one of the day's police-court proceedings when they were going through some notes. Suddenly an arm was thrust between them and a voice said, 'He did not say that,'—it was Major Armstrong who for some reason had not been returned to his cell. This seems extremely unlikely, but Armstrong's 'at homeness' in the courtroom was without parallel.

The author L.C.T. Rolt, who knew Armstrong, wrote in *Landscape With Machines*, '. . .there was never any doubt in my mind that, despite the fact that he murdered "in cold blood", Armstrong was as mad as a hatter. His story is like some monstrous black comedy. No sane man would go about his fell business in so naive and ridiculous a manner.' This is an understandable reaction from someone who had known Armstrong and his wife well enough to picnic with them as neighbours. How could the man who read the lessons in Cusop Church be a vile poisoner without being insane?

Another local person who knew the Major first hand was May Lilwall who was walked home by him from a dance one evening a few weeks before he was arrested. The dance was held by the Red Cross Society in Hay and Miss Lilwall who was staying with friends faced the prospect of over a mile's walk home. 'When the dance was over,' she said, 'Major Armstrong suggested to mother that he should walk home with me. I had made other arrangements, but mother insisted that I accept the Major's offer. I was not pleased. We set out on our long walk, he was wearing his famous khaki great coat with its fur collar. When we left the town behind, he slipped his arm in mine. The road was dark, not a house did we pass, the owls hooted in the tall fir trees which bordered the road, and in the distance the church clock sounded its warning chimes of midnight.'

When Armstrong had reached the pinnacle of infamy by having his effigy stood in Madame Tussaud's Chamber of Horrors, Miss Lilwall went alone to contemplate the wax figure dressed in its brown suit, red tie and British warm. As she stood with the crowd looking at the figure Miss Lilwall said, 'Once again I felt his arm slip into mine. . .A woman in the crowd turned to me and said, "Nasty looking little man isn't he? I shouldn't like to have met him on a dark night." "No," I said, "I don't suppose you would".'

The Reverend Jack Griffiths in a letter to the journal *Criminology*, wrote of an incident in 1939 when as an army chaplain he received a blessing from the Bishop of Hereford, Dr Lisle Carr. As he was leaving the house the Bishop showed him an oar which he had used while rowing for his college at Cambridge. The names of the crew were painted on it; he

pointed to the last, H. ARMSTRONG, and asked Griffiths if
it meant anything to him. It was, of course, the Hay murderer,
'He was our cox,' explained the Bishop, 'and when I heard
that he had been arrested I immediately wrote a letter telling
him I was sure he was not guilty and was looking forward to
learning of his early release. Then something told me not to
send it, and that something kept me from looking extremely
foolish. . .'

Several years later, Griffiths met a member of the Armstrong jury, who was quite sure there was no doubt about
Armstrong's guilt. He added, '. . .More than that, he could
have been found guilty of other murders—but one was
enough.' This expressed a popular view that several other
murders could be laid at Major Armstrong's door, indeed
Bosanquet wrote, '. . .it is quite certain that Martin was not
the only person whom he had tried to murder.' There was
general expectation that other bodies would be exhumed at
Hay. The wildest estimate was seven. Sir Henry Curtis
Bennett was said to have known that the Home Office
considered three possible exhumations.

The most likely candidates were Edmund Hall Cheese,
Armstrong's former partner, and Willi James Davies, a Hereford
Estate Agent. The circumstances of Cheese's death and that
of his wife have already been mentioned. Cheese, of course,
was an old man and had been ailing for some time. Consequently his death in April 1914 came as no great surprise, but
the almost simultaneous demise of Mrs Cheese had the most
fortunate result for Armstrong in that he became heir to the
whole legal practice.

The police made inquiries into Cheese's death and were
particularly keen to establish the date on which he died. They
were obviously looking for a link with Armstrong's arsenic
purchases and were perhaps disappointed to find that the
first recorded purchase was on 2nd May 1914, a week after
Cheese died. Official inquiries on this matter were not pursued
any further.

In the case of Willi James Davies, it seemed to be common
knowledge that he was trying to get money due to one of his
clients from Armstrong. There were those who thought he
tried too hard, for he was taken ill the day following a visit
to Armstrong at Hay. He died in a nursing home on 4th

October 1921, three weeks before Armstrong made his attempt on Oswald Martin's life. The official cause of Davies's death was an appendix abscess, but again it had the beneficial result for Armstrong that temporarily at least he had one less creditor on his back.

In expectation of the police exhuming bodies under cover of darkness, some reporters spent the nights of the trial at Hay churchyard where the Cheeses were buried. This self-imposed discomfort went unrewarded. No further exhumations were ordered but that in no way prevented public curiosity about the matter.

In a sensational murder case, all manner of crimes will be laid at the feet of the accused. This is perhaps particularly so in the case of the poisoner whose cold, premeditated and passionless violence seems worse than that of the frenzied murderer using knife or gun.

The Armstrong case also had its share of inexplicable coincidences. One of the most interesting was noted at the time by Chief Inspector Crutchett. He wrote, 'It may be a coincidence but it is rather remarkable that Mrs Armstrong was the third person that Dr Hincks had certified as insane from Armstrong's house, the other two being a domestic servant and either Mr or Mrs Armstrong's niece.'

Shortly after Armstrong returned to Mayfield following his demobilization in the summer of 1920, his twenty-two-year-old niece, Pearl, came to stay at the house. The idea behind the visit was that the girl might become a companion to Mrs Armstrong. It was odd, therefore, that Mrs Armstrong went to stay with friends soon after her arrival. 'Unfortunately', said Armstrong, 'she [Pearl] developed mental trouble while staying with us and she was taken to an asylum.'

Armstrong referred to his niece in his dairy as 'P' and on 17th June noted, ' "P" queer after Lunch'. The deterioration in the girl's health was duly recorded during the next weeks.

18th June—Slept fairly well
19th   —Slept late, still distraite
20th   —'P' went to bed
28th   —Dr Pugh saw 'P'
30th   —Dr Pugh saw 'P' again
1st July —'P' certified taken Talgarth

Dr Hincks attended the girl at Mayfield and later called in Dr Pugh, the medical superintendent at Talgarth Mental Hospital. Hincks described Pearl's condition as 'mental stupor with extreme hesitancy and slowness of speech. Melancholia and mental depression. For over a week previously she has refused to take food.' Pearl was duly certified as insane and admitted to hospital.

Pearl's departure from Mayfield was not without benefit to Armstrong who the following week was busily having his servants witness the forged will—at least there were no other persons present to complicate his plans.

The girl was undoubtedly in a depressed state when admitted to the asylum but she made a good recovery and was discharged into the care of her sister two months later. Her sister, in fact, told Hincks that Pearl had suffered attacks such as this before.

The ease with which a person could be certified as insane in the 1920s is staggering, and only a month after Pearl's certification from Mayfield, Mrs Armstrong herself was experiencing the same procedure. Although Crutchett mentioned this in his reports, no action seems to have been taken, but it is interesting to speculate that Armstrong may have wanted his niece out of the house in order not to be hindered when completing the forgery of his wife's will.

When the character of a man of some standing is destroyed in court, as Armstrong's was, there are many who seek to blacken it still further. Countless stories were told to point up the cruelty inherent in Armstrong's nature. Some of these probably contained a germ of truth and were related by honest people to justify society's verdict on the man, while others were undoubtedly malicious. A local resident, for example, said that Armstrong was cruel to his dog: he kept a St Bernard at one time and 'used to beat it if he had a bad day at the office.' At any rate the dog died a miserable death by licking off its fur lead paint which someone brushed on the animal at a time when Mayfield was being redecorated.

A similar story, also involving a St Bernard, was related by a person who had been a neighbour of Armstrong's during his youthful days at Liverpool. Armstrong lived with his mother and aunt next door to a doctor who bred St Bernards. There was great distress in the neighbourhood one morning

when one of the dogs, 'Lassie', was found dead. Recalling this
years later, the doctor's daughter, who had known Armstrong
well as a child, said, 'You know that Lassie was Herbert's first
victim. My father always knew that Herbert poisoned her,
only he had no positive evidence'.

On the credit side, another contemporary of those early
days at Liverpool wrote to prosecuting counsel during
Armstrong's trial to point out that it would have been quite
out of character for the Major to hand a piece of food with
his fingers—he was far too polite and even pernickety to do
such a thing. Naturally those who knew Armstrong as a young
man and were impressed by his manners and pleasant behaviour
found it difficult to believe the 'Excuse fingers' episode, but
then they did not appreciate the desperation which drove
him on.

Many articles and stories about Armstrong have appeared
during the last fifty years. For the most part they have either
been wildly inaccurate or extremely novel. One that falls
into the second category was a piece called, 'The Artist
Poisoner' which appeared in the *Sunday Express*:

Master of Arts at Cambridge,
and Master of Arts at Cusop!
Master of all the Arts of Poison!
This subtle-souled country solicitor,
clerk to the justices, churchwarden,
reader of lessons at the Sunday
lectern, is a poisoner as cruel and as
crafty as any of the Borgias. . .

The article went on at some length in a similar vein but
did strike a serious note when referring to the mentality of
the poisoner. It was suggested that the poisoner succumbed
to the lures of cruelty and risk, both intellectual appetites.

* * * * *

Inevitably the Armstrong affair returns to Hay and to the
surroundings which provided the backcloth to the Major's
crimes. Hay has changed little since Armstrong's day. His
office stands in Broad Street opposite that once occupied by

Oswald Martin; both offices are still used by the town's solicitors. Just down the street is the clock tower which, though it never concealed Crutchett and Sharp, could tell a tale or two, as could the Cafe Royal which provided tea and scones for the Major in his day. Tom Hincks's fine old house is no longer the home of the town's doctor, instead there is a new, well-equipped surgery staffed by three doctors. The practice is less demanding, and there is not the need for the sacrifice of health which Hincks made.

Mayfield, now called by another name, set back from the road at Cusop, stands proudly behind its gravel drive. It is a solid, fine-looking house. Up the hill behind it is Cusop Church lying quietly behind its massive yews though the graveyard is less well kept than in former times.

Hay achieved prominence through a citizen who came to occupy a unique position in British criminological history— Major Herbert Rowse Armstrong, the only British lawyer ever to have been hanged for murder. The law's verdict on its own practitioner was unequivocally that he was guilty. Despite the fact that he made no confession, and Edgar Wallace is said to have offered him £5000 on behalf of a newspaper syndicate for just that, there are few who disagree with the verdict.

The case is a remarkable one by any standard. Circumstances and events combined to make an unusual story. The Home Office's initial reluctance to act, the circumstantial nature of the evidence and the prejudice of the trial judge might each have resulted in Armstrong's being let off the hook. But, as it turned out, he damned himself with his arrogance and cleverness. What hanged him was not that he had been caught putting arsenic into his wife's food or on Martin's scone but that he could muster no adequate argument in his own defence to explain his use of arsenic or the reason for carrying it in his pocket. If he had used only a fraction of the arsenic he bought in his garden, and no doubt he did, he could have said, 'Test the soil at Mayfield for arsenic. That will prove I used weed killer in the way I described.' This should not have been difficult for the man who could menace Oswald Martin with the suggestion of another attack of sickness. But his cleverness failed him when he needed it most.

Customarily the police spend a great deal of time looking

for the murder weapon; concealment is a criminal art which has to be matched by the' ever-increasing sophistication of detection methods. But in Armstrong's case there was no concealment. He openly signed for his poison at the nearest chemist's shop and had it lying about the house in all manner of tins, bottles and packets and, most damning of all, in the pocket of his jacket. That packet of arsenic found on him when he was arrested was Armstrong's greatest piece of self-deception. It probably thrilled him to think of the potential havoc it could produce and he was so convinced of his own invulnerability that the thought of detection never crossed his mind. Without that packet, the Attorney General would have had a more difficult time winning a verdict of guilty and Armstrong might have enjoyed both his freedom and his notoriety. Of course, he did not expect when he was charged by the police that he would not be allowed back to Mayfield— he could undoubtedly have put quite a few things right there. Was there a faint cry of the trapped man in his statement when he wrote, 'I shall be able to ascertain by going to my house where the scone and currant loaf were bought.'?

Once he had signed for his arsenic in John Davies's Poison Book he had abandoned all hope of concealment. The astute chemist pressing home his suspicion and the amiable doctor ready to admit his mistake and prepared to put his reputation at risk combined to bring about Armstrong's undoing.

There were many strange contradictions in Armstrong's personality. That a man who sought so actively to attain a position of high esteem as a public figure could see no damage to his image in flirting with girls at local dances might be put down to understandable weakness. But what can be said of a man who every Sunday walked past the grave of the wife he had murdered to read the lesson in church?

Poor Mrs Armstrong, plagued by ill health, could find comfort only in her patent medicines. She was a cold woman whose only influence over her husband was that of the shrew and Armstrong knew not how to tame her. Despite his military affectations there was passion and warmth within Armstrong's breast. He loved his children and wanted affection from his wife. But the responses he got from Katharine were negative ones: no wine, no smoking and no love. His antidote was to kick the dog and make himself foolish by pestering local girls and by consorting with women who gave him venereal disease. It was a short-cut to disaster. When his frustration finally overcome him, he resolved to remove the root cause of his unhappiness. His preparations in most respects were calm, deliberate and premeditated—he committed what might have been a perfect murder. Compare this with the bungling attempt on Martin's life and the subsequent ill-considered cat and mouse game played with teapots and telephones—the two actions hardly seem the product of the same mind. Here perhaps lies the greatest contradiction.

The mental processes whereby Armstrong decided to gain mastery over his own life by murdering his wife were extraordinary. It was said that he changed as a result of his army service. His behaviour bears this out but what is amazingly clear is that in all his secret works as a poisoner he was completely untroubled by any thought of detection. The questions he asked were, 'What is a lethal dose of arsenic?', and he quizzed Dr Hincks to get the answer; 'What is the best method of carrying and administering the poison?', and the chemist's method of putting up powders came to mind. But he never thought that his wife's body would best be cremated as an absolute protection against being found out. Armstrong chose arsenic because it was a most readily available poison. Throughout its administration he seemed completely impervious to the prolonged agony of suffering which it produced in his wife.

Something of this dark brooding comes over in a pen picture of Armstrong provided by Halliday Sutherland in his book, *Arches of the Years*. In 1915, Sutherland was bacteriologist at the Pembroke Naval Hospital and like many of his fellow officers used to spend a good many of his evenings in the bar-parlour of one of the local hotels. 'In this pub', wrote Sutherland, 'I met a sad, silent man named Armstrong. He was a major in the Territorial Army, never drank more than two glasses of beer, and never by any chance ordered a round of drinks. There were rumours of domestic trouble and of an invalid wife who henpecked him. She had appeared one evening on the tennis court and ordered the major home, publicly announcing that it was "his bath night". No wonder the poor man was said to be in love with someone else'. Little did I know of the fires of hell that were burning in the mind of that silent man. Some years later the river of hate overflowed and he poisoned his wife with weed-killer, was convicted and hanged.'

Once his wife was gone Armstrong seemed to have become intoxicated with his secret success. Those places in his mind where the shrewd, careful solicitor resided gave way to the growing demands of his ego. Perhaps he felt that the Greenwood affair would cast a protective cloak around him—lightning does not strike twice in the same place—surely no-one would suspect another solicitor of poisoning his wife with arsenic after Greenwood has been acquitted. At any rate, he cast aside all pretence at stealth in his stupidly contrived attempt to poison Martin whom he saw as a threat. Whether or not he disposed of others whom he similarly imagined threatened him, it is impossible to say, but in all his imaginings he had reckoned without the power of those closest to him. He underrated the perception of Hincks and Davies and thought too little of the legal system of which he had been a practitioner. Far from putting off the authorities, the Greenwood case merely made them try harder next time.

Unique is a much abused word but it truly describes Herbert Rowse Armstrong. The swaggering little Major, blue-eyed, alert and vainglorious inside his British warm, was both laughed at behind his back and genuinely respected. Clerk to the Magistrates, solicitor, retired army officer, Freemason and churchwarden—there could be few attributes to middle-class respectability that he had not acquired. 'But he was our solicitor', seems the only possible response to the revelation that so esteemed a man was a poisoner, a forger and a victim of venereal disease.

Beneath the vanity which was laughed at and the courtesy which was admired, ran a strong current of sly cunning. Armstrong showed that the unemotive poisoner is not as other men—there were no thoughts of detection, no fear, no soul-searching—just blind confidence in his self-determination. More than anything else he wanted to be his own man, but he stepped beyond the bounds of reason. The fateful flaw in the man's nature was that he thought he could be higher than the law. A lawyer who could act on such self-deception must indeed be unique.

Even when confronted with overwhelming evidence of his guilt and during the terrible countdown to the scaffold, he made no hint of confession, gave no glimmer of remorse. He retained for himself, forever, that secret memory of committing the perfect crime. That was Major Armstrong's final triumph, his parting gesture to vanity.

Appendix   STATEMENT MADE BY HERBERT ROWSE ARMSTRONG TO THE POLICE ON 31st. DECEMBER 1921

Broad Street,
Hay.

31st December 1921

I, HERBERT ROWSE ARMSTRONG, after having been cautioned by Chief Inspector Crutchett that anything I may say may be used in evidence hereafter, wish to make the following statement:

Mr Martin is a brother solicitor in Hay. He had been married in June last but owing to ~~a personal breavement~~ my   * wife's death in February last I had been unable to do any entertaining. I asked Mr Martin to have a cup of tea on Wednesday the 26th October 1921. At that time I had two men working in my garden, which had been allowed to get into a very bad state: their names are McGeorge, who was working in the garden, and Stokes who was erecting a fowl-house. They both live in Bear St., Hay.

I had no special reason for inviting Mr Martin to tea other than I had not entertained him since his marriage, and at that time I was not entertaining on a very large scale.

On the day in question Mr Martin arrived at my house about 5 p.m. I had previously gone home to see that every-thing was in order. I took him round the garden and showed him various improvements that I proposed to make. We then entered the drawing room where tea had been laid out by my housekeeper Miss Pearce. As far as I remember the food was placed in three plates on a wicker stand. I ~~can trace~~ remember   * the wicker stand as I have a more ornate one in brass, and my housekeeper had asked which I preferred. The food consisted of buttered scone, buttered currant loaf in slices, and bread and butter. I handed Mr Martin some scone on a plate. He took some, and I also took some which I eat and I afterwards placed the dish of currant bread and butter by his side on the table and asked him to help himself. I shall be able

to ascertain by going to my house where the scone and ~~buttered~~
*   ~~bread~~ currant loaf were bought. I remember Mr Martin saying
that buttered loaf was a favourite dish of his, and I know that he
ate heartily and cleared the dish. Afterwards I asked him to
smoke, and I remember that he was off colour and instead of
having a pipe said that he would smoke a cigarette. At the
time both Mr Martin and I were working at high pressure on
some sales of a Capt. Hope, and this was probably the reason
of his being below par. Mr Martin and I discussed general
office organization, and I remember telling him that I was
under-staffed. I also was feeling the effects of hard work. It
was light when we began tea, but it soon became necessary
for me to light the gas, and as I did so the globe came off and
fell which caused it to break. Mr Martin left about 6 p.m.
and drove home in his own car. All the food which Martin
consumed was prepared by Miss Pearce and was waiting for
us when we entered the drawing room; and either she or the
maid brought the tea and hot water in when we had taken
our seats. Miss Pearce had previously asked if the food (which
was subsequently placed on the table) would be satisfactory,
and I had said 'Yes'.

The following morning I went to Mr Martin's office to get
various documents relating to Capt. Hope's sale which was to
be completed on the 2nd November. It was a big property
sale in which he was acting for several purchasers. I was told
*   ~~that Mr~~ by one of his clerks (I cannot remember which) that
he had been taken ill. I think now that it was Preen as I have a
recollection of him saying that Dr Hincks had been called
and had said that he thought Mr Martin was suffering from
jaundice.

Mr Martin's illness was causing great inconvenience as the
completions were fixed for the following Wednesday, and
there was a great deal to be done. I sent a message to Mr
Martin by one of his clerks (I do not remember which), and
said that if I could assist in any possible way, and he would
authorise his clerks, that I would carry the matter through if
he were not well enough. The next thing that I remember was
that as he was not down at his office on Saturday I called
at his house on the Sunday morning after church. I saw Mrs
Martin, and she told me that he had been very sick but was
better, and would be down at his office on Monday. It was

not necessary for Mr Martin to accept my offer of assistance as he was able to attend his office and carry through the completions by the stated date. After Mr Martin's illness he told me that he had been very sick and that he had had a thorough clean out. Prior to his illness I had chaffed him about his practice of motoring to and from his office saying that if he did not take walking exercise he would be ill. I always walk to my office, not possessing a car.

I am continually meeting Mr Martin professionally and he and his wife have a ~~standing~~ dinner invitation to my house *
when a date can be fixed.

The first time I purchased arsenic was in 1914. ~~I think I~~ *
~~have got the receipt in my garden book.~~ At this time I came across a recipe for weed killer consisting of caustic soda and arsenic which was very much cheaper than the liquid weed killer, which ~~I~~ my gardener had previously been in the habit *
of purchasing. I therefore purchased caustic soda and arsenic from Mr Davies, chemist of Hay, and signed the book. I remember him telling me that the arsenic had to be mixed with charcoal and he mixed it accordingly. I made the weed killer at my house by boiling the caustic soda and arsenic in an old petrol tin. I think I put in all I purchased. It might have been in the proportion of equal parts of each but I don't remember. I think Miss Pearce will remember the preparation. It was all used in the garden as a weed killer. I have always had considerable trouble with weeds on the path of my vegetable garden.

The purchase of ½ lb of arsenic in June 1919, was for the same purpose and was used in exactly the same way.

The liquid and powder weed killer were purchased to my order by Jay of Castle Gardens, Hay (~~my gardener~~) who *
attended to my garden at that time ~~to my order.~~ I don't even *
know how much was purchased and I never saw it. I believe it was kept in the stable.

In January 1921 I made a further purchase of ¼ lb of arsenic at Mr Davies's shop. A small amount of this was used as a weed killer after being boiled with caustic soda by myself. It was not a success which explains why I have some left at my house. When I purchased this arsenic it was mixed with charcoal. I am keeping this to make a further trial later on. I remember talking to Mr Taylor, the Bank Manager of Hay, respecting my recipe for weed killer. I remember being pleased at being able to make my own weed killer at a much cheaper rate than the prepared article, which after the war was very dear and I could not afford it. This last preparation I carried out myself as before by boiling the arsenic with caustic soda in a petrol can. Although I have no motor car I use petrol for a petrol gas installation.

From the 2nd Sept to the 20th Sept 1921 as far as I can trace I did not leave Hay, but on the 21st Sept 1921, I went motoring with Mr Lee, Surveyor of Taxes, of Derby, who took myself and my son to Bath where my son was returning to school. We returned on the Sunday following.

I don't take chocolates myself and have not purchased any of them since I bought a small box for my late wife in August 1920. These I bought in Hay but I can't remember the shop— they were certainly not Fuller's, which I was of the impression were not procurable in Hay.

* During the period between the 2nd and 20th Sept 1921, ~~while~~ I was in Hay transacting business at my office and residing at my house. I did not leave the town. I may have called on friends socially but I do not remember.

I am unable to throw any light upon the finding of arsenic in Mr Martin's urine or as to the cause of his illness after having tea with me on the 26th October 1921. I did not touch the food he ate in any way and partook myself of what was on the same dish. If arsenic got into the food, I cannot account for it being there.

The cupboard where I keep the arsenic at my house contains boot cleaning materials and is unlocked. Nobody in the house as far as I know is aware of the presence of arsenic in the house. This arsenic I speak of is the only poison in my possession anywhere excepting of course any contained in medicine.

* I have a medicine chest in ~~my~~ a bedroom.

I make this statement quite voluntarily, and without being questioned.

31 December 1921   H. Rowse Armstrong

---

* The statement as printed here shows the deletions and alterations made by Armstrong.

The end of Armstrong's statement of 31st December 1921, showing signatures of Chief Inspector Crutchett and Sergeant Sharp.

Bibliography

BOOKS

Abrahams, Gerald:	*According to the Evidence* (Cassell, 1958)
Appleton, Arthur:	*Mary Ann Cotton* (Michael Joseph , 1973)
Arthur, Herbert:	*All the Sinners* (John Long, 1931)
Ashwin, E.A.:	*Sixty Famous Trials* ed. Richard Huson (Daily Express)
Bailey, Guy:	*The Fatal Chance* (Peter Davies, 1969)
Barker, Dudley:	*Lord Darling's Famous Cases* (Hutchinson, 1936)
Bosanquet, Sir Ronald:	*The Oxford Circuit* (Thames Bank Publishing Co., 1936)
Brock, Alan:	*A Casebook of Crime* (Rockliff, 1948)
Brookes, J.A.R.:	*Murder in Fact and Fiction* (Hurst & Blackett, 1926)
Brophy, John:	*The Meaning of Murder* (Ronald Whiting & Wheaton, 1936)
Browne, Douglas G.:	*Rise of Scotland Yard* (Harrap, 1956)
——:	*Sir Travers Humphreys* (Harrap, 1960)
Browne, Douglas G., and Tullett, E.V.:	*Bernard Spilsbury: His Life and Cases* (Harrap, 1951)
Carlin, Francis:	*Reminiscences of a Great Detective* (Hutchinson, 1927)
Coe, S.J.:	*Crimes of Love, Passion and Poison* (John Gifford, 1952)
Cuthbert, C.R.M.:	*Science and the Detection of Crime* (Hutchinson, 1958)
Darling, Lord:	*Musings on Murder* (J.A. Allen, 1925)
——:	*On the Oxford Circuit* (John Murray, 1924)
Davis, Val:	*Gentlemen of the Broad Arrows* (Selwyn & Blount, 1941)

Davis, Val: *Phenomena in Crime*
(John Long, 1941)

Dearden, Harold: *The Mind of the Murderer*
(Geoffrey Bles, 1930)

——:   *Death under the Microscope*
(Hutchinson, 1934)

Dilnot, George: *The Real Detective*
(Geoffrey Bles, 1933)

Duke, Winifred (ed.):   *Trial of Harold Greenwood*
(William Hodge, 1930)

Dunbar, Dorothy: *Blood in the Parlor*
(Thomas Yoseloff, 1964)

Ensor, David: *I was a Public Prosecutor*
(Robert Hale, 1958)

Fairs, G.L.:   *A History of Hay*
(Phillimore, 1972)

Felstead, S.T.   *Sir Richard Muir: a Memoir of a Public
Prosecutor*
ed. Lady Muir
(John Lane, The Bodley Head, 1927)

Glaister, John: *The Power of Poison*
(Christopher Johnson, 1954)

Graham, Evelyn: *Lord Darling and his Famous Trials*
(Hutchinson, 1929)

——:   *Fifty Years of Famous Judges*
(John Long, 1930)

Gribble, Leonard: *Triumphs of Scotland Yard*
(John Long, 1955)

Grice, Edward: *Great Cases of Sir Henry Curtis Bennett, K.C.*
(Hutchinson, 1937)

Haestier, Richard: *Dead Men Tell Tales*
(John Long, 1934)

Henderson, William (ed.):   *Trial of William Gardiner*
(William Hodge, 1934)

Hodge, Harry (ed.):   *Famous Trials 11*
(Penguin, 1948)

Hoskins, Percy: *No Hiding Place*
(Daily Express)

Jackson, Robert: *The Chief: The Autobiography of Gordon
Hewart, Lord Chief Justice of England
1922-40*
(Harrap, 1959)

Jackson, Robert:	*Case for the Prosecution: A Biography of Sir Archibald Bodkin* (Arthur Barker, 1962)
Jesse, F. Tennyson:	*Murder and its Motives* (Heinemann, 1924; Harrap, 1952)
Lambton, Arthur:	*"Thou Shalt Do No Murder"* (Hurst & Blackett, 1930)
Lawrence, John:	*Extraordinary Crimes* (Sampson Low, Marston & Co., 1931)
——:	*A History of Capital Punishment* (Sampson Low, Marston & Co., 1932)
Le Queux, William:	*Things I Know* (Eveleigh Nash & Grayson, 1923)
Logan, Guy B.H.:	*Dramas of the Dock* (Stanley Paul, 1930)
——:	*Wilful Murder* (Eldon Press, 1935)
Lustgarten, Edgar:	*The Judges and the Judged* (Odhams Press, 1961)
Nicholson, Anthony:	*Esprit de Law* (Wolfe, 1973)
Pearson, Edmund:	*Queer Books* (Constable, 1929)
——:	*Masterpieces of Murder* (Hutchinson, 1964)
——:	*Instigation of the Devil* (Charles Scribner's Sons, New York, 1930)
Picton, Bernard:	*Murder, Suicide or Accident* (Robert Hale, 1971)
Randall, Leslie:	*The Famous Cases of Sir Bernard Spilsbury* (Nicholson and Watson, 1936)
Rolt, L.C.T.:	*Landscape with Machines* (Longman, 1971)
Rowland, John:	*A Century of Murder* (Home and Van Thal, 1950) *Poisoner in the Dock* (Arco, 1960) *Murder Revisited* (John Long, 1961)
——:	
Russell, Donn:	*Best Murder Cases* (Faber, 1957)
Russell of Liverpool, Lord:	*Though the Heavens Fall* (Cassell, 1956)

Scott, Sir Harold: *Scotland Yard*
(Andre Deutsch, 1954)

Shew, E. Spencer: *Companion to Murder*
(Cassell, 1960)

Sparrow, Gerald: *The Great Judges*
(John Long, 1974)

——:   *Vintage Murder of the Twenties*
(Arthur Barker, 1972)

Speer, W. Harold: *The Secret History of Great Crimes*
(Arthur H. Stockwell, 1929)

Squire, Robin: *Classic Murders*
(W. Foulsham, 1970)

Sutherland, Halliday: *The Arches of the Years*
(Bles, 1933)

Symonds, Julian: *Crime and Detection*
(Studio Vista, 1966)

Shore, W. Teignmouth,
(ed.):   *Crime and its Detection*
(Gresham, 1931)

Thompson, C.J.S.:   *Poisons and Poisoners*
(Harold Shaylor, 1931)
Poison Mysteries Unsolved
(Hutchinson, 1937)

Tidy, Sir Henry: *Synopsis of Medicine*
(Wright, 1920)

Townsend, W. and L.:   *Black Cap: Murder Will Out*
(Albert E. Marriott, 1930)

Ullyett, Kenneth: *Criminology.*
(Franklin Watts, 1972)

Walter-Smith, Derek: *The Life of Lord Darling*
(Cassell, 1938)

Van Der Elst, Violet: *On the Gallows*
(Doge Press, 1938)

Wallace, Edgar: 'Herbert Armstrong, Poisoner' *in Great Stories of Real Life*
ed. Max Pemberton
(George Newnes, 1923)

——   'The Armstrong Case in *Crime and Detection 1* '
(Tallis Press, 1966)

Wensley, F.P.:   *Detective Days*
(Cassell, 1931)

Willcox, Philip H.A.:   *The Detective Physician: the Life and Work of Sir William Willcox*
(Heinemann, 1970)

Wild, Roland, and Curtis
   Bennett, Derek   *'Curtis': the Life of Sir Henry Curtis Bennett*
                               (Cassell, 1937)

Wilson, Colin, and
   Pitman, Pat: *Encyclopaedia of Murder*
                               (Arthur Barker, 1961)

Young, Filson (ed.):   *The Trial of Herbert Rowse Armstrong*
                               (William Hodge, 1927)

——   *The Case of Major Armstrong*
                               Criminological Studies No.3
                               (George Newnes, 1932)

PAPERS AND JOURNALS

The Hereford Times
Brecon and Radnor Express
The Sunday Express
The Criminologist
John Bull
News of the World
The Lancet
 etc, etc.

Index

Ainslie, Dr William, 86, 199; gives evidence at trial 175-6; 216

Allen, Nurse Eva, 28, 37, 101-2; Gives evidence at trial 148-9; 202

Allaway, Thomas Henry, 125

Armstrong, Joseph, 194

Armstrong, Katharine Mary, Albuminuria 20, 157-8, 159; Analysis for arsenic in exhumed body 90-1; Given arsenical tonic 114-5; 157; Auto-intoxication 152, 159, 173-4; 174; Certified as insane 21-3; Change of life 21, 24; Character 16-18; Children 9, 196-7, 206, 210-11; Coroner's Inquest 88-9, 111, 188; Discoloration of skin 29, 202-3; Exhumation Order 84; Final illness and death 27-32; Funeral 33; Hypochrondria 18, 99, 206, 233; Letters 24-5, 132, 134-5; Marriage 9; Melancholia 173-4; Post mortem 86-8; Progress at Asylum 23-6; Tendencies to suicide 28, 112-13, 160, 163, 167-8, 176, 178, 180, 207 Wills 25, 59, 95, 96, 99, 100, 102, 130-4, 137-9.

Armstrong, Herbert Rowse, Alleged cruelty to animals 230-1; Appeal against sentence of death 189; Army career 10,11-4; Arsenic found in pocket when arrested 4, 76-7, 169-172, 179, 181, 133; Arsenic found in bureau at Mayfield 154-5, 166-7 186; Association with Marion Glassford Gale 119-25, 149, 163, 165, 203, 211; Birth 8; Diary entries 28, 31, 33, 36, 108, 125, 229; Execution 194-196; Financial affairs 134-7, 221-4; Freemason 10, Henpecked 11, 16-19, 234 House searched 61; Inherits wife's money 37, 110; Injections of arsenic 68, 105, 118, 119; Inquest after execution 199; Love letters 121-4; List of symptoms 118; Migraine 119; Notary Public 8, 18-19 Passport description 5, 59; Professional career as solicitor 8-11; Purchases of arsenic 79; Sale of effects at Mayfield 209-10; Syphilis 94, 104, 105 117-19,203, 206, 234; Travels abroad 36; Trial evidence 165-72.

Arsenic, Encysted theory 157, 160, 173, 174-5; Legal requirements 67

Avory, Mr Justice, 189

Baker, Una Mary, 1, 2, 53, 96

Ball, R.L., 177

Bayliss, Mortimer, 64, 92

Bell, Edward A., 225

Bell, Dr James A. 194, 197

Bigham, Hon F. Trevor, 55

Bismuth, Impurities in, 152, 158, 204-5

Black Jones, Dr W., 101, 106

Blackwell, Sir Ernley, 53

Bodkin, Sir Archibald, 55, 59, 60, 77, 129, 214, 219

Bosanquet, Samuel Ronald 141, 142, 143, 187, 193, 195

Brecon and Radnor Express, 33

Brown, Chief Inspector W., 121

Buchanan, Rev C.M., 33, 42

Candy, Lily (see Evans),

Carr, Rev Charles Lisle, 8, 227, 228

Cheese, Edmund Hall, 9, 10, 135, 228

Chevalier, Arthur Edward 8, 20, 25, 28, 34, 110, 130, 191, 210, 220

Chivers, Reginald Henry, 98

Clinical Research Association, 50, 51

Coleridge, Mr Justice, 99

Cremation Act (1902), The, 208

Criminology, 227

Crippen, Hawley Harvey, 115, 142

Crutchett, Chief Inspector Alfred 2, 55, 59, 97, 134, 166, 210, 217-8, 229

Curtis,Bennett, Sir Henry, 143, Trial Opening Speech 162-4; Trial Closing Speech 176-7; 181, 182, 184, 186, 188, 190, 193, 210, 214-5, 228

Daily Mirror, 216

Darling, Mr Justice (later lord) 141, 142; Decision on admissibility of Martin evidence 147; Direction to Trial Jury 179-81; Passes Sentence of Death 183; 187, 200, 204, 213

Davies, Constance, Muriel (see under Martin)

Davies, John Fred, 45, 46, 48, 49, 56, 79-80, 205, 233

Davies, Laura Jesse, 62, 78-9

Davies, Willi James, 228-9

Davis, W.G. Val, 190

Dearden, Harold, 217

Donegal, Lord, 215

Ellis, William, 193, 195, 225

Evans, Supt David, 162

Evans, Lily (nee Candy), 95, 100, 132, 133

Evans, Percy, 63

Evening News, 186

Friend, Ida Bessie, 20, 25, 100-1, 102, 130, 134

Frogley, Horace, 58

Fuller's Chocolates, 3, 58

Gale, Marion Glassford (see under Madame X), 120-5; Love letters 121-4; 149, 163, 165, 203, 211

General Paralysis of the Insane, 117-8

Godson, Edwin Alfred, 144, 193, 221

Grand Jury, 144-5

Gransmore, J.R., 98

Grant, William George, 96

Greenwood, Harold, 59, 62, 125-130, 141, 158, 173, 188, 189, 100, 201, 203, 235

Greenwood, Irene, 127, 128-9

Griffiths, Rev Jack, 227-8

Griffiths, Robert T., 1, 10, 15, 38

Griffiths, Trevor, 33, 38, 60, 197, 210, 211

Griffiths, Dr Thomas R., 127-8

Grout, W.H., 74, 92

Hammonds, Henry John, 100

Harrington, Sir Richard, 145

Heath, Dr Douglas, 118-9

Hereford Times, 88, 184

Hewart, Lord, 189

Hincks, Dr Thomas Ernest Certifies Mrs Armstrong 20-2; Attends Mrs Armstrong's last illness 26-32; 35; Attends Martin's illness 43-6; Suspects the Major 49-55; Gives evidence at the police hearing 103-10; Gives evidence at trial 150-3; 188, 204, 205, 212, 230

Hird, John, 78
Home Office, 51-5
Hopkins, Tom, 146,186-7
Hutchins, Augusta Gertrude, 100, 102, 130, 134

Iredell, S.J.S., 124

James, F.R., 98
James, Lieutenant Col John, 222
Jay, William, 80-1
Jayne, Dr Frederick James, 20, 24, 103, 205
John Bull, 188, 207
Jones, Lewis, 39

Kinsey, Nurse Muriel Gladys, 27, 103, 202

The Lancet, 207
Lee, R.H., 191
Le Queux, William, 225
Lilwall, May, 60, 63, 125, 227
Lloyd, Nurse Lucy Alice, 103
London Gazette, 14
McCardie,Mr Justice, 105
McGeorge, Robert, 41, 87
Madame X (see also under Gale) 109, 119
Marshall Hall, Sir Edward, 128
Martin, Constance Muriel, 44, 48, 57, 75, 220, 221
Martin, Dorothy Harriet Birch, 47-8, 57, 74, 111
Martin, Gilbert Charles, 47-8, 57, 75
Martin, John Osborne, 47, 57
Martin, Oswald Norman, 1-3, 15-6, 37, 38; ill after taking tea with Armstrong 40-6; Suspicious of having been poisoned 48-50; urine analysed 53; Gives evidence at police hearing 70-3; Gives evidence at trial 149-50; 197, 203, 211, 221.

Matthews, Thomas Alfred, 5, 64, 66; Defends Armstrong at police hearing 70-82 and 92-116, 143, 172, 191, 210, 220 226
Micklethwait, St John, Prosecutes at police hearing 67-82 and 93-116; 143
Morning Post, 31

News of the World, 194

Paling, Gerald, 67, 102, 147
Paradise, William, 189-90, 193, 208
Parley, Elizabeth, 130
Pearce, Emily Ellis, 27, 41, 61, 75-6, 95, 112-3, 130, 132-3, 148, 197, 209
Phillips, Arthur, 1, 2, 213
Phillips, Cambridge, 64, 66, 70
Poisons Act, The, 67
Poisoned chocolates, 3, 46-8, 49, 58, 68, 71, 216
Pollock, Sir Ernest, 143; Trial Opening Speech 146-7; Trial Closing Speech 178-9; 215
Preen, Alan, 42, 43, 44, 97
Price, Harriet Elizabeth, 41, 42, 77-8, 111, 135-6

Rangecroft, John Arthur, 96
Reinsch's Test, 159
Rhodes, Henry T.F., 137-9
Rolt, L.C.T., 227
Rosser, Inez, 31, 32, 33, 113, 201-2, 212-3
Russell of Liverpool, Lord, 208

Sampson, A.C., 12
Samuel, Inez (see under Rosser)
Seddon, Frederick Henry, 115, 142
Sefton, Cohen, H. 55
Sharp, Det Sgt Walter, 2, 56,

105, 186, 217, 218, 221
Shearman, Mr Justice, 189
Smith, Dr Janet, 23, 26
Soutar, Dr James, 24
Southall, Eric, 219
Southall, Henry J., 84, 89, 188, 219-20
Speer, W. Harold, 225, 226
Spilsbury, Dr Bernard Henry 85, 90; Gives evidence at police hearing 114-5; 147; Gives evidence at trial 155-8; 216-7
Stanhope, Capt E.S., 55, 92
Steed, Dr John, 176, 216
Stokoe, Fred, 224
Sunday Express, 231
Sutherland, Halliday, 234

The Times, 214
The Times Literary Supplement, 18
Toogood, Dr Frederick Sherman, Gives evidence at trial 173-5; 204; 216
Townsend, Dr Arthur Allen Deykin 23, 24, 83-4, 102-3; Gives evidence at trial 153
Tunnard Moore, Charles, 21, 59, 64
Tunnard Moore, Mary, 141

Vachell, Charles Francis, 143

Velinnewydd Estate, The, 39, 40, 46, 136, 203, 221-4

Waghorne, J, 199
Wallace, Edgar, 207, 232
Wallace, William Herbert, 198
Way, Daisy Alice, 130
Weaver, Supt Albert, 2, 3, 64, 90, 92, 98; Gives evidence at trial 154-155; 162

Webb, Humphrey Vines, 33, 85, 100, 161
Webster, John,52, 90, 115; Gives evidence at trial 158-9
Wensley, Supt Frederick Porter, 56
Western Mail, 141
Westminster Gazette, 142
Whiting, Evelyn, 219, 220
Whyte, Harry, 190, 191, 196
Willcox, Sir William Henry, 59, 115-6, 147; Gives evidence at trial 159-61; 201, 202, 204-5, 216
Williams, Eddie, 16
Williams, Sgt James, 4, 105
Williams, Rees, 89
Williams Vaughan, John, 52, 90, 115, 136, 221, 222
de Winton, Rev John Jeffrys, 33, 191, 197, 220
Worthing, Sgt Walter, 4, 63, 89, 103, 162, 218-9

Young, Filson, 182, 141, 206, 210.